"I put it in the same category as Tawny's *The Acquisitive Society* and Keynes's *Economic Consequences of the Peace.* It is unique, witty and inescapable." —*Malcolm Muggeridge*

"The most brilliant essay in politico-economic criticism in a decade." —*Kermit Gordon*

"Lo, what a man of wit has arisen to do biopsy on what Carlyle called 'the dismal science' of economics." —CHICAGO SUNDAY TRIBUNE

"Galbraith has done an enormous service to the cause of intelligent economic and social debate. In the end, he may have done as substantial a service to the prestige of economics itself."
—NEW REPUBLIC

JOHN KENNETH GALBRAITH was a president of the American Economic Association, a Warburg Professor of Economics at Harvard, and served as United States Ambassador to India from 1961 to June, 1963. He is the author of *A China Passage, Economics, Peace and Laughter, Economics and the Public Purpose, The Liberal Hour,* and *The New Industrial State,* all available in Signet or Mentor editions.

Recommended MENTOR and SIGNET Books

(0451)

☐ **THE AFFLUENT SOCIETY by John Kenneth Galbraith.** Third Revised Edition. The book that added a new phrase to our language, a new classic to literature, and changed the basic economic attitudes of our age. In this new revision, Galbraith has extensively updated the information and widened the perspectives of his basic argument ... "Daring ... a compelling challenge to conventional thought." —*The New York Times* (618947—$2.95)

☐ **THE NEW INDUSTRIAL STATE by John Kenneth Galbraith.** Third Revised Edition. One of our most distinguished economists and author of such bestsellers as *The Affluent Society* offers a comprehensive look at modern economic life and the changes that are shaping its future. (620291—$3.50)

☐ **UNDERSTANDING THE ECONOMY: For People Who Can't Stand Economics by Alfred L. Malabre, Jr.** The U.S. economic scene made easily comprehensible and intensely interesting ... "Millions of readers can learn from this lively book."—Paul Samuelson, Nobel Prize-winning economist. (618009—$1.95)

☐ **UNDERSTANDING FINANCIAL STATEMENTS by John Myer.** A handbook for executives, students and investors presenting samples of each type of accounting statement with full explanation of how the figures may be interpreted and used. Illustrated. Index. (620518—$2.50)

☐ **TAX SHELTERS. A Complete Guide by Robert and Carol Tannenhauser.** In simple, concise language, a top lawyer explains the latest legislation and rulings and tells you which shelters work and which are outmoded. Cash-flow charts plot savings through 1989, and a glossary turns technical terms and IRS-ese into plain English. (110463—$2.75)

THE AFFLUENT SOCIETY

THIRD EDITION, REVISED

by

John Kenneth Galbraith

A MENTOR BOOK
NEW AMERICAN LIBRARY
TIMES MIRROR
NEW YORK AND SCARBOROUGH, ONTARIO

To Emily,
Peter and Jamie

The economist, like everyone else, must concern himself with the ultimate aims of man.

—ALFRED MARSHALL

Contents

Introduction to the Third Edition

Following World War II in the United States, there was what could have been called the free enterprise, possibly the market, revival. It deeply engaged the conservative mind. Our conservatism is normally thought to depend on self-interest, moral indignation, vehement expression and something approximating religious revelation. This is unjust. The influence of ideas is ubiquitous and cannot be excluded anywhere.

The source of the ideas was a rediscovery of the Benthamite world of the nineteenth century as it was applied to economic policy by the classical economists and to sociology and politics by Herbert Spencer and William Graham Sumner. In 1944, it derived a new scholarly sanction from F. A. von Hayek's *The Road to Serfdom*, an alarming tract against socialism and the state, which, as the name implies, it identified extensively with servitude. And, in the years following, it achieved considerably more academic reputability from an energetic group of evangelists and scholars who gathered, along with von Hayek, at the University of Chicago with intellectual outriders in other academic centers.

As I shall notice presently, the academic proponents of the market revival were not imagined by most economists to have a large measure of practical relevance. But they had a strong and even impressive command of the economic theory to which the market (unlike practical public action) lends itself. And they could picture themselves as solidly in descent from the oldest tradition in western economic thought—that of Adam Smith, David Ricardo, John Stuart Mill and Alfred Marshall. Economics, like the law although less so, has a sense of its prophets. Also, as a consequence of its rapid growth, the discipline includes a considerable number of participants who are, intellectually, a trifle insecure—who secretly doubt the depth of the scholarship which, for professional reasons, they avow. Being in an old tradition, the proponents of the market revival had no such doubts. They were reassuring company, men to be treated with respect by those who disagreed. In economics, it is professionally better to be associated with highly respectable error than uncertainly established truth.

The market revival spread rapidly outside the academic world. It was warmly embraced by the editors of *Fortune, The Wall Street Journal,* other business journals and by editorial writers, for whom it was an admirable way of placating socially backward publishers in an unexpectedly sophisticated way. In those years, also, numerous socialists were in retreat from Joseph Stalin. For John Chamberlin, the late William Henry Chamberlin, James Burnham and many others, it meant that the important social decisions would be taken, not by fallible, cruel and egotistical men but by a wholly automatic mechanism which, if also cruel, was impersonally so. Anything that so effectively excluded personal power was obviously an instrument of freedom. From these sources, the market revival went on into politics.

II

In its academic manifestation, the market revival stressed the social efficiency of the unmanaged market. It distributed resources—labor, capital, managerial and technical talent—to various uses in accordance with the ultimate command of the consumer. Any interference was damaging to this allocative efficiency; the most dangerously intrusive agency was the state. The state could interfere with the free movement of prices; it could also intrude services of its own which had not survived the market test. The test of faith in the market, it followed, was the rigor with which one sought to minimize the role of the state.

Not that the efficiency of the market—cruel, as noted, but worth suffering—was the only basis for the academic opposition to government. Here too there was moral and political concern. Here too all who suspected authority, either its competence or its motive, were urged to align themselves with the impersonal market against the state.

In the academic world, there was a certain additional

concern, often obeisant, on occasion actual, with private interference with the market. General Motors and General Electric, it was known, enjoyed no slight power as regards the prices they charged—a power that no prophet of the market economy could tolerate if exercised by the state. For here was authority and here also were both the power and the incentive to impose the restrictions on output (the inferior allocation of resources) associated with monopoly. So, in principle, such firms should be broken up. In principle, also, the ban on government intervention should be comprehensive. It should fall not alone on minimum wage legislation and public housing and support to collective bargaining, things of which conservative businessmen and politicians naturally disapproved, but also on the Federal Reserve System, subsidies to air transportation, and the tariff, of which, often devoutly, they approved. However, the academic doubts about General Motors and those government services needed and hence approved by the businessmen were not, on the whole, damaging to the market revival. Its proponents managed to convey the impression that this part of the program was liturgical, that the deeper enthusiasm lay with the defense of the market, and the attack on more iniquitous forms of government interference such as the welfare system or support to public education. In any case, professors are inconvenient people; it was inevitable that they would exact some rhetorical price for so great a doctrinal blessing. Accordingly, as it moved out into the less literal world of journalism and on into politics, the market revival hardened into a simple prescription against government services. The only exception, apart from those that conservatives needed and hence approved, was expenditures and other action to fight or resist communism. To exclude the war on world communism from the general ban on government activity seemed wholly logical. The communists were the greatest exponents of precisely the opposite system. One rightly invoked a lesser evil against the greater one. Considering the effects of defense expenditures on the economy, there were many reasons for being glad that this could be so.

If one is rich or even well-to-do and self-regarding, any doctrine that makes public services (and therewith taxes) uneconomic, politically regressive and possibly immoral is bound to seem benign. Anything so convenient must be right. But though proof was not needed, exegesis was welcomed and hence there was a considerable demand for prophets of the market. These quickly became available and in the years following World War II, service clubs, sales conventions, even suburban ladies' clubs listened to the gospel as revealed by John Stuart Mill, Herbert Spencer, William Graham Sumner, Friedrich von Hayek and Ludwig von Mises. The last two defenders of the market they could then hear in person. Some of the consequences were not without charm. In 1948, Hubert Humphrey won election to the United States Senate over a man who had become enchanted by Jeremy Bentham. Over the length and breadth of Minnesota, he proclaimed his commitment to Bentham's doctrines until, it was said, some citizens looked for the philosopher's name on the ballot. Humphrey was able to persuade the farmers of the state, quite rightly, that Bentham would have opposed farm support prices. So they chose Humphrey instead.

III

Historical circumstance supported the market revival. The thirties had been a miserable time. Many had lost confidence in the economic system; many more had come to assume that it could endure only as the result of more of the government intervention that had been the hallmark of the New Deal. This was grim news for conservatives. Then came the further great expansion in government controls during World War II. Many of the controls were annoying and even onerous, not alone on businessmen. Equally oppressive, without question, were many of those responsible for their improvisation and administration, of whom I was one. Additionally, shortages of goods and houseroom and restrictions on production and consumption resulting from the war were blamed on the controls. Without price ceilings, rationing, the allocation of scarce materials and restrictions on their less important use, the discomfort resulting from inflation and shortages would have been worse and the war would have been longer. But this was not easy to see. Many people were open to the argument that an obstrusive and intrusive state was deliberately making life difficult.

Meanwhile, with more skill than they have normally manifested in such matters, business spokesmen took credit for the superior industrial performance of the economy during the war. Output had greatly increased. Production of munitions and other requisites of war had been impressive. Not the strong demand, coupled with an improvised but highly rational planning design, but the natural virtuosity of American enterprise and the American market system was given credit for this success. If, after the war, the restrictive hand of the state could be dispensed with, things would be even better. The public, bedeviled by the regulations and regulators, was again in an excellent mood to listen. The 1940 elections were an indication of the attitude. Almost everywhere men ran in opposition to the state. The resulting Congress was the most conservative in modern history. Its more primitive members, so it is said, left behind in Senate closets, washrooms, and in the distant recesses of forgotten basements bronze tools, wall painting and pottery shards, all dubiously symbolizing their religion. The market revival was very much a product of the times.

It had some reverberations in other countries. In Germany in the late forties, weariness with wartime privation and controls was also extreme and with rather more reason. Ludwig Erhard made the recovery of German industry after 1948 the product of the unaided market. This was a remarkable feat of oratory, for it coincided with the Marshall Plan, a vastly publicized effort in public intervention, and took place in a country where industry was extensively regulated and where per capita government expenditures were much higher, and those for welfare about twice as high, as in the avowedly socialist state of Norway (as it then was) where the level individual income was then about the same. The message of the market revival was also carried to other countries by American businessmen who frequently revealed an enthusiasm for exuberant and unfettered price competition that they never displayed at home. In Japan, as also in Germany, it led to the dismantling of the great business trusts in the interest of a more effectively functioning market—a remarkable gift, in many ways, by a victorious to a defeated power. (The Japanese later reassembled the pieces.) The prophets of the revival gathered at intervals in international congresses to proclaim and thus to reinforce their faith. Still, the market revival was mostly an American phenomenon.

IV

The market revival brought no very drastic action. Desirable as sharp curtailment of federal regulation or civilian spending might be in principle, it was something to be approached with circumspection in practice. Only much later, in the presidential campaign of Barry Goldwater, did the ideas of the market revival—the elimination of social security, an end to the farm programs—become a program and many wiser men were prompt to warn their candidate that action was never intended. By the time of the Nixon Administration, it was accepted that the government could simultaneously endorse competition while doing all possible to secure the favored from its effects. The sincerity of such market evangelists as Professors Milton Friedman and George Stigler of the University of Chicago was conceded but it was not imagined that they would be taken too seriously in practical matters. They were meant to be studied, perhaps called on for advice, but not too seriously followed. Still, in Washington and in statehouses, city halls and school districts across the land, the case for public spending became the case against freedom. This added powerfully to the older arguments about the grievous burden of taxes. In the deeper intellectual wastes of Orange and Harris counties, attitudes were more severe. To be for new schools, against air pollution or in favor of stronger zoning laws was to be in support of the first awful step down the steep slippery path to communism.

Meanwhile, and remarkably, these ideas were meeting no very effective attack from liberals. The main thrust of liberal economic thought flowed in different channels. And it was able, in one important aspect, to find common cause with the market revival.

V

In the years following World War II, Keynesian fiscal policy became the *summum bonum* of liberal economic policy. An adequate level of output and employment in the economy was assumed to solve nearly all economic and most social problems. Inadequate production and employment made all other problems insoluble. So not without a sense of strategy, liberal economists concentrated on policies designed to ensure an adequate level of demand and therewith of output and employment.

Acceptance of the Keynesian ideas involved, for conservatives, one of those strange combinations of misapprehension and paradox which make the otherwise tedious study of economics so fascinating. In the broadly liberal view of those who first introduced the Keynesian system to the United States, the regulation of aggregate demand—the total of all spending at any time—required no fundamental revision of the role of the state in the economy. When there was unemployment or an inadequate rate of growth, the government would increase its expenditures for useful purposes without a parallel increase in taxes. When this support to the economy was not needed, it would defer or even reduce expenditures and therewith the deficit. This regulation would be supplemented and reinforced by the automatic increase in some expenditures, notably those for unemployment compensation, welfare and farm price supports, in periods of unemployment and inadequate growth and by the counterpart reduction in periods of high employment and rapid expansion. Over time, the scope and functions of the state would not be changed appreciably.

Since it made the private economy function better without greatly enlarging the role of the state, this model of the Keynesian system should not have too profoundly aroused conservatives. But it did. It required deficit financing on occasion. This, always a symbol of fiscal sloth, became affirmatively wicked. It was seen also as an excuse for a soft policy on public spending. The name of Keynes thus became mildly coordinate with subversion. The Keynesian ideas came to the United States in the thirties primarily by way of apostles at Harvard, most notably Professors Alvin Hansen and Seymour Harris. Following World War II, conservative members of the Harvard governing boards conducted an investigation of the Harvard Department of Economics to see if his influence there was excessive and found it was.[1] Elsewhere too, circumspect scholars were careful to explain that their commitment to Keynes was subject to cautious and intelligent reservations. And then the Keynesian system became respectable and accepted, not through the above-cited balancing measures which left the state small, but by a fundamental enlargement of the role of the state. And this—and this is the paradox—was highly acceptable to conservatives.

The decisive application of Keynesian policy came about in the postwar years as the result of a large increase in public spending supported by a large increase in taxation. This spending was highly reliable, not a subject of serious controversy. And the personal and corporation income taxes by which it was sustained fell with special force on those revenues—corporation profits and surtax income—which increased most in periods of expansion and diminished most with stagnation or contraction. In consequence, the tax system increased its yield more than in proportion in periods of economic expansion and diminished its yield more than in proportion with contraction. The role of the state being large, these effects were quantitatively adequate. And this large role of the state was acceptable to conservatives because it served a function of which conservatives strongly approved, the maintenance of a strong military defense against communism. It was also exceptionally pleasing to those industries which were recipients of the spending involved.

And here was the basis for a coalition—or at least a tacit working arrangement between conservatives and liberals. Liberals did not entirely forget their earlier commitment to the public services—so long a distinguishing feature of American liberalism. But this was now secondary to a successful Keynesian policy. In consequence, the conservative warnings that public education, public housing, better sanitation, control of water and air pollution, improvement of environment were threats to liberty evoked only a modest liberal challenge. Meanwhile, large defense expenditures were underwriting the Keynesian policy and thus accomplishing the major liberal goal. In the early postwar years, Stalin's policy in Eastern Europe and the Korean War made these expenditures seem es-

[1]James B. Conant, then President, rejected the finding. My election to a professorship had also been thought a manifestation of the danger.

sential. Thereafter, they became more or less habitual. Even the man who argued for more domestic outlays prefaced his case by conceding the higher priority of national defense. Liberal uneasiness over the role of defense expenditures in the Keynesian system was assuaged by observing that outlays for domestic purposes would serve just as well. With the Vietnam conflict, military expenditures acquired the further sanciton of war. By 1969, a conservative President could announce his conversion to Keynesian principles with little rebuke.

Such were the ideas, here writ slightly larger than life, that were contending for public attention and belief in the United States in the years after World War II. They were ideas—both the market revival and the Keynesian preoccupation with employment *qua* employment and production *qua* production—that seemed to me damaging. Contemplating them in the early 1950s, I began work on this book.

VI

I had been considerably a part of the environment I was examining. Like others of my generation, I was, in the late thirties and early forties, an aggressive evangelist for the Keynesian system in its standard form. The writing, accordingly, involved a heavy effort to detach myself from my own past beliefs. I discovered how difficult this could be. I have read on occasion that I find a perverse pleasure in attacking the conventional myth. I do not, and on the contrary, it is very hard work. Some day for recreation I intend to write a book affirming fully all the unquestioned economic truths.

I was kept going by the conviction that, in starving our public services and in placing so much of our faith in the general curative powers of increased production, we were inviting grave social ills. (I was less aroused then than later by the imbalance in public outlays, especially those for defense.) It is unwise to reflect excessively on one's foresight, for to do so is to invite critical attention to those other forecasts which bring one's score back to normal. But while there have been many explanations of our urban disasters of recent times, some designed, not without thought, to direct attention away from remedies that would cost money, few can doubt that persistent and continuing underinvestment in needed services is one. Further, while something must be attributed to the fact that some citizens are black and some white, no one has yet shown how to overcome this condition. But we can have good schools and well-paid teachers and ample and attractive housing and clean streets and sufficient and well-trained policemen and plenty of parks and well-supervised playgrounds and swimming pools and adequate divertissement on hot summer nights. These will help even if they will not completely cure and they require only a willingness to tax and pay. Not many would now challenge the efficiency or morality of such outlays. And even the stalwart conservative who dares not venture out in the street at night, pays heavily for private security guards, thinks often about kidnaping and hesitates on occasion to drink the water or breathe the air must, on occasion, wonder if keeping public services at a minimum is really a practical formula for expanding his personal liberty.

That some balance must be maintained between the public and private sectors of the economy—between increased private expenditures and the facilities for removing the waste that results—is now widely agreed, at least in principle. Practical economic policy has also moved in the direction of this book. Few economists would now argue that a sufficiently expanding economy will sweep away other social problems. Since the first edition, there have been many years of expansive Gross National Product. Social tension has, if anything, increased, not lessened. If the expenditure that produces this expansion is for military purposes—for example, for a war in Vietnam—not many will suppose that it will do much to relieve the agony of the urban ghetto. Throughout the Kennedy Administration, there was a friendly but vigorous battle over whether to reduce taxes in order to expand private income and expenditure and therewith employment and economic growth. The alternative was to keep up the level of taxes and press instead for more public spending for social purposes—education, urban renewal and improved welfare standards. Since Congress would be reluctant, this would be slower, so a larger allocation of resources to public purposes would be won at the price of a slower rate of total growth. While I argued the second case, not without some encouragement from the President, the weight of reputable economic opinion was solidly on the other side. The outcome was never really in doubt and, in 1964, taxes were reduced. Now, though the decision in a liberal administration might not be different, it is at least possible that the needs of the public sector would be more strongly pressed.

The more serious error in this book, as first published, was in understatement. A large movement of the poorer rural population to the great urban centers, a still continuing population increase, the public costs of affluence—from managing its automobile traffic to removing its detritus—and the desire, however frustrated, for improved quality in education, public order, public health and sanitation and other public services have all joined to make the modern city, if it is to be agreeable and not just tolerable, an almost unbelievably expensive thing. I did not see how expensive it would be or that the reaction to social imbalance would be far from peaceful. However, this does not matter too much. If, two decades ago, one had foreseen and described the disaster that lay ahead for our urban communities, he would have been dismissed as a professional alarmist.

VII

The main inducement to this book was the market revival and the Keynesian conviction that nearly all social ills could be cured by more production. But it had another source which, though reflected in the book, was, to my discomfort, extensively overlooked. For quite a few years prior to publishing *The Affluent Society*, I had been concerned with the problems of agriculture. This had led me to wonder, as it had others, why year in and year out, decade after decade, islands of egregious poverty persist in the rural United States. Many have difficulty in imagining the depth of this deprivation. I recall in subsequent years the surprise of Jawaharlal Nehru when I once suggested to him that in some areas of the United States—in mountain counties of West Virginia, eastern Kentucky, eastern Tennessee, the Ozark plateau— the standard of rural living was almost certainly lower, and life by any test more meager, than in the comparatively prosperous Punjab. In the early nineteen-fifties, I obtained a small grant from the Carnegie Corporation to study the causes of this continuing poverty in the United States. In the strictest sense, this was the beginning of this book; the title I had then in mind was "Why People Are Poor."

In a world where everyone is poor, there is nothing very remarkable about poverty. It becomes remarkable, and also less forgivable, in a community where the great majority of people are well-to-do. And the explanation for poverty in the well-to-do society must be sought in the general and not the particular aspects of the case—not in the nature of the society of the poor but in the nature of a society of the rich which allows or requires some to stay so poor. This also led on to the preoccupation with production and to our neglect of the government services—education, health, welfare and urban existence generally—by which the poor (or their children) might hope for escape from their plight.

I never explained this transmigration of my thoughts. And as the book progressed, the specific conclusions on how the affluent society excludes numerous people from its endowment were, with conclusions in general, pushed along to the end. A considerable number of readers, including a fair number of reviewers, never got so far. They complained that, carried away by the vision of affluence, the book ignored the fact that there were still a great many poor people in the United States. Some, more censorious than others, said it was hardhearted. All used my seeming oversight as an excuse for continuing with their accustomed beliefs and preoccupations. "It will be time to stop worrying about production when there aren't so many poor people who need it." I could have protected myself, and saved less diligent reviewers from error, by hinting somewhere near the beginning that this subject did come up. But it is my impression, confirmed by such as Michael Harrington, the *The Affluent Society* helped direct attention to the continuing scandal of great deprivation amidst the great wealth of the United States and to the eventual decision, alas more rhetorical than real, to mount a direct attack on poverty. The basic situation has, unhappily, not changed much since this book first appeared nearly twenty years ago.

I must pause here to settle another score. The thrust of this book is that increased production is not the final test of social achievement, the solvent for all social ills. Thus, it challenged the very foundation of Keynesian policy with its nearly total emphasis on the expansion of economic output and income. A common Keynesian reaction was: How can Galbraith be so callous when a named percentage of our people have a disposable personal income of less than the necessary minimum? When everyone has that minimum, it will be time to worry about the problems of social balance. Everyone then entered the minimum income level which reflected either the state of his personal generosity or the statistics he had at hand. A few especially perceptive critics added that my own social vision was being clouded by an eccess of personal income of my own.

In retrospect, I have some difficulty in seeing why this reaction caused me annoyance, though it did. In social matters, critics are an interim phenomenon. Given a little time, circumstances will prove you either right or wrong. Perhaps it was the obtuseness of the argument. To suggest that we cannot consider how we use our wealth until everyone or nearly everyone reaches a certain minimum is to say that such consideration should be postponed forever, for the seemingly decent minimum will rise along with the increase in wealth. And anyone who wants to postpone the discussion can do so by raising the minimum standard that must first be reached. But most important, to refuse to consider how we use our wealth is to fail to see why some people remain permanently poor. For underinvestment in education, housing, health, recreation, community decency and order are, as we have now come largely to agree, a prime cause of this deprivation. The critics were asking that we postpone consideration of the causes of poverty until no one was poor.[2]

Let me now turn to slightly less portentous matters.

---

[2] A variant was to point to the millions of needy people elsewhere in the world as the case for continuing to emphasize production. This argument was advanced, I believe, only by those who did not read the book. The book shows that wants are expanded by the very process that increases production. This being so, more production does not create a larger surplus over domestic need for dispatch to India or Bolivia and although output has increased, in most recent years it has, in fact, become progressively more difficult to spare product for the poorer countries.

VIII

I have been asked hundreds of times where I got the eventual title, *The Affluent Society*. And I have received no slight applause for inventing a phrase which, as it is said, has passed into the language. The truth is less grand. For a long while after I discarded "Why People Are Poor" as undescriptive of the whole book, I called it "The Opulent Society." Opulent has a greasy, unattractive sound. Presently I could stand it no longer. One morning in Switzerland, while seeking as all writers do to postpone the moment when the typewriter faces you and asks for intelligent response, I looked up the synonyms. The first was affluent. It is wrong to attribute to inventive genius what is properly explained by the possession of Webster's Collegiate Dictionary. I remember wondering if I could sell so dry a title to my publisher.

For a year or so before the book appeared, I found myself giving thoughtful consideration to its eventual reception. I had no high hopes; in the climate of the time, I feared it would be dismissed as another semi-socialist case for public spending and by my Keynesian friends as apostasy. Then in the autumn of 1957, the Soviets sent up the first Sputnik. No action was ever so admirably timed. Had I been younger and less formed in my political views, I would have been carried away by my gratitude and found a final resting place beneath the Kremlin Wall. I knew the book was home. A vastly less productive society had brought off a breathtaking and also, who could tell, very alarming achievement. It couldn't be because they had more wealth—more automobiles, more gasoline, more elegantly packaged food, or anything comparable in depilatories and deodorants. Surely they were using their more meager resources more purposefully. So, people would be asking, what of their education? What of their ability to concentrate their lesser scientific and engineering resources more effectively to their chosen ends? Could anyone now be sure that either the Benthamite or the Keynesian world had the answer? Certainly no one could say that it was because the socialist Soviets eschewed public spending.

In any case, the Sputnik meant we were in for one of those orgies of anguished soul-searching which are a recurrent and distinctive feature of our spirtual history. Whether they lead to action is uncertain but their immediate and incontrovertible effect is to cause people to read, or at least to buy, books. Except when dealing with his publisher, modesty combined with the deepest pessimism about the ability of people to appreciate his work is the only acceptable posture of an author. After the first Sputnik, I was able to sustain this pose only with effort. I expected, in fact, that the book would be a major success.

Once only was I mildly shaken. In the spring of 1958, as it was poised for publication, I accepted an invitation to lecture in Poland (and also Yugoslavia). Medicine, botany, even pediatrics are easy in these countries but economics is a sensitive subject. I was, I was told to my delight, the first economist with no avowed reputation as a communist or socialist to be asked to lecture in a communist country. I returned to London on the day of publication and, at the newsstand of the hotel, searched for American journals with reviews. *Time* magazine, in a manner of speaking, favored me. It had relegated its comment to the business pages: "vague essay with the air of worried dinner-table conversation" was the concluding line. The editors, had they known my reaction, would have been pleased. Perhaps the book could be dismissed. As I was so reflecting, I became aware, to my horror, that someone was reading the same review over, or by, my shoulder. It was John Steinbeck. His comment cheered me greatly. "Unless a reviewer has the courage to give you unqualified praise, I say ignore the bastard." Generally speaking, as I learned a little later by telephoning my wife, the reviewers had shown courage. On arriving in New York, I told my publisher it would be a success as these things are measured. He told me, gently, I was insane. No work on economics became a best seller. We bet the most expensive procurable dinner on the subject. I won. Despite the fact that I drank willingly in those days, I was amazed to learn how difficult it is to spend any really important money on a meal. Publishers rarely lose.

IX

The early chapters of this edition, the third, remain almost unchanged from the first. The later chapters where I apply these ideas to the issues of the time are much more extensively changed. Most of the issues, alas, are still relevant. But on some matters, there has been progress. Thus, when I wrote the book, the Cold War was being fought with undiluted enthusiasm; and it was urgently proclaimed that nothing counted so much in this combat as our ability to sustain a greater rate of increase in production than the Russians. "The ultimate survival of the free nations may well turn on their ability to develop their productive power. The Soviet leaders are counting heavily on the economic growth of the Soviet Union," my distinguished colleague, Professor Robert Richardson Bowie, then an Assistant Secretary of State, said in 1956 in a thoughtful articulation of established belief. The book attacked this doctrine. The affluent society increases its wants and therewith its consumption *pari passu* with its production. This consumption is not easily forgone in the event of war; it is more vulnerable to military attack than old-fashioned, less specialized production; the plant that supplies it is of little wartime utility; and in any case, these considerations apply to old-fashioned war, following a leisurely mobilization, and have nothing to do with the sudden and total obliteration of nuclear conflict. All of this now seems obvious. Perhaps my argument helped a little to make it so—I always felt that so brittle and vulnerable were the clichés associating military power with the rate of increase in Gross National Product that a single onslaught, sufficiently replete with ridicule, could destroy them. In any case, though I liked the chapter on The Illusion of National Security and miss it as a favorite child, I deleted it from the second edition.

In other instances, I have changed my mind or have had it changed. Thus, when I wrote this book, I did not think we were likely soon to develop public measures for stabilizing the wage and price spiral as an alternative to this source of inflation. And the notion of a guaranteed income as a way of breaking the nexus between production and income for those who could not find a role in production was not even a glimmer on the horizon. Now both are the subject of serious policy discussion. Since the second edition, wage and price control has been used, although under the auspices of the Nixon Administration and of men who did not believe in it save, perhaps, for getting by an election. In the first edition, I proposed that we be more tolerant of unemployment in order to take the pressure off wages and prices and thus prevent inflation. And I suggested that we make unemployment more tolerable and also self-limiting by a system of unemployment compensation, Cyclically Graduated Compensation—in which benefits increased as unemployment increased. This is an inferior alternative to what is now politically feasible and I have dropped it. The measures just mentioned reflected my feeling then and indeed before, that, inflation, no less than unemployment and depression, would be a problem of the modern affluent economy and one for which the solutions would be both less evident and less pleasant. Events since have amply supported my case and against, I can't help adding, the weight of the cautiously reputable economic opinion. However, I did not then see fully the reason for the severity of the inflation problem, one that is still far from appreciated. It arises, ultimately, from the unwillingness of large groups in the modern society to believe that they are meant to consume less. In past times it was accepted that there would be a hierarchy in consumption. Owners of property and recipients of profits should have the highest living standards; business executives would be next in line; these would then be followed in order by professional workers, teachers and civil servants, white-collar workers and blue-collar workers. Blacks and other minorities would be contentedly or hopelessly at the bottom.

But no longer. Increasingly and with increasing effect those at the bottom assert their belief that they are entitled to as much as those above. Consumption is losing its class stratification. One result is the persistent upward pressure of wage claims. Another is a stronger aggregate of demand for both public and private goods. Thus inflation; thus also a stronger pressure on the productive capacity of the affluent society than I earlier saw. It does not alter my point that this society manufactures or otherwise contrives the demand for the private goods by which it is sustained. It affirms the point that consumption is imitative in much of its origin. The problems of social balance between public and private goods become, if anything, more acute. So does the contrasting poverty. It does make the pressure on output a good deal more acute than I realized when I worked on the earlier editions.

In this edition, I have further revised what I modernized before. Still, every book belongs to its particular time as well as place, and that is true of this one. In taking out or changing what would strike the reader as obviously obsolete, I have not hoped or sought to leave the impression that it all was written in the bicentennial year of 1976 or even the year before. I could even wish that the reader might remember that much of this was put on paper a full two decades ago.

A great deal could be said by way of addition to what is argued in this book. That however, I have said elsewhere. For as I have told on other occasions, before I had finished writing *The Affluent Society,* I had come to the conclusion that I had written only a part of a larger book. Back of affluence were its causes—technology, a large use of capital heavily specialized to a particular product, a long gestation period in production and, withal, great specialization and vast organization. And from these comes the need to control or plan the environment in which organization functions. Beyond the ability to manage the market behavior of the affluent consumer here described was the need to make his market reaction reliable and thus to make him the instrument of the economic organizations that have been created to serve him. And beyond this are further questions. This economic system, by its nature, requires a large educational and scientific establishment. Will these people long be content with the rather mundane goal of ever-increasing affluence which the system espouses as the highest aim of man? Might there not one day be discontent with a society in which there is single-minded concentration or the goal of economic success? Might there not one day be suspicion of leadership and prestige that are so universally associated with economic achievement? Might not one wish for such a revolt? These were the questions, as I have said, to which *The Affluent Society* was as a window to a room. That room I inhabited for much of the next decade as I worked on *The New Industrial State* and then the final summary volume, *Economics and the Public Purpose.*

CHAPTER I

The Affluent Society

Wealth is not without its advantages and the case to the contrary, although it has often been made, has never proved widely persuasive. But, beyond doubt, wealth is the relentless enemy of understanding. The poor man has always a precise view of his problem and its remedy: he hasn't enough and he needs more. The rich man can assume or imagine a much greater variety of ills and he will be correspondingly less certain of their remedy. Also, until he learns to live with his wealth, he will have a well-observed tendency to put it to the wrong purposes or otherwise to make himself foolish.

As with individuals so with nations. And the experience of nations with well-being is exceedingly brief. Nearly all, throughout all history, have been very poor. The exception, almost insignificant in the whole span of human existence, has been the last few generations in the comparatively small corner of the world populated by Europeans. Here, and especially in the United States, there has been great and quite unprecedented affluence, which until now has been the accepted future.

The ideas by which the people of this favored part of the world interpret their existence, and in measure guide their behavior, were not forged in a world of wealth. These ideas were the product of a world in which poverty had always been man's normal lot, and any other state was in degree unimaginable. This poverty was not the elegant torture of the spirit which comes from contemplating another man's more spacious possessions. It was the unedifying mortification of the flesh—from hunger, sickness and cold. Those who might be freed temporarily from such burden could not know when it would strike again, for at best hunger yielded only perilously to privation. It is improbable that the poverty of

1

the masses of the people was made greatly more bearable by the fact that a very few—those upon whose movements nearly all recorded history centers—were very rich.

No one would wis hto argue that the ideas which interpreted this world of grim scarcity would serve equally well for the contemporary United States. Poverty was the all-pervasive fact of that world. Obviously it is not of ours. One would not expect that the preoccupations of a poverty-ridden world would be relevant in one where the ordinary individual has access to amenities—foods, entertainment, personal transportation, and plumbing—in which not even the rich rejoiced a century ago. So great has been the change that many of the desires of the individual are no longer even evident to him. They become so only as they are synthesized, elaborated and nutured by advertising and salesmanship, and these, in turn, have become among our most important and talented professions. Few people at the beginning of the nineteenth century needed an adman to tell them what they wanted.

It would be wrong to suggest that the economic ideas which once interpreted the world of mass poverty have made no adjustment to the world of affluence. There have many adjustments, including some that have gone unrecognized or have been poorly understood. But there has also been a remarkable resistance. And the total alteration in underlying circumstances has not been squarely faced. As a result, we are guided, in part, by ideas that are relevant to another world; and as a further result, we do many things that are necessary, some that are unwise, and a few that are insane. Some are a threat to affluence itself.

II

The foregoing tells the purpose of this book. The first task is to see the way our economic attitudes are rooted in the poverty, inequality and economic peril of the past. Then the partial and implicit accommodation to affluence is examined. The next task is to consider the devices and arguments, some elaborate, some meretricious, some in a degree dangerous, by which, in vital matters, we have managed to maintain an association with the older ideas which stemmed from a world where nearly all were poor. For no one should suppose that

2

there is anything convenient or agreeable about the assumption of affluence as an economic fact. On the contrary, it threatens the prestige and position of many important people. And it exposes many of us to the even greater horror of new thought. We face here the greatest of vested interests, those of the mind.

Finally, as we escape from the obsolete and contrived preoccupations associated with the assumption of poverty, we are able to see for the first time the new tasks and opportunities that are before us. This is not as reassuring as it sounds. One of the best ways of avoiding necessary and even urgent tasks is to seem to be busily employed on things that are already done.

Such is the purpose. But first there is some preparatory work. For we have not clung to obsolete and impalpable assumptions concerning our society purely as the result of obtuseness and ignorance. Powerful as these influences may be, they are not that strong. On the contrary, in matters of social discussion, there are active and pervasive influences which bind us to the past and which, on occasion, even cause us to try to recover the moribund. We must first be aware of our captivity by these forces if we are later to engineer an escape. That is the task of the next chapter.

III

No one will think this an angry book. Some may think it lacking in that beguiling modesty which is so much in fashion in social comment. The reader will soon discover that I think very little of certain of the central ideas of economics. But I do think a great deal of the men who originated these ideas. The shortcomings of economics are not original error but uncorrected obsolescence. The obsolescence has occurred because what is convenient has become sacrosanct. Anyone who attacks such ideas must seem to be a trifle self-confident and even aggressive. Yet I trust that judgments will not be too hasty. The man who makes his entry by leaning against an infirm door gets an unjustified reputation for violence. Something is to be attributed to the poor state of the door.

Originality is something that is easily exaggerated, especially by authors contemplating their own work. There are few thoughts in this essay, or so I would imagine, which have not occurred to other economists. The reaction of many will be to welcome the elaboration of ideas which evidence has already brought them. But these are also days in which even the mildly critical individual is likely to seem like a lion in contrast with the general mood. These are the days when men of all social disciplines and all political faiths seek the comfortable and the accepted; when the man of controversy is looked upon as a disturbing influence; when originality is taken to be a mark of instability; and when, in minor modification of the scriptural parable, the bland lead the bland. Those who esteem this world will not enjoy this essay. Perhaps they should return it to the shelf unread. For there are negative thoughts here, and they cannot but strike an uncouth note in a world of positive thinking.

IV

No student of social matters in these days can escape feeling how precarious is the existence of that with which he deals. Western man has escaped for the moment the poverty which was for so long his all-embracing fate. The unearthly light of a handful of nuclear explosions would signal his return to utter deprivation if, indeed, he survived at all. I venture to think that the ideas here offered bear on our chances for escape from this fate. Illusion is a comprehensive ill. The rich man who deludes himself into behaving like a mendicant may conserve his fortune although he will not be very happy. The affluent country which conducts its affairs in accordance with rules of another and poorer age also forgoes opportunities. And in misunderstanding itself, it will, in any time of difficulty, implacably prescribe for itself the wrong remedies. This this reader will discover is, to a disturbing degree, our present tendency.

Yet it would be a mistake to be too gravely depressed. The problems of an affluent world, which does not understand itself, may be serious, and they can needlessly threaten the affluence itself. But they are not likely to be as serious as those of a poor world where the simple exigencies of poverty preclude the luxury of misunderstanding but where, also and alas, no solutions are to be had.

CHAPTER II

The Concept
of the Conventional Wisdom

The first requirement for an understanding of contemporary economic and social life is a clear view of the relation between events and the ideas which interpret them. For each of these has a life of its own and, much as it may seem a contradiction in terms, each is capable for a considerable period of pursuing an independent course.

The reason is not difficult to discover. Economic like other social life does not conform to a simple and coherent pattern. On the contrary, it often seems incoherent, inchoate and intellectually frustrating. But one must have an explanation or interpretation of economic behavior. Neither man's curiosity nor his inherent ego allows him to remain contentedly oblivious to anything that is so close to his life.

Because economic and social phenomena are so forbidding, or at least so seem, and because they yield few hard tests of what exists and what does not, they afford to the individual a luxury not given by physical phenomena. Within a considerable range, he is permitted to believe what he pleases. He may hold whatever view of this world he finds most agreeable or otherwise to his taste.

As a consequence, in the interpretation of all social life, there is a persistent and never-ending competition between what is right and what is merely acceptable. In this competition, while a strategic advantage lies with what exists, all tactical advantage is with the acceptable. Audiences of all kinds most applaud what they like best. And in social comment, the test of audience approval, far more than the test of truth, comes to influence comment. The speaker or writer who addresses his audience with the proclaimed intent of telling the hard, shocking facts invariably goes on to expound what the audience most wants to hear.

Just as truth ultimately serves to create a consensus, so in the short run does acceptability. Ideas come to be organized around what the community as a whole or particular audiences find acceptable. And as the laboratory workers devotes himself to discovering scientific verities, so the ghost writer and the public relations man concern themselves with identifying the acceptable. If their clients are rewarded with applause, these artisans are deemed qualified in their craft. If not, they have failed. By sampling audience reaction in advance, or by pretesting speeches, articles and other communications, the risk of failure can now be greatly minimized.

Numerous factors contribute to acceptability of ideas. To a very large extent, of course, we associate truth with convenience—with what most closely accords with self-interest and personal well-being or promises best to avoid awkward effort or unwelcome dislocation of life. We also find highly acceptable what contributes most to self-esteem. Speakers before the United States Chamber of Commerce rarely denigrate the businessman as an economic force. Those who appear before the AFL-CIO are prone to identify social progress with a strong trade union movement. But perhaps most important of all, people approve most of what they best understand. As just noted, economic and social behavior are complex, and to comprehend their character is mentally tiring. Therefore we adhere, as though to a raft, to those ideas which represent our understanding. This is a prime manifestation of vested interest. For a vested interest in understanding is more preciously guarded than any other treasure. It is why men react, not infrequently with something akin to religious passion, to the defense of what they have so laboriously learned. Familiarity may breed contempt in some areas of human behavior, but in the field of social ideas it is the touchstone of acceptability.

Because familiarity is such an important test of acceptability, the acceptable ideas have great stability. They are highly predictable. It will be convenient to have a name for the ideas which are esteemed at any time for their acceptability, and it should be a term that emphasizes this predictability. I shall refer to these ideas henceforth as the conventional wisdom.

II

The conventional wisdom is not the property of any political group. On a great many modern social issues, as we shall see in the course of this essay, the consensus is exceedingly broad. Nothing much divides those who are liberals by common political designation from those who are conservatives. The test of what is acceptable is much the same for both. On some questions, however, ideas must be accommodated to the political preferences of the particular audience. The tendency to make this adjustment, either deliberately or more often unconsciously, is not greatly different for different political groups. The conservative is led by disposition, not unmixed with pecuniary self-interest, to adhere to the familiar and the established. These underlie his test of acceptability. But the liberal brings moral fervor and passion, even a sense of righteousness, to the ideas with which he is most familiar. While the ideas he cherishes are different from those of the conservative, he will be no less emphatic in making familarity a test of acceptability. Deviation in the form of originality is condemned as faithlessness or backsliding. A "good" liberal or a "tried and true" liberal or a "true blue" liberal is one who is adequately predictable. This means that he forswears any serious striving toward originality. In both the United States and Britain, in recent times, liberals and their British counterparts of the left have proclaimed themselves in search of new ideas. To proclaim the need for new ideas has served, in some measure, as a substitute for them. The politician who unwisely takes this proclaimed need seriously and urges something new will often find himself in serious trouble. To have done this may well have been the misfortune of George McGovern in 1972.

We may, as necessary, speak of the conventional wisdom of conservatives or the conventional wisdom of liberals.

The conventional wisdom is also articulated on all levels of sophistication. At the highest levels of social science scholarship, some novelty of formulation or statement is not resisted. On the contrary, considerable store is set by the device of putting an old truth in a new form, and minor heresies are much cherished. And the very vigor of minor debate makes it possible to exclude as irrelevant, and without seeming to be unscientific or parochial, any challenge to the framework itself. Moreover, with time and aided by the debate, the accepted ideas become increasingly elaborate. They have a large literature, even a mystique. The defenders are able to say that the challengers of the conventional wisdom have not mastered their intricacies. Indeed, these ideas can be appreciated only by a stable, orthodox and patient man—in brief, by someone who closely resembles the man of conventional wisdom. The conventional wisdom having been made more or less identical with sound scholarship, its position is virtually impregnable. The skeptic is disqualified by his very tendency to go brashly from the old to the new. Were he a sound scholar, he would remain with the conventional wisdom.

At the same time, in the higher levels of the conventional wisdom, originality remains highly acceptable in the abstract. Here again the conventional wisdom makes vigorous advocacy of originality a substitute for originality itself.

III

As noted, the hallmark of the conventional wisdom is acceptability. It has the approval of those to whom it is addressed. There are many reasons why people like to hear articulated that which they approve. It serves the ego: the individual has the satisfaction of knowing that other and more famous people share his conclusions. To hear what he believes is also a source of reassurance. The individual knows that he is supported in his thoughts—that he has not been left behind and alone. Further, to hear what one approves serves the evangelizing instinct. It means that others are also hearing and are thereby in process being persuaded.

In some measure, the articulation of the conventional wisdom is a religious rite. It is an act of affirmation like reading aloud from the Scriptures or going to church. The business executive listening to a luncheon address on the immutable virtues of free enterprise is already persuaded, and so are his fellow listeners, and all are secure in their convictions. Indeed, although a display of rapt attention is required, the executive may not feel it necessary to listen. But he does placate the gods by participating in the ritual. Having been present, maintained attention, and having applauded, he can depart feeling that the economic system is a little more secure. Scholars gather in scholarly assemblages to hear in elegant statement what all have heard before. Again, it is not a negligible rite, for its purpose is not to convey knowledge but to beatify learning and the learned.

With so extensive a demand, it follows that a very large part of our social comment—and nearly all that is well regarded—is devoted at any time to articulating the conventional wisdom. To some extent, this has been professionalized. Individuals, most notably the great television and radio commentators, make a profession of knowing and saying with elegance and unction what their audience will find most acceptable. But, in general, the articulation of the conventional wisdom is a prerogative of academic, public or business position. Thus, any individual, on being elected president of a college or university, automatically wins the right to enunciate the conventional wisdom. It is one of the rewards of high academic rank, although such rank itself is a reward for expounding the conventional wisdom at a properly sophisticated level.

The high public official is expected, and indeed is to some extent required, to expound the conventional wisdom. His, in many respects, is the purest case. Before assuming office, he ordinarily commands little attention. But on taking up his position, he is immediately assumed to be gifted with deep insights. He does not, except in the rarest instances, write his own speeches or articles; and these are planned, drafted and scrupulously examined to ensure their acceptability. The application of any other test, e.g., their effectiveness as a simple description of the economic or political reality, would be regarded as eccentric in the extreme.

Finally, the expounding of the conventional wisdom is the prerogative of business success. The head of almost any large corporation—the United States Steel Corporation, General Motors, the Radio Corporation of America—is entitled to do so. And he is privileged to speak not only on business policy and economics but also on the role of government in the society, the foundations of foreign policy, and the nature of a liberal education. In recent years, it has been urged that to expound the conventional wisdom is not only the privilege but also the obligation of the businessman. "I am convinced that businessmen must write as well as speak, in order that we may bring to people everywhere the exciting and confident message of our faith in the free enterprise way of life . . . What a change would come in this struggle for men's minds if suddenly there would pour out from the world of American business a torrent of intelligent, forward-looking thinking."[1]

IV

The enemy of the conventional wisdom is not ideas but the march of events. As I have noted, the conventional wisdom accommodates itself not to the world that it is meant to interpret, but to the audience's view of the world. Since the latter remains with the comfortable and the familiar, while the world moves on, the conventional wisdom is always in danger of obsolescence. This is not immediately fatal. The fatal blow to the conventional wisdom comes when the conventional ideas fail signally to deal with some contingency to which obsolescence has made them palpably inapplicable. This, sooner or later, must be the fate of ideas which have lost their relation to the world. At this stage, the irrelevance will often be dramatized by some individual. To him will accrue the credit for overthrowing the conventional wisdom and for installing the new ideas. In fact, he will have only crystallized in words what the events have made clear, although this function is not a minor one. Meanwhile, like the Old Guard, the conventional wisdom dies but does not surrender. Society with intransigent cruelty may transfer its exponents from the category of wise man to that of old fogy or even suffed shirt.

This sequence can be illustrated from scores of examples, ancient and modern. For decades prior to 1776, men had been catching the vision of the liberal state. Traders and merchants in England and in the adjacent Low Countries, and in the American colonies, had already learned that they were served best by a minimum of government restriction

[1]Clarence B. Randall, *A Creed for Free Enterprise* (Boston: Atlantic-Little, Brown, 1952), pp. 3, 5.

rather than, as in the conventional wisdom, by a maximum of government guidance and protection. It had become plain, in turn, that liberal trade and commerce, not the accumulation of bullion, as the conventional wisdom held, was the modern source of national power. Men of irresponsible originality had made the point. Voltaire had observed that "It is only because the English have become merchants and traders that London has surpassed Paris in extent and in the number of its citizens; that the English can place 200 warships on the sea and subsidize allies."[2] These views were finally crystallized by Adam Smith in the year of American independence. *The Wealth of Nations,* however, continued to be viewed with discontent and alarm by the men of the older wisdom. In the funeral elegy for Alexander Hamilton in 1804, James Kent complimented his deceased friend on having resisted the "fuzzy philosophy" of Smith. For another generation or more, in all western countries, there would be solemn warnings that the notion of a liberal society was a reckless idea.

Through the nineteenth century, liberalism in its classical meaning having become the conventional wisdom, there were solemn warnings of the irreparable damage that would be done by Factory Acts, trade unions, social insurance and other social legislation. Liberalism was a fabric which could not be raveled without being rent. Yet the desire for protection and security and some measure of equality in bargaining power would not down. In the end, it became a fact with which the conventional wisdom could not deal. The Webbs, Lloyd George, La Follette, Roosevelt, Beveridge and others crystallized the acceptance of the new fact. The result is what we call the welfare state. The conventional wisdom now holds that these measures softened and civilized capitalism and made it tenable. There have never ceased to be warnings that the break with classical liberalism was fatal.

Another interesting instance of the impact of circumstance on the conventional wisdom was that of the balanced budget in times of depression. Almost from the beginning of organized government, the balanced budget or its equivalent has been the *sine qua non* of sound and sensible management

---

[2]"Tenth Philosophical Letter." Quoted by Henri Sée, *Modern Capitalism* (New York: Adelphi, 1928), p. 87.

of the public purse. The spendthrift tendencies of princes and republics alike were curbed by the rule that they must unfailingly take in as much money as they paid out. The consequences of violating this rule had always been unhappy in the long run and not infrequently in the short. Anciently it was the practice of princes to cover the deficit by clipping or debasing the coins and spending the metal so saved. The result invariably was to raise prices and lower national self-esteem. In modern times, the issue of paper money or government borrowing from the banks had led to the same results. In consequence, the conventional wisdom had emphasized strongly the importance of an annually balanced budget.

But meanwhile the underlying reality had gradually changed. The rule requiring a balanced budget was designed for governments that were inherently or recurrently irresponsible on fiscal matters. Until the last century, there had been no other. Then in the United States, England and the British Commonwealth, and Europe, governments began to calculate the fiscal consequences of their actions. Safety no longer depended on confining them within arbitrary rules.

At about the same time, there appeared the phenomenon of the truly devastating depression. In such a depression, men, plant and materials were unemployed en masse; the extra demand from the extra spending induced by the deficit— the counterpart of the extra metal made available from the clipped coinage—did not raise prices uniquely. Rather, it mostly returned idle men and plant to work. The effect, as it were, was horizontally on production rather than vertically on prices. And such price increases as did occur were far from being an unmitigated misfortune; on the contrary, they retrieved a previous, painful decline.

The conventional wisdom continued to emphasize the balanced budget. Audiences continued to respond to the warnings of the disaster which would befall were this rule not respected. The shattering circumstance was the Great Depression. This led in the United States to a severe reduction in the revenues of the federal government; it also brought pressure for a variety of relief and welfare expenditures. A balanced budget meant increasing tax rates and reducing public expenditure. View in retrospect, it would be hard to imagine a better design for reducing both the private and the public demand for goods, aggravating deflation, increasing unemployment, and adding to the general suffering. In the conventional wisdom, nonetheless, the balanced budget remained of paramount importance. President Hoover in the early thirties called it an "absolute necessity," "the most essential factor to economic recovery," "the imperative and immediate step," "indispensable," "the first necessity of the Nation," and "the foundation of all public and private financial stability."[8] Economists and professional observers of public affairs agreed almost without exception. Almost everyone called upon for advice in the early years of the depression was impelled by the conventional wisdom to offer proposals designed to make things worse. The consensus embraced both liberals and conservatives. Franklin D. Roosevelt was also elected in 1932 with a strong commitment to reduced expenditures and a balanced budget. In his speech accepting the Democratic nomination in 1932, he said, "Revenue must cover expenditures by one means or another. Any government, like any family, can for a year spend a little more than it earns. But you and I know that a continuation of that habit means the poorhouse." One of the early acts of his Administration was an economy drive which included a horizontal slash in public pay. Mr. Lewis W. Douglas, through a distinguished life a notable exemplar of the conventional wisdom, made the quest for a balanced budget into a personal crusade and ultimately broke with the Administration on the issue.

In fact, circumstances had already triumphed over the conventional wisdom. By the second year of the Hoover Administration, the budget was irretrievably out of balance. In the fiscal year ending in 1932, receipts were much less than half of spending. The budget was never balanced during the depression. But not until 1936 did both the necessities and advantages of this course begin to triumph in the field of ideas. In that year, John Maynard Keynes launched his formal assault in *The General Theory of Employment Interest and Money*. Thereafter, the conventional insistence on the balanced budget under all circumstances and at all levels of

---

[8] Arthur M. Schlesinger, Jr., *The Crisis of the Old Order* (Boston: Houghton Mifflin, 1956), p. 232.

economic activity was in retreat. Keynes, as we shall see presently, was on his way to being the new fountainhead of conventional wisdom. By the late sixties a Republican president would proclaim himself a Keynesian. It would be an article of conventional faith that the Keynesian remedies, when put in reverse, would be a cure for inflation, a faith that circumstances would soon be undermining.

V

In the following pages, there will be frequent occasion to advert to the conventional wisdom—to the structure of ideas that is based on acceptability—and to those who articulate it. These references must not be thought to have a wholly invidious connotation. (The warning is necessary because, as noted, we set great ostensible score by intellectual innovation though in fact we resist it. Hence, though we value the rigorous adherence to conventional ideas, we never acclaim it.) Few men are unuseful and the man of conventional wisdom is not. Every society must be protected from a too facile flow of thought. In the field of social comment, a great stream of intellectual novelties, if all were taken seriously, would be disastrous. Men would be swayed to this action or that; economic and political life would be erratic and rudderless. In the communist countries, stability of ideas and social purpose is achieved by formal adherence to an officially proclaimed doctrine. Deviation is stigmatized as "incorrect." In our society, a similar stability is enforced far more informally by conventional wisdom. Ideas need to be tested by their ability, in combination with events, to overcome inertia and resistance. This inertia and resistance the conventional wisdom provides.

Nor is it to be supposed that the man of conventional wisdom is an object of pity. Apart from his socially useful role, he has come to good terms with life. He can think of himself with justice as socially elect, for society in fact accords him the applause which his ideas are so arranged as to evoke. Secure in this applause, he is well armed against the annoyance of dissent. His bargain is to exchange a strong and even lofty position in the present for a weak one in the future. In the present, he is questioned with respect, if not at great length, by Congressional Committees; he walks near the head of the academic processions; he appears on symposia; he is a respected figure at the Council on Foreign Relations; he is hailed at testimonial banquets. He risks being devastated by hostile events. But by then he may be dead. Only posterity is unkind to the man of conventional wisdom, and all posterity does is bury him in a blanket of neglect. However, somewhat more serious issues are at stake.

VI

No society seems ever to have succumbed to boredom. Man has developed an obvious capacity for surviving the pompous reiteration of the commonplace. The conventional wisdom protects the community in social thought and action; in the immediately following chapters, we shall see how great this continuity is. But there are also grave drawbacks and even dangers in a system of thought which by its very nature and design avoids accommodation to circumstances until change is dramatically forced upon it. In large areas of economic affairs, the march of events—above all, the increase in our wealth and popular well-being—has again left the conventional wisdom sadly obsolete. It may have become inimical to our happiness. It has come to have a bearing on the large questions of civilized survival. So while it would be much more pleasant (and also vastly more profitable) to articulate the conventional wisdom, this book involves the normally unfruitful effort of an attack upon it. I am not wholly barren of hope, for circumstances have been dealing with the conventional wisdom a new series of heavy blows. It is only after such damage has been done, as we have seen, that ideas have their opportunity.

Keynes, in his most famous observation, noted that we are ruled by ideas and by very little else. In the immediate sense, this is true. And he was right in attributing importance to ideas as opposed to the simple influence of pecuniary vested interest. But the rule of ideas is only powerful in a world that does not change. Ideas are inherently conservative. They yield not to the attack of other ideas but, as I may note once more, to the massive onslaught of circumstance with which they cannot contend.

CHAPTER III

Economics and the Tradition of Despair

Economics, not entirely by accident, became a subject of serious study at an important turning point in the history of western man. This was when the wealth of national communities began, for the first time, to show a steady and persistent improvement. This change, which in advanced countries like England and Holland came some time in the eighteenth century, must be counted one of the momentous events in the history of the world. "From the earliest times of which we have record—back, say, to two thousand years before Christ—down to the beginning of the eighteenth century, there was no very great change in the standard of living of the average man living in the civilized centers of the earth. Ups and downs certainly. Visitations of plague, famine and war. Golden intervals. But no progressive violent change."[1]

Some of the intervals had been extended. For something over a century in late medieval England—from perhaps 1380 ot 1510—workers or at any rate skilled artisans seem to have enjoyed a period of considerable prosperity. But as always before, the good times came to an end; by the close of the sixteenth century, the purchasing power of an artisan's wage had fallen by more than half. It remained low through the disorders of the Civil War, and progress was uncertain for a long time thereafter. Then early in the last century these wages began the rise which, with slight interruption, has since continued.[2]

[1] J. M. Keynes, "Economic Possibilities for Our Grandchildren," *Essays in Persuasion* (London: Macmillan, 1931), p. 360.
[2] E. H. Phelps Brown and Sheila V. Hopkins, "Seven Centuries of the Prices of Consumables, Compared with Builders' Wage Rates." *Economica*, New Series, Vol. XXIII, No. 92 (November 1956).

There were reasons for the age-old stagnation as there were also reasons for the change. The productivity of an economy based on agriculture and household industry had inherent limits. And before the appearance of the national state, any surplus that might be accumulated was subject to the spoliation of armed marauders and might, in fact, be what would attract their attention.

In the latter part of the eighteenth century, the factory began to replace the household at an accelerating rate as the center of productive activity. Output per man-hour was no longer limited by the simple technology and the small capital of the household and by the need to rely mostly on human or animal power. The new national states had begun to make effective the guarantee of internal order. Armies would still cross national frontiers and with considerable capacity for doing damage where they fought and trod. But the economic consequences of national armies in the age of nationalism have been almost infinitely small as compared with the damage wrought by feudal, marauding or crusading armies in the centuries before. Within a few years following the two World Wars, the standard of living of Western Europe countries, even those that were defeated and devastated, was higher than ever before. The economic life of the Middle East never recovered from the imaginative destruction, pillage and massacre of Genghis Khan. In contrast with recent experience, Germany required a hundred years to recoup the destruction and disorganization of the Thirty Years' War. However, a future national war using nuclear weapons would assuredly bring destruction abreast of the ancient art.

But it would have been surprising if, as the conditions of life gradually improved in the eighteenth and nineteenth centuries, man had quickly forsaken the lessons of all the preceding ages and supposed this improvement to be permanent. This was all the more improbable, for, in the early years of the Industrial Revolution, the rewards of increased efficiency were distributed very unequally. It was the wealth of the new entrepreneurs, not that of their workmen which was everywhere celebrated. Those who owned the new factories, or the raw materials or railroads or banks that served them, lived in the mansions by which the nineteenth century is still remembered. Their workers lived in dark and

17

noisome hovels, crowded on dirty and unpaved streets along which missionaries and social reformers ventured with some sense of their own courage. And in the factories themselves, the old and the very young worked from early to late and for a pittance. In England, in the first half of the nineteenth century, both total production and output per person were rising rapidly. The number of people of means was increasing. So, too, as the mid-century approached, were real wages. But the improvement in the position of the masses were far less evident than the increase in industrial and mercantile wealth. If the poor were becoming less poor, this change was slight as compared with the growing contrast between the rich and the poor.

Economic ideas began to take their modern form in the late eighteenth and early nineteenth centuries. It was against this background of centuries-old stagnation relieved now by increasing wealth, but wealth not of the many but the few, that they were first worked out and offered. Economists would indeed have been indifferent to both history and environment had they not taken the privation and economic desolation of the masses for granted. In economics, misfortune and failure were normal. Success, at least for more than the favored few, was what had to be explained. Enduring success was at odds with all history and could not be expected. This was the legacy of circumstances to ideas. As we shall see, it has enjoyed a remarkable vitality.

II

In the history of economic thought, Adam Smith (1723–1790), the first great figure in the central economic tradition,[3] is counted a hopeful figure. In an important sense, he was. His vision was of an advancing national community not a

[3]I have used the phrase "central tradition" to denote the main current of ideas in descent from Smith. The more common reference to the "classical tradition" is ruled out by a difference of opinion, in my view, a rather futile one, as to whether classical economics should or should not be considered to have ended with John Stuart Mill and J. E. Cairnes. Another possible reference is to the orthodox tradition. But this, by implication, excludes those like Keynes who, though working in the same current of ideas, have taken sharp issue with accepted conclusions.

stagnant or declining one. His title, *An Inquiry into the Nature and Causes of the Wealth of Nations,* had an obvious overtone of opulence and well-being. He offered an all but certain formula for economic progress. This was the liberal economic society in which regulation was by competition and the market and not by the state, and in which each man, thrown on his own resources, labored effectively for the enrichment of the society.

But it was of aggregate wealth that Smith spoke. He had little hope that the distribution between merchants, manufacturers and landlords on the one hand, and the working masses on the other, would be such as much to benefit the latter. Smith regarded this distribution as depending in the first instance on relative bargaining strength. And he did not believe it difficult "to foresee which of the two parties must upon all ordinary occasions have the advantage in the dispute." In an admirably succinct comment on the balance of eighteenth-century economic power, he added: "We have no acts of Parliament against combining to lower the price of work; but many against combining to raise it."[4] So in the normal course of events, the income of the working masses would be pressed down and down. There was a floor below which they would not fall. "A man must always live by his work, and his wages must at least be sufficient to maintain him. They must even upon most occasions be somewhat more; otherwise it would be impossible for him to bring up a family, and the race of such workmen could not last beyond the first generation."[5]

But this obviously was not much. On the contrary, although Adam Smith is rarely identified with the idea, this was one of the beginnings of perhaps the most influential and certainly the most despairing dictum in the history of social comment, the notion that income of the masses of the people—all who in one way or another worked for a living and whether in industry or agriculture—could not for very long rise very far above the minimum level necessary for the survival of the race. It is the immortal iron law which, as

[4]*Wealth of Nations,* Ch. VIII. (There are so many editions of this famous work that it seems idle to cite the pages of the particular edition one happens to use.)
[5]*Wealth of Nations,* Ch. VIII.

19

stiffened by Ricardo and refashioned by Marx, became the chief weapon in the eventual ideological assault on capitalism.

Smith was not categorical about the iron law—he was categorical about almost nothing, and ever since, economists have always been at their best when they adhered to his example. Thus, he conceded that a scarcity of workers might keep wages above the subsistence level for an indefinite time. Under conditions of rapid economic growth, wages would also rise. Growth was much more important than wealth *per se* in its effect on wages. "It is not the actual greatness of national wealth, but its continual increase, which occasions a rise in the wages of labor. . . . England is certainly, in the present times, a much richer country than any part of North America. The wages of labor, however, are much higher in North America than in any part of England."[6]

III

Smith's two great successors in the central tradition were David Ricardo (1772–1823) and Thomas Robert Malthus (1766–1834). With Adam Smith, they were the founding trinity of economics, at least as the subject is known in the English-speaking countries. As the man who first gave economics its modern structure—who looked at the factors determining prices, rents, wages and profits with a sense of system that has served economists ever since—Ricardo has a special claim to have bent the twig. Marxians and non-Marxians are equally in his debt.

With Ricardo and Malthus, the notion of massive privation and great inequality became a basic premise. These conclusions were never wholly unqualified. But the qualifications were only qualifications. It was to Ricardo and Malthus that Carlyle alluded when he spoke in 1850 of the "Respectable Professors of the Dismal Science" and gave to economics a nature that it has never quite escaped because it was never quite undeserved.

Of Malthus, it is necessary to say only a word. Through

[6]*Wealth of Nations*, Ch. VIII. Smith observes that this was written in 1773 before "the commencement of the late disturbances," meaning the American Revolution.

the nineteenth century and to our own day, he has been intimately and all but exclusively identified with his *Essay on Population*. Though he had other and important things to say on economics which have been the subject of a latter-day rediscovery, it is for his views on population that he will be always known.

The number of people who can live in the world is obviously limited by the number that can be fed. Any increase in the supply of food would bring, in Malthus' view, an increase in the number of people to consume it. Nothing but stark need limits the numbers who are propagated and who endure. As a result, men will forever live on the verge of starvation. In the later editions of the *Essay*, Malthus hedged somewhat; the increase in response to a surplus over subsistence might be tempered by "moral restraint" and also, somewhat more ambiguously, by "vice." In other words, people might indefinitely protect their standard of living at a level above subsistence, and this would become all the more likely once both restraint and vice were abetted by effective contraceptive techniques. But as also with Ricardo, Malthus' qualifications were lost in the sweep of his central proposition. This was the inevitability of mass poverty. There was also the considerable fact that for a large part of the world, the central proposition was valid and the qualifications were unimportant. So it was and so it remains in much of Asia. Malthus, it may be noted, was professor of political economy in Haileybury College, an institution maintained by the East India Company for training in India.

Since most men had always been poor, it is hardly surprising that Malthus was, on the whole, unperturbed by his conclusions and that he did not feel called upon to propose any remedy. (He confined himself to urging the postponement of marriage and to recommending that there be incorporated into the marriage a warning that the husband and not the state would be responsible for the children of the union so that if these were excessive, the parents could expect to be punished by want.) "The note of gloom and pessismism which distinguished so much of the economic doctrine of the nineteenth century is in no small measure the legacy of Malthus."[7]

[7]Alexander Gray, *The Development of Economic Doctrine* (London: Longmans, Green, 1931), p. 163.

IV

Both Adam Smith and Malthus had an instinct for national aggregates—for the forces which acted to enrich the nation. While Malthus was concerned with showing how increased national wealth might be used up in the explosive impulse to procreate, neither was centrally concerned with how different individuals and classes might share in what the economy produced. This to David Ricardo was of primary interest. What were the laws which governed the distribution of product or income between the landlords, entrepreneurs and workers who had claim to it? "Political Economy you think is an enquiry into the nature and causes of wealth—I think it should rather be called an enquiry into the laws which determine the division of the produce of industry amongst the classes who concur in its formation."[8] These laws, as Ricardo formulated them, worked with ferocious inequality.

Like Malthus, Ricardo regarded population as a dependent variable—it "regulates itself by the funds which are to employ it, and therefore always increases or diminishes with the increase or diminution of capital."[9] Advancing wealth and productivity thus bring more people; but they do not bring more land from which to feed these people. As a result, those who own land are able to command an ever greater return, given its quality, for what is an increasingly scarce resource. Meanwhile, in Ricardo's view, profits and wages were in flat conflict for the rest of the product. An increase in profits, other things being equal, meant a reduction in wages; an increase in wages must always come out of profits. "Every rise of profits," on the other hand, "is favourable to the accumulation of capital, and to the further increase of population, and therefore would, in all probability, ultimately lead to an increase in rent."[10] The effect of these compact relationships will be clear. If the country is to have increasing capital and product, profits must be good. But then as product expands,

[8]Letter to Malthus, October 9, 1820. In *The Works and Correspondence of David Ricardo*, ed. by Piero Sraffa (Cambridge University Press, 1951), Vol. VIII, p. 278.
[9]Letter to Malthus, Vol. I, p. 78.
[10]Letter to Malthus, Vol. I, p. 411.

the population will increase. The food requirements of the population will press on the available land supply and force up rents to the advantage of the landowner. In other words, capitalists must prosper if there is to be progress and landlords cannot help reaping its fruits. The victims of this inescapable misfortune are the people at large. Ricardo summarized that prospect in, perhaps, the most quoted passage in economic literature: "Labour, like all other things which are purchased and sold, and which may be increased or diminished in quantity, has its natural and its market price. The natural price of labour is that price which is necessary to enable the labourers, one with another, to subsist and perpetuate their race, without either increase or diminution."[11]

This was the iron law of wages. As with Smith (and Malthus on population), Ricardo followed the proposition with qualifications. In an "improving" society, the market wage might be above the natural wage for an indefinite period and were Ricardo still alive, he could show with little difficulty that the conditions necessary for the rule of the iron law have been in abeyance ever since the nineteenth day of April, 1817, when *On the Principles of Political Economy and Taxation* was published. But although the truth rarely overtakes falsehood, it has winged feet as compared with a qualification in pursuit of a bold proposition. The iron law, in its uncompromised clarity, became part of the intellectual capital of the world.

Moreover, as with Mauthus, nothing could be done about it. Ricardo brought his analysis to a close with the unbending observation that "These then are the laws by which wages are regulated, and by which the happiness [a word to be duly noted] of far the greatest part of every community is governed. Like all other contracts, wages should be left to the fair and free competition of the market, and should never be controlled by the interference of the legislature."[12] Nor may anyone be blamed. On a number of occasions, Ricardo complained that Malthus was unfairly accusing him of being hostile to landlords—"one would suppose from his language

[11]Letter to Malthus, Vol. I, p. 93.
[12]Letter to Malthus, Vol. I, p. 105.

that I considered them enemies of the state."[13] The landlords were merely the passive and natural beneficiaries of their great good fortune. This was the nature of things. Such was the Ricardian legacy.

There were many contradictions and ambiguities in Adam Smith. There were also flaws in the Ricardian logic as it applied to the Ricardian world. His treatment of capital and profits left much to be desired. And he preoccupied himself with land at almost the point in history when, because of the opening of a new world, it had begun to lose its ancient preoccupying importance. Yet is is hard to think that economists ever came much closer to interpreting the world in which they lived than did Smith, Ricardo and Malthus. None was committed to preconceived doctrine. They had broken decisively with the conventional wisdom of the traditionalist and mercantilist society. They had no public opinion to appease. The result was a formidable interpretation of, and prescription for, the world as they found it.

In the world that had for so long been so poor, nothing was so important as to win an increase in wealth. The prescription—to free men from the restraints and protection of feudal and mercantilist society and put them on their own—was sound, for it was already proving itself. This was not a compassionate world. Many suffered and many were destroyed under the harsh and unpredictable rule of competition and the market. But many had always perished for one reason or another. Now some were flourishing. This was what counted. One looked not at the peril and misfortune, for there had always been peril and misfortune, but at the opportunity. In any case, nothing could be done about the inequality, for it was not rooted in mutable social institutions but in biology. This was fortunate, for the state was excluded from intervention by its prior commitment to freedom of enterprise.

Remarkably little that concerned contemporary economic society was left unbuttoned. It is hardly surprisingly that a system seemingly so complete and practical and so subject to test against the realities of the world made an indelible dent on men's minds.

[13]Letter to Malthus, Vol. II, p. 117.

V

For thirty years following the death of Ricardo, the development of economics continued firmly in the tradition he had established. Lesser men, together with the conscientious and immeasurably learned John Stuart Mill, refined, developed and organized the ideas. Their thoughts remained centered on the liberal economic society—that in which economic life was regulated by the market and not by the state. On the continent, men did talk about socialism but in England and in the Anglo-Saxon tradition, they took the market very nearly for granted.

Then, at mid-century, the economic ideas in descent from Ricardo came to the great divide. The central tradition continued in its course. It continued to provide the skeletal framework for economic ideas down to our own day. In so doing, it gave them system and continuity and went far to make economic life comprehensible. But now, branching off to the left but with a common debt to Ricardo, was the revolutionary tradition of Karl Marx. Henceforth, in shaping attitudes toward economic life, it was both a massive competitor of, and a powerful influence on, the central tradition.

The purpose of these chapters is not to trace the evolution of the individual ideas. That is the task of other volumes and even more of other authors. Rather, it is to see what economics assumed in its origins about the ordinary individual and his fate. As between the early Ricardian world and that of Marx, there was in this respect no difference. For both, the prospect, given the uninterrupted working out of the underlying forces, combined peril with hopelessness. The difference was that Ricardo and his immediate followers expected the system to survive and Marx did not. But, for Ricardo, the system survived not because it served the ordinary man. Obviously it did not. It survived only because there was no evident alternative and certainly none that was better. Any effort to modify it made it less efficient.

In time, the case for the continuation of the liberal economic society changed. Its superior efficiency was still argued. But, by almost imperceptible degrees, it came to be argued, or at least implied, that it was also tolerable. It provided a reasonable prospect for the ordinary man and something better for the individual of exceptional capacities. This was widely taken as ushering in an age of optimism on man's material prospects. On closer examination, to which we now turn, we shall see how much of the natal pessimism survived.

CHAPTER IV

The Uncertain Reassurance

As it was left by Malthus and Ricardo, the economic prospect for the ordinary individual was remarkably dull. His normal expectation was to live on the edge of starvation. Anything better was abnormal. Progress would enhance the wealth of those who, generally speaking, were already rich but not that of the masses. Nothing could be done about it. And these are more than the casual conclusions of two men. They have claim to be considered the propositions on which modern economic thought was founded.

In the usual view, from the middle of the nineteenth century on, economists became more sanguine, even optimistic. England was the center of the influential discussion. She was in her great era of commercial and industrial expansion. Real wages were rising. There was a clear and apparently enduring margin over mere substistence. In Western Europe and America, the Malthusian horror was also receding, although it was still possible to suppose that this was the temporary result of the opening, all in a few decades, of the North American prairies and plains, the Pampas and the Veld, the New Zealand pastures and the endless Australian outback. These could rescue the world once but not twice. When population had caught up with these new areas, population would again press upon the food supply. In time, this fear receded, especially in the affluent world. Men came to worry more about surpluses of farm products than about a shortage of food. But it has not yet been extirpated. The ghost of Malthus still hovers over India, Bangladesh, Indonesia and other countries of what is called the Third World. And not everyone is certain that the rich countries are assured of enduring abundance.

In the more specific realm of economic theory, the latter half of the last century saw the rejection of the iron law. For a time, the income of those who worked was thought to be limited by the amount of working capital somehow dedicated to the employment of labor in agriculture and industry. This was the famous wages fund which John Stuart Mill once espoused and then rejected. Doubts then began to arise as to whether a single generalization on wages would suffice. Education and special skills came to be regarded as having costs of production that had to be paid for. Special abilities, it was concluded, would, like land, command a rent. Finally, by the end of the century, the worker's return—bearing always in mind that by this is meant the income of the masses of the people—was being related to the value of his marginal product; i.e., to what he added to the value of his employer's product. Were he paid less than the value of his contribution, it would be open to a competitor to offer him more, for in a competitive world there would be other employers whose product he could increase by more than his wage. As a result—a result that might be greatly aided by effective bargaining by a union—wages would tend to be equated with the marginal productivity. This might be high if workers were scarce or highly productive and low if they were redundant or incompetent. But obviously this was a long distance from the iron law, and the break became complete when it no longer seemed certain that well-being brought a self-liquidating flood of children.

With the development of the marginal productivity theory, the effort to construct a general theory of remuneration came pretty much to an end. Having satisfied themselves, as it were, that poverty for those who toiled was not the natural order of things, economists turned to other questions. Most recent work has concerned itself with unions and with the bargaining power which Adam Smith, a notably prescient man, identified as the real problem.

Yet it would be a great mistake to suppose that economics in the central tradition had escaped from its history. For one thing, the notion of an upper limit on the incomes of the masses of the people died very slowly; perhaps these incomes might not be pressed remorselessly down to the floor but they would still be under a ceiling. At the end of the last century, Alfred Marshall (1842–1924), whose *Principles* educated the older members of the present generation of economists, was still impelled to argue that if "economic conditions of the country remain stationary sufficiently long . . . both machines and human beings would earn generally an amount that corresponded fairly with their cost of rearing and training, conventional necessaries as well as those things which are strictly necessary being reckoned for."[1] In other words, wages would cover the cost of producing the children, as these costs are conventionally reckoned, and no more. As with Ricardo, the tendency was still to a minimum. In the United States in the early decades of the present century, the leading figure in the central tradition and the most respected teacher of his time was Professor Frank W. Taussig of Harvard. His summary of the prospect for the ordinary individual which he republished as late as 1936 was as follows: "The usual rate of wages for ordinary labor in the United States was during the first decade of the twentieth century not far from $800 a year. This is much better than savagery . . . [but] . . . If no more is in prospect, the institution of private property stands not only on the defensive but in a position that cannot long be defended. Yet something better is by no means incompatible with the system."[2] He was not yet prepared to assert categorically that something better was wholly compatible with the system.

II

There remained down to our own time, in short, the lingering conviction that while economic life for the masses might not be intolerable, it would not be very good. In this degree Ricardo still ruled. He ruled in another respect. For it was also believed that if men were poor, not much could be done about it. By skill, diligence and training, the individual could

---

[1] Alfred Marshall, *Principles of Economics*, 8th ed. (London: Macmillan, 1927), p. 577. The highly infelicitous expression is exceptional in Marshall.
[2] F. W. Taussig, *Principles of Economics*, 3d ed. (New York: Macmillan, 1936), p. 223. The first edition was published in 1911.

raise his marginal product and hence the wage he could claim. As the most obvious avenue of escape for the individual from poverty, this became a factor of great importance in shaping economic attitudes. There will be occasion to return to it later. But if a worker's wage was low, it was because his marginal product had remained low. To raise his wage without raising his marginal productivity would be to put his pay above his contribution. This would make it profitable for his employer to fire him. Thus, the alternative to low wages was unemployment. Nor is this an antique view. "Each worker receives the value of his marginal product under competition. If a minimum wage is effective, it must therefore have one of two effects: first, workers whose services are worth less than the minimum wage are discharged (and thus forced into unregulated fields of employment or into unemployment . . .) or, second, the productivity of low-efficiency workers is increased."[3] The second likelihood was discarded. The legislation was thus shown to be damaging to those for whom it was designed.

The marginal productivity theory, moreover, provided no reassurance on the other malign tendancy of the Ricardian system, which was for the rich to become very rich indeed. Capital, like labor, was compensated at a rate corresponding to its marginal product. However appropriate and just this arrangement of things might be, it followed that if the capital were owned in large amounts by few individuals, it would be to these that its income would accrue. The resulting inequality might be very great. Observation suggested that this would be the case. In the half century following the Civil War in the United States, men accumulated fortunes of incredible size. Between 1892 and 1899, John D. Rockefeller's personal dividends from Standard Oil amounted to between $30 million and $40 million. In 1900, Andrew Carnegie had an income from his steel companies of $23 million.[4] These revenues were not subject to tax, and the dollar then was worth

---

[3] G. J. Stigler, "The Economics of Minimum Wage Legislation," *American Economic Review*, Vol. XXXVI, No. 3 (June 1946), p. 358. This position is still being advanced by Professor Stigler and his colleagues.
[4] *New York Times*, March 4, 1957.

rather more than now. In addition to oil and steel, railroads, real estate, copper, banking and other pursuits returned vast rewards. While some of it represented a return on capital, some could readily be related to a strategic grip on "original and (not perhaps entirely) indestructible powers of the soil" and of the subsoil from which, precisely, Ricardo expected vast wealth would be derived.

There was uneasiness in the central tradition over this inequality. The inheritance of wealth was a special source of discomfort. Perhaps one could justify riches as the reward for the skill, diligence, foresight and cunning of the original creator. None of this justified its highly fortuitous devolution on the individual who happened to be his son. Monopoly was also regarded with grave misgiving. This rewarded not production but the ability to control production. Moreover, the rule of competition, a point to be emphasized in a moment, was fundamental. Nothing else so completely and utterly underwrote the logic of the system. Inequality resulting from monopoly might be the warning of fatal flaws in the system itself.

Those who might themselves be subject to equalization have rarely been enthusiastic about equality as a subject of social comment. As a result, there has anciently been a muted quality about debate on the subject. Still, the economists in the central tradition started their position with some clarity. There is, Marshall observed, "no moral justification for extreme poverty side by side with great wealth. The inequalities of wealth, though less than they are often represented to be, are a serious flaw in our economic organisation."[5] In the United States, Taussig was more specific. "No stretch of psychological analysis concerning the spur of ambition, the spice of constant emulation, the staleness and flatness of uniformity, can prevail against the universal conviction that the maximum of human happiness is not promoted by great, glaring, permanent inequality."[6]

---

[5]Marshall, *Principles of Economics*, p. 714.
[6]Taussig, *Principles of Economics*, p. 207.

III

The economy of the central tradition presupposed competition. This, also, was a source of misgiving—a misgiving that was often elaborately disguised but nonetheless acute.

The role of competition in the central tradition was fundamental and it became increasingly precise. Numerous firms competed to supply markets at prices which none controlled. The efficient and the progressive were rewarded with survival and growth. The inefficient and unprogressive were penalized by extinction. The employees obviously were involved in the rewards and penalties of their employers and had something of the same inducements to efficiency.

Competition was also the instrument of change. As the tastes of the sovereign consumer altered, the demand for some products rose and so did their prices. The demand and prices of products that were less in vogue declined. Firms in the areas favored by the new demand expanded and others were attracted in. Where demand was shrinking, firms would close down or lay off workers and contract operations. To the extent that it might be possible, some would follow the market into the areas of expanding demand. Capital as well as labor and entrepreneurial talent was distributed according to need by the same process.

In the closing decades of the last century and the early years of the twentieth century, economists became increasingly preoccupied with the operation of the model of a competitive society. As it was developed and idealized, it was a thing of precision and symmetry, almost of beauty. The hold which it came to exercise on men's minds has often been noted.[7] There was no equally explicit appreciation of the fact that it committed men to a remarkable measure of uncertainty. The penalty for falling behind in the race for increased efficiency was bankruptcy. This could also be the penalty of mere bad luck in the case of the producer whose

---

[7] I have so observed at more length in *American Capitalism: The Concept of Countervailing Power* (Boston: Houghton Mifflin, 1952, 1956), especially Chapter II.

product was no longer wanted. And in the case of the worker, the component of luck, as opposed to the role of penalty and reward for performance, was multiplied. The most oaken worker could turn up in the employ of an inadequate entrepreneur. The just misfortunes of the employer would then be visited quite irrationally upon his faithful servant. He could lose his job and his livelihood equally through his own shortcomings and those of others. Needless to say, the competitive model had no place for individuals who, as the result of age, infirmity, industrial injury or congenital incompetence, had only a low or negligible marginal productivity.

These misfortunes did not go entirely unperceived. It was ever necessary to assert that they were "part of the system." And it was also made clear by the prophets of the competitive model, not without a certain ruthless logic, that to seek to mitigate the risks and uncertainties of the system would be to undermine the system itself. The race for increased efficiency required that the losers should lose. If consumers were to rule, there must be rewards for those producers who were in the path of current tastes and penalties for those who were left behind. To seek to mitigate the penalities was to undermine the incentives—to separate the stick from the carrot.

Abridgment of the rigors of competition might even be unjust and immoral. "The traders or producers, who find that a rival is offering goods at a lower price than will yield them a good profit, are angered at his intrusion, and complain of being wronged; even though it may be true that those who buy the cheaper goods are in greater need than themselves, and that the energy and resourcefulness of their rival is a social gain."[8] Indeed, there is a curious likelihood that the competitive model, as it was adumbrated by the textbooks, was intrinsically more insecure and dangerous than anything produced by competition in real life. In the real world, competition was abridged by custom, monopoly, trade unions, torpor, legislation and even a degree of compassion. Thus, the penalties for falling behind in the race were exacted less relentlessly in practice than in principle.

8Marshall, *Principles of Economics*, p. 8.

The basic impact of these ideas will be clear. The economic system pictured in the central tradition was a thing of peril for those who participated in it and so, *pro tanto*, was economic life at large. This peril was a virtue, and the purer the peril, the better the performance of the system. Yet the intrinsic insecurity was disturbing and in two respects. The vulnerability of the weakest members of the society could not entirely be ignored. An economic system which of constitutional necessity was so unfeeling, so intolerant of weakness, was troubling. Even in the best of causes, compassion is difficult to control. And equally disturbing was the unwillingness of ordinary men—businessmen, farmers, workers, reformers—to live with that peril. At every turn, they showed their inclination to press collectively or with the aid of government for measures designed to make their life more secure. Even if the insecurity of the competitive model was not a damaging flaw, the efforts at self-protection that it induced almost certainly were.

In addition, there was the ganwing doubt as to whether competition, in fact, existed. As the nineteenth century wore along, both firms and fortunes grew. Control over economic life seemed to be passing into fewer hands—a development which was heralded by Marx as marking the system's ultimate collapse. As the notion of competition became intellectually more precise, the behavior of the economy became empirically more at odds with the competitive model. Where the latter called for many firms in a market, there were in real life often few. Where the competitive model called for a price that no firm controlled, in real life some firms, at least, seemed to have quite considerable discretionary power over price. And unions were not without power of their own.

In the twentieth century, economists in the central tradition began to accommodate the competitive model to these seeming facts of life. Instead of pure competition, there was monopolistic competition or imperfect competition. With this came more doubts. Who could be sure that a blending of competition and monopoly would be benign? Might not such oddly assorted parents produce a misshapen progeny?[9]

---

[9] I have also dealt with this source of uneasiness, which I regard as of prime importance, in *American Capitalism*.

IV

There was a final source of disquiet in the central tradition. That was the serious depression. Depression through the nineteenth and the first decades of the twentieth centuries had become ever more difficult to ignore. Business suffered a sharp setback in the seventies following the resumption of specie payment after the Civil War. There was a period of comparative stagnation in the nineties and a brief interruption following the financial panic in 1907. There was a short but severe depression following World War I. Then came the vast disaster of the nineteen-thirties. What was the meaning of these recurring misfortunes for the future of the system? Perhaps men might not starve amidst Malthusian scarcity, but might it not still be their fate to starve amidst an abundance of goods that they could not buy? Was it not a fair conclusion that by whatever means they were predestined to to poverty?

Notthing in the history of social ideas is more interesting than the treatment of the so-called business cycle in the central tradition of economic thought. Its study was isolated in a separate compartment until very recent times. Prices, wages, rents and interest, all of which were profoundly affected by depressions, were studied very largely on the assumption that depressions did not occur. Normal conditions were assumed; normal meant stable prosperity. In the separate study of the business cycle, emphasis was placed on the peculiar and nonrecurring conditions which lay back of each depression—the retirement of the greenbacks prior to 1873, the readjustments following World War I, the breakdown of international trade and capital movements and the collapse of the stock market in 1929. But, paradoxically, there was an equal emphasis—sometimes in the same work—on the rhythmic and normal character of the succession of good times and bad. The etymology emphasized the rhythm—as noted, the study was not of depressions but of the business cycle which served to remind everyone that just as bad times followed good, so good times would follow the bad. Even the word depression itself was the terminological product of an effort to soften the connotation of deep trouble. In the last century, the term crisis was normally employed. With time, however, this acquired the connotation of the misfortune it described. And Marx's reference to the "capitalist crisis" gave the word an ominous sound. The word panic, which was a partial synonym a half century ago, was no more reassuring. As a result, the word depression was gradually brought into use. This had a softer tone; it implied a yielding of the fabric of business activity and not a crashing fall. During the Great Depression, the word depression acquired from the event it described an even more unsatisfactory connotation. Therefore, the word recession was substituted to connote an unfearsome fall in business activity. But this term eventually acquired a foreboding quality and a recession in 1953–1954 was widely characterized as a rolling readjustment. By the time of the Nixon Administration, the innovative phrase "growth recession" was brought into use.

To view the business cycle as a normal rhythm was to regard it as self-correcting. Hence, nothing needed to be done about it. Remedies are unnecessary if the patient is certain to recover, and they are also unwise. Writing in 1934, Joseph A. Schumpeter, then with Wesley C. Mitchell one of the world's two most eminent authorities on the business cycle, surveyed the experience of the preceding century and concluded, "In *all* cases . . . recovery came of itself . . . But this is not all: our analysis leads us to believe that recovery is sound only if it does come of itself. For any revival which is merely due to artificial stimulus leaves part of the work of depressions undone and adds, to an undigested remnant of maladjustment, new maladjustments of its own."[10]

Had depressions always remained mild, the notion of a normal rhythm, which wisdom required be undisturbed, would have been reassuring. But as depressions became more violent, such a view was the very reverse of reassuring. Workers lost their jobs. Farm prices fell and some farmers lost

10J. A. Schumpeter, *Essays,* ed. by Richard V. Clemence (Cambridge, Mass.: Addison-Wesley, 1951), p. 117. This essay was originally published in 1934 in *The Economics of the Recovery Program* (New York: Whittlesey House, McGraw-Hill). The italics are in the original.

their farms. Investors lost their savings and some businessmen, more particularly the smaller ones, went bankrupt. And all this was insouciantly described as normal. The conclusion was inevitable: there must be something very wrong with a system in which such faults were normal. Especially in the early thirties, the ideas in the central tradition acted powerfully to breed such doubts. And those who were immune to such uneasiness had another reason for disquiet. Although it was unwise to do anything about depressions, ignorance and popular passion might easily force some action. This could only serve to make things worse. In face of a really bad depression, the notion of a normal self-correcting cycle was calculated to provide uneasiness tailored for every temperament.

There is little need to stress the consequences. To the lingering fear that poverty might be normal, the increasing conviction that inequality was inevitable and the sense of individual insecurity which was inherent in the comeptitive model, the orthodox view of the business cycle added a much more general sense of disquiet. This was the insecurity of a householder who is told that, in the normal and regular course of events, he must expect his house to catch fire and his property to be partially or wholly destroyed. The fire cannot be prevented or arrested for it has its work to do; to call for a fire department is to invite an attempt to drown the flames by drenching them with gasoline.

Such was the legacy of ideas in the great central tradition of economic thought. Behind the façade of hope and optimism, there remained the haunting fear of poverty, inequality and insecurity. Partly latent, partly in the suppressed background of conviction, these doubts could easily be aroused by such an occurrence as the Great Depression.

But the reader will surely ask if there was not a more confident stream of ideas—one more completely purged of all traces of the Ricardian gloom. The question will occur especially to Americans: surely in the American tradition, there must have been a more consistently optimistic current. Here there must have been some who rejected doubt—who reflected an indigenous and abounding confidence. Perhaps among those who neither read nor wrote there was such confidence. But those who gave voice to the American ideas were also far from confident.

CHAPTER V

The American Mood

Only within very narrow limits can one speak of a separate American tradition in economics. Ideas do not respect national frontiers, and this is especially so where language and other traditions are in common. The precepts of the central tradition were accepted equally by Englishmen and Americans. It was from Smith, Ricardo, Mill and Marshall that American economic ideas were derived. The ideas were written by Americans into textbooks and enlarged or amended as to detail. But, in the last century, not much was added by American theorists. Just as the ideas were common to both countries, so were the worries, uncertainties and doubts which the ideas engendered.

This is not to say there were no distinctively American figures but, as compared with the majestic authority of the central tradition, their influence was comparatively small. There would be a measure of agreement on who were the three that were most heard. They were not the total of the American voice but they were also far more than a mere sample. Of the three, two did nothing to offset the presumption of privation and the sense of foreboding which lingered in the central tradition. On the contrary, they did a good deal to accentuate it.

The exception was Henry Charles Carey (1793–1879) who did voice the buoyant optimism which one is obliged to think appropriate to the new republic. Ricardo, he observed, had never seen from his window the progress of a new settlement; had he done so, he would have had a different view of the prospects for mankind. Drawing on such observation, he argued that, with the passage of time, men were not forced, as Ricardo claimed, to poorer and poorer land with ever lower return to their labor and, for any land that was better than

39

the worst, ever higher rents to the landlords. On the contrary, they first cultivated the thin but unencumbered soil on top of the hills. Then at a later period they tackled the thick vegetation in the valleys; having cleared away the trees, they proceeded to work this richer alluvial soil. The returns to the toil were not less but more. In his first book, in 1835, which, like those of his English contemporaries, centered on the problem of wages and thus as ever on the mass prospect for poverty or well-being, he argued that real wages during the previous forty years had shown a tendency to rise. This, too, was in contrast with Ricardian expectations.

But even Carey was not an unqualified optimist. He more than half agreed with Malthus on the procreative power of mankind and, in his earlier books, he hazarded the guess that the time might come when "there will not even be standing room."[1] And the influence of Carey, whether as an optimist or pessimist, was not great. Of this, he himself was aware. He complained bitterly of the small attention that was paid to his ideas in his own country. In Europe, he felt that he was discussed more seriously, and this may well have been so.[2] Little or nothing of Carey passed into the tradition of American economic thought. His books moldered and died. In the last fifty years, he has been mentioned only as a curiosity— an early American economist who had the fortitude to disagree with Ricardo on rent and wtih Adam Smith on the virtues of free trade.

II

The two other distinctively American figures had more enduring, influence. These were Henry George and Thorstein Veblen. But so far from manifesting the exuberant attitudes of the frontier, both were prophets of a gloom that was, in some respects, more profound than that of Ricardo. Henry George (1839–1897) was, like Marx, the founder of a faith, and the faithful still assemble to do honor to their prophet. Like Adam Smith, he made clear his view of the social prospect in

---

[1]Quoted by Alexander Gray, *The Development of Economic Doctrine* (London: Longmans, Green, 1931), p. 256.
[2]See Joseph Dorfman, *The Economic Mind in American Civilization*, 1606–1865 (New York: Viking, 1946), p. 804.

the title of his remarkable book: *Progress and Poverty. An Inquiry into the Cause of Industrial Depressions and of Increase of Want with Increase of Wealth*. In the opening chapter, he posed his basic questions: Why in a time of general economic advance—he was writing in the depression years following 1873—should so much labor "be condemned to involuntary idleness," should there be so much "want, suffering and anxiety among the working classes"?[3] Why, to press things further, should there be so little gain to the poorest classes from increased productive power? "Nay, more," why should its effect be "still further to suppress the condition of the lower classes"?[4]

The reason for this perverse aspect of progress was again part of the almost infinite legacy of Ricardo. Labor and capital increased in productivity; the land supply remained constant in quality and amount. Rents, as a result, increased more than proportionately and made the landlords the undeserving beneficiaries of advance. The anticipation of rent increases and attendant speculation in land values were also the cause of depression. (It is worth recalling that the nineteenth century was marked by recurrent outbreaks of real estate speculation, especially in the American West, and that Henry George spent much of his life in California. Economic ideas, as ever, have their nexus with their environment.) So long as there was private property in land, poverty and depressions were the prospect. Progress would make them worse.

In one respect, Henry George was radially more optimistic than Ricardo. On his title page were the further words *The Remedy*; this phrase had no place in the Ricardian lexicon. If land were nationalized—more precisely, if a tax were imposed equal to the annual use value of real property *ex* its improvements, so that it would now have no net earnings and hence no capital value of its own—progress would be orderly and its fruits would be equitably shared. But this, obviously, was a very drastic prescription. Were the remedy not applied, and this was a reasonable propect given the predictable reac-

[3]Henry George, *Progress and Poverty*, Fiftieth Anniversary ed. (New York: Robert Shalkenbach Foundation, 1933), p. 5.
[4]*Progress and Poverty*, p. 9.

tion of property owners to the proposal, then the consequence would be continuing poverty combined with increasing inequality and increasing insecurity. If this was the American dream, it had little to commend it as compared with the meager classical prospect. And, in fact, the mood of Henry George's followers was often one of misanthropic or frustrated radicalism.

III

In the tradition of American popular radicalism, there were other influential figures besides Henry George—Henry Demarest Lloyd and Edward Bellamy come especially to mind as important figures of the latter decades of the last century. Their conclusions, however, were broadly similar: great inequality and great poverty were inevitable in the absence of great reform. And unlike Henry George, their words mostly died with them. There remains, however, the man whom many regard as the uniquely American economist, Thorstein Veblen (1857–1929).[5]

For the eager search for reassurance that followed the Ricardian gloom, Veblen substituted a grandiloquent inconoclasm. Ricardo had forecast a disagreeable fate for most of mankind. His followers hoped against hope that it might not be. Veblen took a position above the debate. The fate of man was something with which, at least for purposes of posture, he chose not to identify himself. But he also made clear his view that those who talked of progress were mostly feckless optimists or frauds.

To this end, he made specific many of the misfortunes that lurked in the background of the central tradition. Poverty, or

[5] A case might be made for the influence of three other men who were generally outside the central tradition: namely, Simon N. Patten (1852–1922), John R. Commons (1862–1945), and Wesley C. Mitchell (1874–1948). However, Patten, a singularly interesting and original figure, has joined Carey in the neglect reserved for American heretics. Commons and Mitchell, as a matter of principle or method, largely avoided any overall theoretical formulation of man's economic prospect and hence contributed little to the attitudes with which we are here concerned.

more accurately both the moral and material debasement of man, was part of the system and would become worse with progress. There is an inescapable conflict between industry and business—between the "excessive prevalence and efficiency of the machine industry" and its "deplorable" tendency to overproduce and thus to threaten the basic goal of business which is to make money.[6] In this conflict, business always wins. Monopolistic restrictions are imposed where, on purely technical grounds, there could be abundance. This channels income to the owners. The public pays with relative impoverishment.

The economic costs of progress are, however, even less severe than its cultural consequences. Machine industry does not necessarily call for less intelligence on the part of the workers. But it does require a peculiarly narrow and mechanical process of thought and it discourages all other. It also undermines family and church and (here the unions play a key role) the ancient foundations of law and order. The massing together of the workers is a great inducement to "socialist inconoclasm" which is the threshold to anarchy.

Serious depressions are not accidental misfortunes. They are inherent in the conflict between industry and business and hence are organic aspects of the system. They occur "in the regular course of business."[7]

Finally, in his immortal *The Theory of the Leisure Class,*[8] Veblen dramatized, as no one before or since, the spectacle of inequality. The rich and successful were divorced from any serious economic function and denied the dignity of even a serious or indignant attack. They became, instead, a subject for detached, bemused and even contemptuous observation. One watches the struggle between hens for social pre-emi-

---

[6]Thorstein Veblen, *The Theory of Business Enterprise,* 1932 ed. (New York: Scribner), p. 234.
[7]The conclusions sketched above are principally developed in *The Theory of Business Enterprise.* The quote is on p. 183.
[8]Originally published in 1899. There is a new edition, to which I contributed an introduction published in 1973 (Boston: Houghton Mifflin).

nence in the chicken yard as an interesting phenomenon but, in so doing, one does not do much to underwrite the social values of the birds. So with Veblen on the rich.

But equally with Ricardo, wealth and poverty were made inherent. And so, moroever, were their least ingratiating aspects. The ostentation, waste, idleness and immorality of the rich were all purposeful: they were the advertisements of success in the pecuniary culture. Work, by contrast, was merely a caste mark of inferiority. "During the predatory culture labour comes to be associated in men's habits of thought with weaknesses and subjection to a master. It is, therefore, a mark of inferiority, and, therefore, comes to be accounted unworthy of man in his best estate."[9] In the central tradition, the worker was accorded the glory of honest toil. Veblen denied him even that.

Nor was there any hope for change. These things were part of the pecuniary culture. Where Marx looked forward hopefully to revolutionary reconstruction, Veblen did not. In his latter years, he comforted himself only with the thought that the evolving economic society was destroying not only itself but all civilization as well. Such was the view of the greatest voice from the new America.

There will always be debate as to how influential Veblen was. He is the indubitably indigenous figure in American economic thought. This has always commended him to those who—failing to see the enormous authority of the orthodox-classical tradition—have supposed that the dominating influence in American thought must be American.[10] This must still be true even though, as in the case of Veblen, no one could worse fit the cultural stereotype of the optimistic, extrovert American. In fact, Veblen's strictly economic conclusions were not widely read or taught. They never entered the textbooks in competition with the ideas of the central tradition. Yet he was no Carey. He influenced a generation of scholars, writers and teachers. These, in turn, brought some-

[9]*The Theory of the Leisure Class*, p. 41.
[10]This is a criticism which, I think, can fairly be made of Professor Commager. Cf. his discussion of Veblen in *The American Mind* (New Haven: Yale University Press, 1950), pp. 227–246.

thing of his iconoclasm to the ideas of the time. Teachers influenced by Veblen taught the doctrines of the central tradition but they brought to it a disbelief, even a contempt, for the notion that economic progress could much benefit the masses or, indeed, that there was such a thing. Veblen thus precipitated the doubts and pessimism which lurked in the central tradition. In American social thought before the Great Depression, there was a strong feeling, manifested for example in such liberal journals as *The Nation* and *The New Republic*, that the hard-headed intellectual was never beguiled by notions of reform or advance under capitalism. These when offered were either a façade, a trap or an illusion which would quickly bring disenchantment. These attitudes faded with the New Deal, but not until after the Roosevelt reforms had been similarly and repeatedly discussed and dismissed. These attitudes were in no small measure the legacy of Veblen.

IV

Such was the distinctively American contribution. However, we must take note of the impact of another set of social ideas—ideas which, though not American in origin, came almost uniquely to root in the American soil. Toward the close of the last century and in the early years of this, they deeply influenced attitudes on the fate of the ordinary man. These were the doctrines of the Social Darwinists.

Ricardo and Malthus did not conceal from anyone that theirs was a world of struggle. In that struggle, some, and perhaps many, succumbed and there was no hope in public measures to ameliorate the lot of those who were to fall. Speaking of the poor laws, then supported by a fund subscribed by each parish for the support of the indigent, Ricardo concluded that no scheme for their amendment "merits the last attention, which has not their abolition for its ultimate object," adding that "the principle of gravitation is not more certain than the tendency of such laws to change wealth and power into misery and weakness."[11]

[11]David Ricardo, *Principles of Political Economy* (Cambridge, England: University Press for the Royal Economic Society, 1951), pp. 107–108.

However, Ricardo's case for leaving everything to the market—for not allowing compassion to interfere with economic process—was essentially functional. Idleness not being subsidized and substance not being wasted, more was produced and the general well-being would thus be raised. Struggle and misfortune were not themselves to be welcomed.

The position of the Social Darwinists was different. Economic society was an arena in which men met to compete. The terms of the struggle were established by the market. Those who won were rewarded with survival and, if they survived brillantly, with riches. Those who lost went to the lions. This competition not only selected the strong but developed their faculties and ensured their perpetuation. And in eliminating the weak, it ensured that they would not reproduce their kind. Thus, the struggle was socially benign and, to a point at least, the more merciless, the more benign its effects, for the more weaklings it combed out.

The birthplace of these ideas was nineteenth-century England, and their principal source and protagonist was Herbert Spencer (1820–1903). It was Spencer and not Charles Darwin who gave the world the phrase, "the survival of the fittest." Spencer believed that acquired as well as inherited traits were genetically transmitted.

He was a decidedly uncompromising exponent of a very uncompromising creed. He opposed state ownership of the post office and the mint. He was opposed to public education, for it interfered with parental choice between different schools and, indeed, with the choice between wisdom and ignorance for their children. Public aid to the needy and even public sanitation tended to perpetuate the more vulnerable members of the race.

> *Partly by weeding out those of lowest development, and partly by subjecting those who remain to the never ceasing discipline of experience, nature secures the growth of a race who shall both understand the conditions of existence and be able to act up to them. It is impossible in any degree to suspend this discipline by stepping in between ignorance and its consequences, without, to a corresponding degree, suspending the prog-*

ress. If to be ignorant were as safe as to be wise, no one would become wise.[12]

Spencer was restrained from a condemnation of all private charity only by the disturbing thought that this would abridge the liberty of the giver as surely as it would winnow out the weaklings of the race. Misery and misfortune are not misery and misfortune alone but the rungs of a ladder up which man makes his ascent. To seek to mitigate misery was to put in abeyance the fundamental arrangements by which nature ensured progress. "What can be a more extreme absurdity than that of proposing to improve social life by breaking the fundamental law of social life."[13]

Although Spencer was an Englishman, Social Darwinism had much of its greatest success in the United States. Here, in William Graham Sumner (1840–1910) of Yale, it found its major prophet. Here too it found a host of minor ones. Spencer's own books were widely read, or at least widely discussed, in the closing decades of the nineteenth century and the opening years of the present one. When he visited the United States in 1882, he was accorded a welcome by the faithful befitting a messiah. In 1904, when the Supreme Court struck down a New York State law limiting the hours of labor of bakers to ten a day, Justice Holmes observed that "The Fourteenth Amendment does not enact Mr. Herbert Spencer's Social Statics."[14] It was a dissenting opinion.

There were a number of reasons for this popularity in the new republic. By the time of Spencer, England was already moving away from the unhampered rule of the market. Unions, factory inspection, the regulation of the hours of women and children had gained acceptance. In the United States, the race was still being more ruthlessly improved.

And there were many who wished to see the improvement continue with all it implied for those who had been selected.

[12]Herbert Spencer, *Social Statics* (New York: D. Appleton, 1865), p. 413.
[13]Herbert Spencer, *Principles of Ethics*, Vol. II (New York: D. Appleton & Co., 1897), p. 260.
[14]Lochner v. New York, 1904.

"The peculiar condition of American society," Henry Ward Beecher told Spencer as early as 1866, "has made your writings far more quickening here than in Europe."[15] In fact, ideas were never more marvelously in the service of circumstance.

The rise of Social Darwinism in the United States coincided with the rise of the great fortunes. It was a time not only of heroic inequality but of incredible ostentation. Great limestone mansions were rising in New York. Even more stately pleasure domes were being built in Newport. Mrs. William K. Vanderbilt gave her $250,000 ball in 1883. That of the Bradley Martins in 1897 was rather more lavish. For this, the ballroom of the old Waldorf-Astoria was transformed into a replica of Versailles. One guest appeared in a suit of gold-inlaid armor valued at an estimated $10,000. A little earlier at Delmonico's—where Spencer had been entertained—guests were given cigarettes wrapped in hundred-dollar bills which they lighted with a legitimate sense of affluence.

It was also a time of widespread poverty and degradation. The distant workers who supported this wealth lived in noisome slums. There were numerous beggars near at hand. Nor could it always be said that the wealth was being acquired without cost to others. The techniques were sometimes very rude. But none of this need lie on anyone's conscience. Natural selection was at work. The rich could regard themselves as the product of its handiwork—as Chauncey Depew was pleased to remind those who attended one of the great dinners of the successful in New York. So, an important point, could their sons, for the superior qualities were genetically transmitted. This legitimized inherited wealth, for it blessed only the biologically superior. The problem of poverty, meanwhile, was being solved by the only means by which it could be solved. The unfit were being weeded out. Public and even private succor, which if compelled by compassion could be inconveniently expensive, was banned not by callousness but by a perceptive adherence to the laws of nature. "The law of the survival of the fittest was not

[15]Quoted by Richard Hofstadter, *Social Darwinism in American Thought* (Boston: Beacon Press, 1955), p. 31.

made by man. We can only by interfering with it produce the survival of the unfittest."[16] How much better to resist taxation and charity and, incidentally, keep one's money. To this day, the man who refuses a beggar and righteously observes, "I'm told it's the worst thing you can do," is still finding useful the inspired formula of Spencer and Sumner.

Nor need one reflect, uncomfortably, on the methods by which growth had been achieved and wealth acquired. As John D. Rockefeller explained to a fortunate Sunday School class: "The growth of a large business is merely the survival of the fittest . . . The American Beauty rose can be produced in the splendor and fragrance which bring cheer to its beholder only by sacrificing the early buds which grow up around it." As with the rose, so with the Standard Oil Company. "This is not an evil tendency in business . It is merely the working-out of a law of nature and a law of God."[17] This did align God and the American Beauty rose with railroad rebates, exclusive control of pipelines, systematic price discrimination, and some other remarkably aggressive business practices.

V

In 1956, the retiring president of the National Association of Manufacturers called solemnly in the name of Herbert Spencer on the working men of the country to reject the slavery of their unions and on businessmen to renounce the paternalism of Washington. Concerning the latter, he said in a dynamic sentence: "Before we can build solidly into the glorious future that is another unsound part of our structure which we'll have to get rid of, even though it causes severe pain to us businessmen to forgo the federal crutches we have been leaning on." Neither workers nor businessmen took any concrete steps in response to his plea.

In fact, the name of Spencer and Sumner had long since ceased to evoke response. Both democracy and the modern corporation had dealt crippling blows. The masses of the

---

[16]William Graham Sumner, *Essays in Political and Social Science* (New York: Henry Holt, 1885), p. 85.
[17]Hofstadter, *Social Darwinism in American Thought*, p. 45.

people had shown a marked unwillingness to vote for the self-denying policies which would contribute to their own combing out. Individuals were always coming forward with ideas for abridging the struggle and then winning elections on this platform. Those who toyed, however cautiously, with Spencerian virtue, as Barry Goldwater learned in 1964, suffered massive rejection. If Social Darwinism was to work, there all too obviously had to be some curtailment of popular government. To endorse acquiescence in misfortune, there also needed to be a constabulary whose loyalty, most likely, could only be ensured by social security and seniority.

The corporation dealt a different kind of blow. The competitive struggle, as a device for separating the strong from the weak, at least had elements of plausibility in the world of the individual entrepreneur. And conceivably the rugged traits which permit of survival in this contest are passed on to strengthen the generations that follow. It is not so easy to apply this reasoning to the case of General Electric or General Motors. These show marked indications of immortality. And it is not clear how selection works through reproduction to bring a new generation of young and vigorous companies reflecting the strong bloodlines of their corporate parents. Perhaps it could be argued that natural selection operates to bring to the top those who are most effective in the struggle for promotion—that jt rewards with survival those who are most skilled in the tough, complex and ingenious talents that such advance so often requires. If so, then Social Darwinism would work just as selectively in government where the bureaucratic struggle is reputedly severe. This could not be.

Yet Social Darwinism bore importantly on the attitudes which Americans brought into the age of affluence. This was the country where wealth was increasing most rapidly. It was the one where the reassurance of the central tradition might seem to be most plausible. Here, if anywhere, the ordinary man had a chance. Perhaps he did, but he also had to face the fact that all economic life was a mortal struggle. He might win but he also might lose, and for him to accept the full consequences of loss—hunger, privation and death—was a social necessity. Poverty and insecurity thus became inherent in the economic life of even the most favored country. So, of course, did inequality, and this was firmly sanctified by the fact that those who enjoyed it were better. If observation suggested that economic life might be less severe in the United States, Social Darwinism emphasized the contrary.

It had another lasting effect. American thought has always been prone to attribute a special mystique to the market. More than mere efficiency is involved in an uninhibited operation of supply and demand. Other values are at stake. The Social Darwinists identified the vigor of the race with the market. This notion eventually withered and disappeared. But others identified yet other and equally extraneous values with the market and warned, accordingly, of the pervasive consequences of anything which, in the name of welfare or compassion, might interfere with the free play of market forces. Biological progress is no longer threatened by measures which lessen the perils of economic life for the individual. But liberty still is. So, in one fairly substantial view, is Christianity as opposed to secular socialism or communism. To a considerable degree, it was Social Darwinism which led the way in so broadening the claim for the market. In so doing, it narrowed the scope for social measures designed to rescue the individual from the privation or to protect him from the hazards of economic life.

VI

One would not care to claim that this chapter exhausts the influences which have borne distinctively on American economic attitudes. As noted, the frontier and the West had their own expansive mood. So, on the whole, did a good deal of American political debate in the latter part of the last century and the early decades of the present one. Without question, much of this expressed the conviction that any American—at a minimum, any properly energetic American of Anglo-Saxon and Protestant antecedents—could by his own efforts be comfortably opulent. But the ideas which were taught and read, and by which the properly qualified were guided, were far from sanguine. The most influential critics were either misanthropic or committed to the need for massive reform. The established and reputable men of the right pictured and praised a struggle that improved on that of Ricardo only in being more heroic and spectacular and in rejoicing over the immolation of the unfortunate.

CHAPTER VI

The Marxian Pall

In the descent from Ricardo, the Social Darwinists were an eddy to the right. Marx was a massive eruption to the left. But the roots of Marx were deep in the central tradition. There were socialists before Marx, but there have been a great many more since. One reason is that Marx built socialism on Ricardo's orderly arrangement of economic ideas and, in particular, on his bold conception of the problem of income distribution. At least partly as a result, his work carried an authority and conviction that were incomparably greater than any of his socialist predecessors'.

For seventy-five years following his death, Ricardo's admirers were concerned to defend him from the charge, leveled among others by Ruskin, that he was a cold-blooded stockbroker who took a totally detached view of the misery he foresaw for all eternity. The charge may have been unfair, but no one has suggested that Ricardo was a man of passion. Karl Marx (1818–1883) was a man of passion and of Jovian wrath, and this is a matter of first importance. For the Ricardian conclusions—the inevitable impoverishment of the masses, the progressive enrichment of those who own the natural means of production, the inevitable conflict between wages and profits and the priority of the latter for progress—could become, in the hands of an angry man, a call to revolution. As noted, Marx's conception of capitalism was no more gloomy than that of Ricardo or of Malthus. But unlike Ricardo and Malthus, Marx's mission was to identify fault, place blame, urge change and, above all, to enlist disciplined belief. In the latter, his success exceeded that of any man since Mohammed.

53

II

The iron law of wages continued in Marx but in a modified form. The worker is kept on the margin of destitution less because he breeds up to this point than because of his utter weakness in dealing with the capitalist employer and because the system won't work if he is well paid. On occasion, he may get more than the bare minimum, but it is for the same reason that the dairyman feeds his cows more than the maintenance ration—they give him more milk. The bargaining position of the worker vis-à-vis the employer is the same as that of the cows vis-à-vis the dairyman.

This is partly so because the labor force is a reservoir into which, with the passage of time, independent craftsmen and farmers are also forced. Helplessness is assured by the industrial reserve army—by the rising and falling but enduring margin of unemployment which is part of the system. Any worker at any time can be flushed into this reserve, which ensures that he will be cooperative and will accept the wage that is offered him.

The advance of the arts and the accumulation of capital bring no benefit to the average men. On the contrary, in some of Marx's characteristic prose, they ". . . mutilate the labourer into a fragment of a man, degrade him to the level of appendage of a machine, destroy every remnant of charm in his work and turn it into hated toil . . . drag his wife and child beneath the Juggernaut . . . [bring] misery, agony of toil, slavery, ignorance, mental degradation . . ."[1]

Resorting to a device which many others have found useful, Marx dug up a candid opponent to help him make his case. A prominent conservative, Destutt de Tracy, had observed: "In poor countries the people are comfortable, in rich nations they are generally poor."[2]

Further, and in its ultimate influence perhaps the most important of all, the system had an inherent tendency to devastating depression. Sismondi, the great Swiss historian, philosopher and economist, had published at the beginning of

[1]Karl Marx, *Capital* (London: William Gliesher, 1918), pp. 660–661.
[2]*Capital*, p. 664.

the century a book which reflected much of the hopeful attitude of Adam Smith. Then, sixteen years later and after extensive travels over Western Europe, he returned to the subject impressed by the importance of industrial crises and persuaded that they would get worse. The trouble was that the purchasing power of the workers did not keep abreast of what they produced. As a result, goods accumulated for which there were no buyers. A crisis became inevitable. Marx's view of depressions, which he was still working out when he died, was roughly similar and so, in recent times, has been that of almost everyone.

However, Marx stressed other causes too. As capital accumulated, the rate of return would fall. This would weaken incentives and lead to periods of torpor and stagnation. Also, in boom times, the industrial reserve army—the unemployed—would be reduced, and the resulting competition for labor would force up wage rates, and hence costs of production, and this would bring the boom to an end.[3] Nothing so well suggests Marx's intransigent pessimism on the outlook for the worker under capitalism as this. A temporary betterment of his position is the cause of a prompt worsening of it. Depressions are caused both by the poverty of the workers (and their insufficient purchasing power) and equally by temporary improvements in their well-being.

Since the government, for Marx, was the handmaiden of the bourgeoisie, there was small likelihood that it would be impelled to succor the unemployed by making jobs for them. But were it to do so, the effect would be only to reduce the industrial reserve army, raise wage costs, and cause a depression. To correct the deficiency of purchasing power—the deficiency that kept workers from buying the products of their labor—by public measures to put more purchasing power in the hands of the people, as by spending for public works, would be futile for the same reasons. Also, there are deeper disorders in the process of "production and reproduction" which such superficialities leave untouched and which

[3]Marx's explanation of the business cycle is scattered through his work and is in some respects, as Professor Schumpeter has observed, rather casual. This summary owes much to Mrs. Joan Robinson's indispensable book, *An Essay on Marxian Economics* (London: Macmillan, 1952).

render them worthless.[4] This point is one of considerable importance to Marx and even more to his followers. Were it possible to prevent depressions by compensating for the deficient purchasing power of the worker with, say, public spending, then capitalism might be workable. Instead of revolution, there would be a budget deficit. Acute Marxians have seen the danger and denied the possibility of such an easy escape. In one of those developments which make economics such an engaging study in odd bedfellows, the Marxists were, for a long time, joined in this contention by the most stalwart conservatives.

With the longer-run Marxian prospect, almost everyone is familiar. Capitalist concentration proceeds; productive plant and resources come to be owned by ever fewer people of ever greater wealth. The Marxian capitalist has infinite shrewdness or cunning on everything except matters pertaining to his own ultimate survival. On these, he is not subject to education. He continues willfully and reliably down the path to his own destruction. The worker, by contrast, whom he degrades and beats to a hopeless pulp, is gifted with quick perception and the capacity to learn. He is reinforced by ". . . fresh elements of enlightenment and progress" from the sections of the ruling class who are extruded by the process of capitalist concentration.[5] In the end, the centralization of production produces hopeless weakness in face of the masses of the workers who by now have become a disciplined industrial army. Then the knell sounds and the expropriators are expropriated. At the next stage, Marx joins the optimists. The path is now open to a laissez-faire more complete by far than that of Ricardo. For government was occasioned by the needs of capitalism and the acquisitive mentality which capitalism produced. With no further need to police the masses or curb the larceny which is the manifestation of acquisitive modes of thought, the state can begin to wither away. But first, unhappily, there was the revolution. A very large number of people were never able to

---

[4] I should, perhaps, remind the reader that I am here concerned with a characterization of the Marxian position and of its impact on attitudes and not with a critique. Marxian critiques are still very, very long.
[5] Karl Marx, *Communist Manifesto*.

project their minds much beyond this discomforting prospect. And as Marx billed it—". . . the forcible overthrow of all existing social condition. Let the ruling classes tremble . . ."[6]—it was discomforting.

III

Nothing has ever been so badly understood as the influence of Marx. That he seized the minds of millions is, of course, agreed. But it is widely supposed that Marx's influence ends with these faithful. In the conventional wisdom, his ideas are a kind of infection like smallpox. Either men get it and are permanently scarred, or they escape it because of some effective inoculation and are untouched. Nothing could be further from the truth. Marx profoundly affected those who did not accept his sytsem. His influence extended to those who least supposed they were subject to it.

In part, this was the result of the breathtaking grandeur of Marx's achievement as an exercise in social theory. No one before, or for that matter since, has taken so many strands of human behavior and woven them together—social classes, economic behavior, the nature of the state, imperialism and war were all here and on a great fresco which depicted from deep in the past to far into the future. On class conflict, or imperialism, or the causes of national war, Marx was bound to be influential, for he was the only man who had offered an explanation which was at all integrated with the rest of human experience. Thus, all American thought has been deeply influenced by a Marxian view of imperialism. The break with British imperialism came on economic issues. The principal alternative to explaining imperialism in terms of economic self-interest is to argue the benevolence of the imperial power, its commitment to the white man's burden, its feelings that the natives are not ready for independence, its need to protect them from communism. Although this latter view had a brief and damaging run in Indochina, even there the suspicion that there might be economic motive behind the American intervention was never quite stilled.

"As an economic theorist Marx was first of all a very

[6]*Communist Manifesto.*

learned man."[7] His goals were those of a revolutionist, but his method was that of a scholar and scientist. Accordingly, his concepts helped all social scientists in their perception of reality. In a world but little removed from poverty, and where great store was set by wealth, it was inevitable that most conflict would have an economic cause. Nothing else was nearly so worth quarreling about. Even where there were some other ostensible cause—love, honor, patriotism or religion—a more penetrating or cynical view could be expected to discern some economic motive. This, in simple outline, was Marx's materialistic conception of history. Though it was not original with Marx—as he made clear—he made it famous. It is something that even, perhaps especially, the modern conservative accepts. When he sees someone agitating for change, either at home or abroad, he inquires, almost automatically: "What is there in it for him?" He suspects that the moral crusades of reformers, do-gooders, liberal politicians, and public servants, all their noble protestations notwithstanding, are based ultimately on self-interest. "What," he inquires, "is their gimmick?"

Marx foresaw, in the process of capitalist concentration, the tendency for the control of the capital resources of the community to pass into fewer and fewer hands. As the materialistic view of human motivation is fundamnetal in American conservatism, so capitalist concentration is a prime tenet of American liberalism. It is Marx, in considerable measure at least, who agitates year in and year out for the enforcement of the antitrust laws.

In the central tradition of economic theory, the existence of social classes—of capitalists, middle class and proletarians—was only surreptitiously conceded if at all. Yet classes obviously existed; so did something that looked suspiciously like class conflict. For a perception of these matters, the world had also to rely on Marx.

Finally, Marx gained influence by heralding the truly terrifying depression. In the central tradition, as noted, the depression was a routine affliction. For Marx, it was an increasingly devastating fact of capitalist life. In the end, a de-

[7]Joseph A. Schumpeter, *Capitalism, Socialism and Democracy*, 2d ed. (New York: Harper, 1947), p. 21.

pression would destroy (or at least mark the destruction of) the system. On this, of all matters, it was difficult to say that Marx was wrong, for plainly, by the nineteen-thirties, depressions were not routine. In 1934, in the third year of the Great Depression, the late John Strachey, then the most articulate contemporary English Marxist, surveyed the current economic situation and concluded, not without satisfaction, that "the whole capitalist world is on its way to barbarism."[8] But the judgment of the most orthodox of English economists in the same year, except in being tinged with regret, was not different. Sir Arthur Salter concluded that "the defects of the capitalist system have been increasingly robbing us of its benefits. They are now threating its existence."[9]

IV

Had Marx been mostly wrong, his influence would quickly have evaporated. The thousands who have devoted their attention to demonstrating his errors would have turned their attention elsewhere. But on much he was notably right, especially in relation to his time. The latter point is worth emphasizing. Most economic philosophers needed only to be right as regards their own time. No one defends Adam Smith in his conviction that corporations—joint stock companies—had no future. But the Marxists require that Marx, with some adjustment, be right not only for his own time but for all time. This is a truly formidable test.

And it was because Marx was so manifestly right on some things that few could suppress the insistent question: Might he not be right on other things—including the prospect for capitalism itself? Might it be that Marx faced facts while others sought the dubious shelter of wishful thinking? Such thoughts, as much as the convictions of his converts, were the measure of Marx's influence. In those who resisted belief, he still had an unparalleled capacity to inspire doubts. Lurking just beneath the surface in the mind of every non-Marxian—

---

[8]John Strachey, *The Coming Struggle for Power*, 4th ed. (London: Gollancz, 1934), p. 8.
[9]Arthur Salter, *Recovery: The Second Effort* (London: G. Bell & Sons, 1934), p. 209.

everyone at least who was sensitive to any form of thought—was the question: Am I a Pangloss?

And to this doubt the converts also contributed. Whereas those who remained in the central tradition of economics wondered, the Marxists did not. They were certain. No wish for a comfortable and nonviolent future fathered *their* thoughts. They were willing to face the prospect of the progressive immiseration of the masses, worsening economic crises and, in the end, bloody revolution. The unloveliness of these prospects, and the fact that they were being faced, established the Marxist as the profound realist, the man who was entirely without illusion. This evident realism was reinforced by moral passion. "The religious quality of Marxism . . . explains a characteristic attitude of the orthodox Marxist toward opponents. To him, as to any believer in a faith, the opponent is not merely in error but in sin. Dissent is disapproved of not only intellectually but also morally."[10] The man who argues with a Marxist has always been assaulting a rock fortress with a rubber flail.

Lastly, it was always possible to dismiss those who believed Marx wrong as being guilty of a failure of understanding. Marx is not easy to understand. Those who thought him wrong had failed to do so. Thus, one of Marx's reasons for the capitalist crisis, as noted, was the tendency for the rate of profit to fall with continuing capital accumulation. Marx was as insistent on the importance of profit for investment and production as any president of the National Association of Manufacturers. The falling rate of profit would lead to recurrent interruptions of expansion and these would be of increasing severity and duration.

In this century, profits have shown no tendency to fall, and capital accumulation has continued apace. As a result, the declining rate of profit cannot be taken seriously as cause of

---

[10]Schumpeter, *Capitalism, Socialism and Democracy*, p. 5. In the central tradition, by contrast, such passionate belief was thought inconsistent with scientific rationalism. Not exclusively, to be sure. Marx once observed with some justice that "Economists are like theologians . . . Every religion other than their own is the invention of man, whereas their own particular brand of religion is an emanation from God." (From *The Misery of Philosophy*, quoted by Strachey in *The Coming Struggle for Power*.)

depression. One of Marx's sympathetic modern interpreters has been moved to conclude that "his explanation of the falling tendency of profits explains nothing at all."[11] But few Marxists make this concession. Marx was not in error; nor was it because he based his observation on the last century when the rate of return seemed to be showing a tendency to fall. Rather, the dissenter has failed to see the full subtlety and complexity of Marx's argument. He has somehow over-simplified or vulgarized Marx's position.

Much has been written of the appeal of Marx to intellectuals. How, in particular, can a doctrine that has so obviously acquired the standing of a dogma be attractive to inquiring, rational minds? The answer is a complex one. Apart from the obvious fact that Marx for Marxists is the conventional wisdom, there is the seeming realism, the certainty and security of the defenders and the large component of vivid truth. But much of Marx's strength has always been in the contention of his followers that those who thought him wrong were really themselves obtuse, simple- or literal-minded. These are terrible charges; innumerable intellectuals have been unwilling to risk them. How much better to persuade oneself and others of one's ability to see below the surface. This might mean agreeing that Marx meant what he did not say, but it was proof that one wasn't incapably dull. Thus, acceptance of Marx became not a matter of willingness to follow dogma into obvious unreality and error. Rather, it was a question of whether the individual was willing to adventure into the subtle and inverted as distinct from the surface implications of Marx's words, and had the ability to do so. For intellectuals, the lure was strong. This too was a source of Marx's influence.

V

The time has come for a summing up. Up to, say the middle years of the nineteen-thirties, the broad impact of economic ideas is clear. It could not but leave a man with a sense of

[11]Joan Robinson, *An Essay on Marxian Economics*, p. 42. For a different modification see Paul Baran and Paul M. Sweezy, *Monopoly Capital* (New York: Monthly Review Press, 1966).

the depth, pervasiveness and burden of the economic problem and, on the whole, with the improbability of a happy outcome. "Depend on it," Dr. Johnson observed, "when a man knows he is going to be hanged in a fortnight, it concentrates his mind wonderfully."[12] For the same reasons, men's minds were focused on the perils of economic life.

In particular, although it was no longer the lesson of the central economic tradition that men would starve, neither was it the lesson that they would do very well. Privation was still normal. Men might lift themselves by lifting their marginal product; with increasing efficiency and increasing supplies of capital, marginal productivity and hence wages might rise. But no one could suppose that the result could be more than barely adequate. Certainly no one could suggest that any opportunity for such improvement could be overlooked. On the contrary, to relax such effort in the slightest would be extreme social dereliction. The privation, already great, would be greater—and unnecessarily so. The man of conscience and compassion must see that efficiency is increased by all possible means. To do less was to be profoundly callous, even cruel.

Privation is also enhanced by the intransigent inequality of the income. The miserable consumption of the poor is partly the result of the ostentatious demands of the rich. There isn't enough for both, and the latter get far more than they need. If possible, something should be done about inequality, for no sensitive man could be indifferent to the social strains and conflicts that it was producing and seeming likely to produce as the proletariat became increasingly conscious of its inferior position. But could anything serious really be done about it?

Finally, there was the nerve-wracking problem of insecurity. The competitive model made episodic unemployment for the worker, and occasional insolvency for the farmer or businessman, a part of the system.

This insecurity was enhanced by the growing severity of depressions and then in the thirties by the most devastating depression of all. This latter was especially troublesome be-

---

[12]The saying owes its modern fame to Winston Churchill, who noted that his mind had been so focused by the prospect of the invasion of Britain in 1940.

cause the contemporary theory dismissed it as self-correcting. If self-correcting it was inevitable, and if inevitable it was intolerable.

Clearly there was much to bring productivity, inequality and insecurity to the center of men's minds and to make them a preoccupying concern. And if there was any tendency in the central tradition of economics to conclude that all might in the end work out for the best, there were also voices from the wings to say it couldn't be so. From the right was the echo of the Social Darwinists saying struggle is not only inevitable but good. From the Marxist world, in tones of thunderous conviction, came the warning that the inequality and the insecurity would increase and increase until, in the end, their victims would destroy the whole edifice and, by implication, quite a few of its favored inhabitants.

These—productivity, inequality and insecurity—were the ancient preoccupations of economics. They were never more its preoccupations than in the nineteen-thirties as the subject stood in a great valley facing, all unknowingly, a mountainous rise in well-being. We have now had that mountainous rise. In very large measure, the older preoccupations remain. We should scarcely be surprised. This pre-eminently is an occasion when we would expect the conventional wisdom to lose touch with the reality. It has not disappointed us.

That is not to say that the change has had no effect on conventional attitudes. Especially on inequality and insecurity there have been important modifications. To these we now turn.

CHAPTER VII

Inequality

Few things have been more productive of controversy over the ages than the suggestion that the rich should, by one device or another, share their wealth with those who are not. With comparatively rare and usually eccentric exceptions, the rich have been opposed. The grounds have been many and varied and have been principally noted for the rigorous exclusion of the most important reason, which is simply the unwillingness to give up the enjoyment of what they have. The poor have generally been in favor of greater equality. In the United States this support has been tempered by the tendency of some of the poor to react sympathetically to the cries of pain of the rich over their taxes and of others to the hope that one day soon they might be rich themselves.

As the last chapters have shown, the economic and social preoccupation with inequality is deeply grounded. In the competitive society—the society of the central tradition of economics in descent from Ricardo—there was presumed to be a premium on efficiency. The competent entrepreneur and worker were automatically rewarded. The rest, as automatically, were punished for their incompetence or sloth. If labor and capital and land were employed with high efficiency then, *pro tanto*, nothing more, or not much more, could be obtained from the economy in the short run by way of product. And longer-run progress did not necessarily benefit the average man; in the original doctrine, its fruits accrued to others.

So if people were poor, as in fact they were, their only hope lay in a redistribution of income, and especially that which was the product of accumulated wealth. Much though Ricardo and his followers might dissent, there were always some—and the number steadily grew—who believed that redistribution might be possible. (Ricardo and those who followed him in the central tradition were never immune from the suspicion that they were pleading a special interest.) All Marxists took the need for a drastic redistribution for granted. Consequently, throughout the nineteenth century, the social radical had no choice but to advocate the redistribution of wealth and income by one device or another. If he wanted to change things, this was his only course. To avoid this issue was to avoid all issues.

The conservative defense of inequality has varied. There has always been the underlying contention that, as a matter of natural law and equity, what a man has received save by proven larceny is rightfully his. For Ricardo and his immediate followers, the luxurious income of landlords and of capitalists was the inevitable arrangement of things. One could tamper with it but only at the eventual price of disrupting the system and making the lot of everyone (including the poor) much worse.

This was essentially the passive defense. With time (and agitation), the case for inequality became a good deal more functional. The undisturbed enjoyment of income was held to be essential as an incentive. The resulting effort and ingenuity would bring greater production and greater resulting rewards for all. In recent times this tenet has been canonized in the federal tax limit of 50 percent on earned income; no man should ever receive less than half the fruit of his labor or what passes for labor.

Inequality has also come to be regarded as almost equally important for capital formation. Were income widely distributed, it would be spent. But if it flowed in a concentrated stream to the rich, a part would certainly be saved and invested.

There are other arguments. Excessive equality makes for cultural uniformity and monotony. Rich men are essential if there is to be an adequate subsidy to education and the arts. Equality smacks of communism and hence of atheism and therefore is spiritually suspect. In any case, even the Russians have abandoned egalitarianism as unworkable.

The cultural misfortunes from excessive equality cannot be pressed too far. As Tawney observed: "Those who dread a dead-level of income or wealth . . . do not dread, it seems, a dead-level of law and order, and of security of life and property. They do not complain that persons endowed by nature with unusual qualities of strength, audacity, or cunning are prevented from reaping the full fruits of these powers."[1] And in fact, in the conventional wisdom, the defense of inequality does rest primarily on its functional role as an incentive and as a source of capital.

Thus, the limited egalitarianism of the present federal income-tax structure has long been held to be seriously dampening to individual effort, initiative and inspiration or in danger of becoming so. It "destroys ambition, penalizes success, discourages investment to create new jobs, and may well turn a nation of risk-taking entrepreneurs into a nation of softies . . ."[2] "It destroys the incentive of people to work . . . It makes it increasingly difficult, if not impossible, for people to save . . . It has a deadening effect on the spirit of enterprise . . . which has made America."[3]

However, this case is not impeccably consistent. Not many businessmen wish to concede that they are putting forth less than their best efforts because of insufficient pecuniary incentive. The typical business executive makes his way to the top by promotion over the heads of his fellows. He would surely endanger his chance for advancement if he were suspected of goldbricking because of his resentment over the inadequacy of his after-tax income. He is expected to give his best to his corporation, and usually he does.

To give individuals large incomes to encourage savings also has elements of illogic. The rich man saves because he is able to satisfy all his wants and then have something over. Such saving, in other words, is the residual after luxurious consumption. This obviously is not an especially efficient way to promote capital formation. Moreover, the empirical evidence on the effect of egalitarianism on capital formation is uncertain. England is often cited as an unfortunate example.

[1] R. H. Tawney, *Equality*, 4th ed., rev. (London: Allen & Unwin, 1952), p. 85.
[2] "Taxes and America's Future." Address by Fred Maytag II, before the National Association of Manufacturers, December 1, 1954.
[3] "The Relation of Taxes to Economic Growth." Address by Ernest L. Swigert, before the National Association of Manufacturers, December 6, 1956.

But Norway, an even more egalitarian country, had, following World War II, one of the highest rates of capital formation and of economic growth of any country in the non-communist world.[4] The Latin American republics, with a highly unequal income distribution, have no remarkable record for capital formation.

The *formal* liberal attitude toward inequality has changed little over the years. The liberal has partly accepted the view of the well-to-do that it is a trifle uncouth to urge a policy of soaking the rich. Yet, on the whole, the rich man remains the natural antagonist of the poor. Economic legislation, above all tax policy, continues to be a contest, however unequal, between the interests of the two. No other question in economic policy is ever so important as the effect of a measure on the distribution of income. The test of the good liberal is still that he is never fooled, that he never yields on issues favoring the wealthy. Other questions occupy his active attention, but this is the constant. Behind him, always challenging him, is the cynical Marxian whisper hinting that whatever he does may not be enough. Despite his efforts, the wealthy will become wealthier and more powerful. They lose battles but win wars.

II

However, few things are more evident in modern social history than the decline of interest in inequality as an economic issue. This has been particularly true in the United States. And it would appear, among western countries, to be the least true of the United Kingdom. While it continues to have a large ritualistic role in the conventional wisdom of conservatives and liberals, inequality has ceased to preoccupy men's minds. And even the conventional wisdom has made some concessions to this new state of affairs.

On the fact itself—that inequality is of declining concern—it is only necessary to observe that for many years

4Alice Bourneuf, *Norway: The Planned Revival* (Cambridge, Mass.: Harvard University Press, 1958).

no serious effort has been made to alter the present distribution of income.[5] Although in the semantics of American liberalism there is often a tactful silence on the point, since nothing so stirs conservative wrath, the principal public device for redistributing income is the progressive income tax. But the income tax in the years since World War II has greatly regressed as an instrument for income redistribution.

The decline in concern for inequality cannot be explained by the triumph of equality. Although this is regularly suggested in the conventional wisdom of conservatives, and could readily be inferred from the complaints of businessmen, inequality is still great. In 1970, the one-tenth of families and unattached individuals with the lowest incomes received before taxes about 2 percent of the money income of the country; the tenth with the highest incomes received 27 percent of the total, which is to say their incomes averaged 14 times as much as the lowest tenth. The half of the households with the lowest incomes received, before taxes, only 23 percent of all money income. The half with the highest incomes received 77 percent. In 1972, only about 7 percent of all family units had incomes before taxes of more than $25,000. They received, nonetheless, 21 percent of total income. At the other extreme, 17 percent had before-tax incomes of less than five thousand and received only 4 percent of the income.[6] Present laws are notably favorable to the person who has wealth as opposed to the individual who is only earning it. With a little ingenuity, the man who is arleady rich can ordinarily take his income in the form of capital gains and limit his tax liability accordingly. In addition, unlike the man who must earn, he is under no compulsion to acquire a capital stake, either for old

[5]The so-called war on poverty of the Johnson Administration is instructive: Income redistribution was to be limited to the very poor. The more important improvement in the incomes of the poor was to come from the increased productivity of that group. The ability of all shades of political opinion to endorse aspects of this program suggests the mildness of the effort.

[6]U.S. Department of Commerce, *Statistical Abstract of the United States.* The 1970 figures are from p. 324 of the 1972 edition; the 1972 figures from p. 382 of the 1974 edition.

age, family, or the mere satisfaction it brings, since he already has one. Accordingly, he need not save. Yet none of these matters nor the numerous more egregious loopholes in the federal income tax arouse the kind of concern which leads on from rhetoric to action.

III

The first reason inequality has faded as an issue is, without much question, that while it has continued and increased, it has not been showing the expected tendency to get violently worse. And thus the Marxian prediction, which earlier in this century seemed so amply confirmed by observation, no longer inspires the same depth of fear. It no longer seems likely that the ownership of the tangible assets of the republic and the disposal of its income will pass into a negligible number of hands. In the absence of alarm, inequality is more easily accepted than social reformers in the past have supposed. Emulation or, when this is frustrated, envy has long played a large role in the common view of human motivation.[7] So long as one individual had more than another, the second was presumed to be dissatisfied with his lot. He strove to come abreast of his more favored contemporary; he was deeply discontented if he failed. However, these disenchanting traits are less cosmic than has commonly been supposed. Envy almost certainly operates efficiently only as regards near neighbors. It real income is rising, the fact that unknown new New York-is not directed toward the distant rich. If the individual's own ers or Texans are exceedingly wealthy is not, probably, a matter of prime urgency. It becomes easy, or at least convenient, to accept the case of the conventional wisdom, which is that the rich in America are both functional and also much persecuted members of the society. And, as noted, to comment on the wealth of the wealthy, and certainly to propose that it be reduced, has come to be considered bad taste. The individual whose own income is going up has no real reason to incur the opprobrium of this discussion. Why

[7]See Chapter XI.

should he identify himself, even remotely, with soapbox orators, malcontents, agitators, communists, and other undesirables?

IV

Another reason for the decline in interest in inequality, almost certainly, is the drastically altered political and social position of the rich in recent times. Broadly speaking, there are three basic benefits from wealth. First is the satisfaction in the power with which it endows the individual. Second is that in the physical possession of the things which money can buy. Third is the distinction or esteem that accrues to the rich man as the result of his wealth. All of these returns to wealth have been greatly circumscribed in the last fifty years and in a manner which also vastly reduces the envy or resentment of the well-to-do or even the knowledge of their existence.

As recently as a half century ago, the power of the great business firm was paramount in the United States and the firm, in turn, was the personification of the individual who headed it. Men like Morgan, the Rockefeller executives, Hill, Harriman and Hearst had great power in the meaningful sense of the term, which is to say that they were able to direct the actions and command the obedience of countless other individuals.

In the last half century, the power and prestige of the United States government have increased. If only by the process of division, this has diminished the prestige of the power accruing to private wealth. But, in addition, it has also meant some surrender of authority to Washington. Furthermore, trade unions have invaded the power of the entrepreneur from another quarter. But most important, the professional manager or executive has taken away from the man of wealth the power that is implicit in running a business. Fifty years ago Morgan, Rockefeller, Hill, Harriman and the others were the undisputed masters of the business concerns they owned, or it was indisputably in their power to become so. Their sons and grandsons still have the wealth, but with rare exceptions the power implicit in the running of the firm has passed to professionals.[8] Nor has any equivalent new generation of owning entrepreneurs come along.

When the rich were not only rich but had the power that went with active direction of corporate enterprise, it is obvious that wealth had more perquisites than now. For the same reasons, it stirred more antagonism. J. P. Morgan answered not only for his personal wealth but also for the behavior of the United States Steel Corporation which he had put together and which ultimately he controlled. As a man of corporate power, he was also exceedingly visible. Today shares of the United States Steel Corporation are still the foundation of several notable fortunes. But no sins of the Corporation are visited on its owners, for they do not manage the company and almost no one knows who they are. When the power that went with active business direction was lost, so was the hostility.

The power that was once joined with wealth has been impaired in a more intimate way. In 1194, the crusading knight, Henry of Champagne, paid a visit to the headquarters of the Assassins at the castle at al-Kahf on a rugged peak in the Nosairi Mountains. The Assassins, though a fanatical Moslem sect, had, in general, been on good terms with the Christians, to whom they often rendered, by arrangement, the useful service of resolving disputes by eliminating one of the disputants. Henry was sumptuously received. In one of the more impressive entertainments, a succession of the loyal members of the cult, at a word from the Sheik, expertly immolated themselves. Before, and ever since, the willing obedience of a household coterie has been a source of similar satisfaction to those able to command it. Wealth has been the most prominent device by which it has been obtained. As may indeed have been the case at al-Kahf, it has not always endeared the master to the men who rendered it.

In any case, such service requires a reservoir of adequately

[8]More precisely, to the aggregation of technical and planning talent which I have elsewhere called the technostructure. Cf. *The New Industrial State*, 2nd ed., rev. (Boston: Houghton Mifflin, 1971), Chs. VI, VII and *Economics and the Public Purpose* (Boston: Houghton Mifflin, 1973).

obedient or servile individuals. The drying up of this reservoir, no less than the loss of wealth itself, can rob wealth of its prerogatives. The increase in the security and incomes of Americans at the lower income levels has effectively reduced—indeed, for many purposes, eliminated—the servile class. And again the reciprocal is that those who no longer work for the rich (or who have done so or who fear that they might be forced to do so) no longer feel the resentment which such dependence has induced.

V

The enjoyment of physical possession of things would seem to be one of the prerogatives of wealth which has been little impaired. Presumably nothing has happened to keep the man who can afford them from enjoying his Rembrandts and his home-grown orchids. But enjoyment of things has always been intimately associated with the third prerogative of wealth which is the distinction that it confers. In a world where nearly everyone was poor, this distinction was very great. It was the natural consequence of rarity. In England, it is widely agreed, the ducal families are not uniformly superior. There is a roughly normal incidence of intelligence and stupidity, good taste and bad, and morality, immorality, homosexuality, and incest. But very few people are dukes or even duchesses, although the latter have become rather more frequent with the modern easing of the divorce laws. As a result, even though they may be intrinsically unexceptional, they are regarded with some residual awe. So it has long been with the rich. Were dukes numerous, their position would deteriorate irretrievably. As the rich have become more numerous, they have inevitably become a debased currency.

Moreover, wealth has never been a sufficient source of honor in itself. It must be advertised, and the normal medium is obtrusively expensive goods. In the latter part of the last century in the United States, this advertisement was conducted with virtuosity. Housing, equipage, female adornment and recreation were all brought to its service. Expensiveness was keenly emphasized. "We are told now that Mr. Gould's '$500,000 yacht' has entered a certain harbor, or that Mr.

Morgan has set off on a journey in his '$100,000 palace car,' or that Mr. Vanderbilt's '$2,000,000 home' is nearing completion, with its '$50,000 paintings' and its '$20,000 bronze doors.' "[9] The great houses, the great yachts, the great balls, the stables, and the expansive jewel-encrusted bosoms were all used to identify the individual as having a claim to the honors of wealth.

Such display is now passé. There was an adventitious contributing cause. The American well-to-do have long been curiously sensitive to fear of expropriation—a fear which may be related to the tendency for even the mildest reformist measures to be viewed, in the conservative conventional wisdom, as the portents of revolution. The depression and especially the New Deal gave the American rich a serious fright. One consequence was to usher in a period of marked discretion in personal expenditure. Purely ostentatious outlays, especially on dwellings, yachts and associated females, were believed likely to incite the masses to violence. They were rebuked as unwise and improper by the more discreet. It was much wiser to take on the protective coloration of the useful citizen, the industrial statesman, or even the average guy.[10]

However, deeper causes were at work. Increasingly, in the last quarter century, the display of expensive goods, as a device for suggesting wealth, has been condemned as vulgar. The term is precise. Vulgar means: "Of or pertaining to the common people, or to the common herd or crowd." And this explains what happened. Lush expenditure could be afforded by so many that it ceased to be useful as a mark of distinction. An elongated, richly upholstered and extremely high-powered automobile conveys no impression of wealth in a day when such automobiles are mass-produced by the

---

9Matthew Josephson, *The Robber Barons* (New York: Harcourt, Brace, 1934), p. 310. Josephson is paraphrasing W. A. Croffut, Commodore Vanderbilt's biographer, writing in 1885.

10Cf. C. Wright Mills, *The Power Elite* (New York: Oxford University Press, 1956), p. 117. Mr. Mills suggests that in the depression years this effort to provide protective coloration led to the recruiting of technicians and corporate managers as front men behind whom the well-to-do could survive in peace. Not uncharacteristically, I think, Mr. Mills read too much contrivance into such change.

thousands. A house in Palm Beach is not a source of distinction when the rates for a thousand hotel rooms in Miami Beach rival its daily upkeep. Once a sufficiently impressive display of diamonds could create attention even for the most obese and repellent body, for they signified membership in a highly privileged caste. Now the same diamonds are afforded by a television star or a talented harlot. Modern mass communications, especially the movies and television, ensure that the populace at large will see the most lavish caparisoning on the bodies not only of the daughters of the rich but also on the daughters of coal miners and commercial travelers who have struck it rich by their own talents or some facsimile thereof. In South America, in the Middle East, to a degree in socialist India, and by travelers therefrom in Nice, Cannes and Deauville, ostentatious display by those of wealth is still much practiced. This accords with expectations. In these countries, most people are still, in the main, poor and unable to afford the goods which advertise wealth. Therefore, ostentation continues to have a purpose. In not being accessible to too many people, it has not yet become vulgar.

The American of wealth is not wholly without advantages in his search for distinction. Wealth still brings attention if devoted to cultural and technical pursuits or to hobbies with a utilitarian aspect. A well-to-do American may gain in esteem from an admirably run farm, although never from an admirably manicured estate. Although wealth aids a public career, those who too patently rely on it are regarded as slightly inferior public citizens. A Rockefeller or a Kennedy who is elected to public office enjoys a prestige far in excess of an Aldrich or an Annenberg whose appointment to an ambassadorial position, however justified on merit, might have been less certain in the absence of sizable campaign contributions. In sum, although ostentatious and elaborate expenditure, in conjunction with the wealth that sustained it, was once an assured source of distinction, it is so no longer. The effect on attitudes toward inequality will be evident. Ostentatious expenditure focused the attention of the poor on the wealth of the wealthy, for this of course was its purpose. With the decline of ostentation, or its vulgarization, wealth and hence inequality were no longer flagrantly advertised.

Being less advertised, they were less noticed and less resented. The rich had helped to make inequality an issue. Now they were no longer impelled to do so.

There were similar consequences from the fact that the rich man now had to compete for esteem. Once the intellectual, politician or man of general ambition saw the rich man achieve distinction without effort and in contrast with his own struggle. He reacted by helping to focus the resentment of the community as a whole. Now he saw the man of wealth forced to compete for his honors. In this competition, the rich man retained undoubted advantages, but he did not automatically excel. Nothing could operate more effectively to dry up the supply of individuals who otherwise would make an attack on inequality a career. By graduating into the ranks of the professional managers, and after making his way up through the hierarchy of the modern corporation, the ambitious man could expect to compete on tolerably equal terms with the grandson of the founder.

It would be idle to suggest that the man of wealth has no special advantages in our society. Such propositions are the one-day wonders of the conventional wisdom, and those who offer them have a brief but breathtaking reputation as social prophets. This itself suggests that such findings assuage some sense of guilt. But it does seem clear that prestige and power are now far more intimately identified with those who, regardless of personal wealth, administer productive activity. The high corporate official is inevitably a man of consequence. The rich man can be quite inconsequential and often is. His need to achieve success in the nominally popular profession of government is instructive.

VI

In the Ricardian world, as noted, progress required profits, and its fruits accrued to the landlords. Economic advance—expanding output—did not ordinarily help the common man. His only hope lay in reforms that Ricardo and his followers would have considered highly destructive or, alternatively, in a drastic overthrow of the system. Economic advance still holds little promise of betterment for the average man in many countries. On Andean haciendas, it matters little to the man who tills the land whether the product increases. His own share is minute; an increase in product is not important if all but a minute fraction goes to someone else. And matters may be worse: any surplus over the barest need may be absorbed, as the result of an *ad hoc* revision of the rules, by the landlord, merchant or moneylender. This is still the Ricardian world, and in it the obvious hope for improvement lies in a different distribution of income based on a different social structure. For the same reason, until the share of the ordinary man in the product is increased, his incentive to increase production—to adopt better methods of cultivation, for example—is slight or nil. The people of numerous of the poor countries have frequently heard from their presumptively more advanced mentors in the economically more advanced lands that they should be patient about social reform, with all its disturbing and even revolutionary implications, and concentrate on increasing production. It can be remarkably inappropriate advice. Reform is not something that can be made to wait on productive advance. It may be a prerequisite to such advance.

In the advanced country, in contrast, increased production is an alternative to redistribution. And, as indicated, it has been the great solvent of the tensions associated with inequality. Even though the latter persists, the awkward conflict which its correction implies can be avoided. How much better to concentrate on increasing output, a program on which both rich and poor can agree, since it benefits both.

That among those who might be subject to redistribution this doctrine has something approaching the standing of divine revelation is perhaps not entirely surprising. For many years, the relationship of businessmen to economists in the United States was characterized by a degree of waspishness. The economist had shown a predisposition to favor low tariffs, the income tax, the antitrust laws and, quite frequently, trade unions. This made him, at a minimum, an inconvenient friend. But increased output as a substitute for greater equality was the basis for a notable rapprochement. "From a dollars-and-cents point of view it is quite obvious that over a period of years, even those who find themselves at the short end of inequality have more to gain from faster growth than from any conceivable income redistribution."[11]

These statements still arouse some suspicion. Over the centuries, those who have been blessed with wealth have developed many ingenious and persuasive justifications of their good fortune. The instinct of the liberal is to look at these explanations with a rather unyielding eye. Yet, in this case, in the advanced countries, the facts are inescapable. It is the increase in output in recent decades, not the redistribution of income, which has brought the great material increase in the well-being of the average man. And, however suspiciously, the liberal has come to accept the fact. As a result, the goal of an expanding economy has also become deeply embedded in the conventional wisdom of the American left. The beneficent effects of such an economy, moreover, are held to be comprehensive. Not only will there be material improvement for the average man, but an end to poverty and privation for all. This latter is untrue. Increasing aggregate output leaves a self-perpetuating margin of poverty at the very base of the income pyramid. This goes largely unnoticed, because it is the fate of a voiceless minority.[12] And liberals have long been accustomed to expect the poor to speak in the resounding tones of a vast majority. To these matters, it will be necessary to return.

For the moment, we need only notice that, as an economic and social concern, inequality has been declining in urgency, and this has had its reflection in the conventional wisdom. The decline has been for a variety of reasons, but, in one way or another, these are all related to the fact of increasing production. Production has eliminated the more acute ten-

11 "Learning To Multiply and To Divide." Address by Roger M. Blough, Chairman of the Board of the United States Steel Corporation, quoting Professor Henry C. Wallich of Yale University, latterly of the Board of Governors of the Federal Reserve System, January 15, 1957.

12 Although to the extent that it is associated with race, a more militant minority than here suggested. It seems fair to attribute to the discussion following the first publication of this volume and the later work of Michael Harrington, Robert Lampman, Charles C. Killingsworth and those associated with the Office of Economic Opportunity some influence in making this poverty less anonymous than it was in 1958. However, the evident decline of poverty as a source of concern in the nineteen-seventies is not very encouraging.

sions associated with inequality. And it has become evident to conservatives and liberals alike that increasing aggregate output is an alternative to redistribution or even to the reduction of inequality. The oldest and most agitated of social issues, if not resolved, is at least largely in abeyance, and the disputants have concentrated their attention, instead, on the goal of increased productivity. This is a change of far-reaching importance. Our increased concern for production in modern times would be remarkable in itself. But it has also preempted the field once occupied by those who disputed over who should have less and who should have more.

CHAPTER VIII

Economic Security

Few matters having to do with economic life have been so much misunderstood as the problem of economic security. And, in remarkable degree, the misunderstanding persists.

In the model of the competitive society, such insecurity was inherent. The individual producer or worker might, at any time, suffer a sudden decline in his fortunes. This could be the result of laziness or incompetence which would lose him his customers or his job. But the best of men might suffer from a sudden change in consumer tastes or as the result not of their own inadequacy but of that of their employer. These unpredictable changes in fortune were both inevitable and useful. They were inevitable, for they were part of the capacity of the system to accommodate itself to change. As requirements and wishes changed, men were employed in new places and disemployed in the old. Capital was sought in the new industries and written off as a loss in the old. The insecurity was useful, for it drove men—businessmen, workers, the self-employed—to render their best and most efficient service, for severe punishment was visited impersonally on those who did not.

However, this insecurity, valuable though it seemed in principle, was cherished almost exclusively either in the second person or in the abstract. Its need was thought urgent for inspiring the efforts of other persons or people in general. It seldom seemed vital for the individual himself. Restraints on competition and the free movement of prices, the principal source of uncertainty to business firms, have been principally deplored by university professors on lifetime appointments. Their security of tenure is deemed essential for fruitful and unremitting thought. The preoccupation of workers with unemployment insurance or old age pensions has usually seemed most supine and degenerate to business executives who would be unattracted by companies in which they were subject to arbitrary discharge or which lacked adequate pension arrangements. Farmers have been regularly reproached for their lack of fealty to the free price system by entrepreneurs whose own prices have not suffered reduction for some years.

In the conventional wisdom of conservatives, the modern search for security has long been billed as the greatest single threat to economic progress. These fears were strongest at a time when great advances in social security were coinciding with great economic progress. For older liberals, the prospect for finding new forms of social protection with wide appeal to the masses remains the highest hope both for winning social progress and political success. When politicians in the United States deplore, as they regularly do, their lack of new ideas, they have reference, almost invariably, to the lack of new and politically attractive forms of social security. This is disconcerting to conservatives who also suppose that an endless number of new ideas for protecting the individual from economic misfortune are lurking just around the corner. There have been few really new proposals for many years.

II

The first step in penetrating this bedlam is to recognize that while risk was indeed inherent in the economic society of the central tradition, it has long been regarded with equanimity by almost no one. And all who were subject to insecurity sooner or later set about eliminating it as it affected themselves. In large measure, they were successful. The devices by which they did so have varied much. This has led those who were using one device to see it as a necessary precaution while they deplored the iniquitous measures devised by others. And, as will by now be scarcely surprising, while insecurity was eliminated in the real world, it survived more or less intact in the ideological underpinning of the conventional wisdom and continued therein to play its all but indispensable role.

The elimination of economic insecurity was pioneered by the business firm in respect of its own operations. The greatest source of insecurity, as noted, lay in competition and the free and unpredictable movement of competitive market prices. From the very beginning of modern capitalist society, businessmen have addressed themselves to the elimination or the mitigation of this source of insecurity. Monopoly or the full control of supply, and hence of price, by a single firm was the ultimate security. But there were many very habitable halfway houses. Price and production agreements or cartels, price-fixing by law, restrictions on entry of new firms, protection by tariffs or quotas, and many other devices have all had the effect of mitigating the insecurity inherent in the competitive economy. Most important, where the number of firms is small, a characteristic feature of the modern industry, interdependence is recognized and respected, and firms stoutly avoid price behavior which would enhance uncertainty for all.

These efforts have been long and widely remarked. However, the tendency of these measures to focus directly or indirectly on price, which, as stated, is the greatest source of uncertainty, has led economists to regard the management of prices as being of unique importance. And they have far more frequently related such management to the maximization of profits than to the minimization of risks. The specter that has haunted the economist has been the monopoly seeking extortionate gains at the public expense. This has dominated his thoughts. The less dramatic figure, the businessman seeking protection from the vicissitudes of the competitive economy, has been much less in his mind. That is unfortunate, for the development of the modern business enterprise can be understood only as a comprehensive effort to reduce risk. It is not going too far to say that it can be understood in no other terms.

Specifically, it falls within the power of the modern large corporation to mitigate or eliminate many of the more important risks to which business enterprises have anciently been subject. Consumer taste and demand may shift. The modern large corporation resists this by its advertising. Consumer taste is thereby brought at least partly under its control. Size makes possible a diversified line. This provides further protection. There is danger that technological change will render obsolete a product or method of production. The modern corporation is able, through its research and technological resources, to ensure that it will be abreast of such change. Therefore, technological change will occur under its own auspices or within its reach. A measure of control over prices means a measure of control over earnings. This means at least partial independence of the capital market for funds. Size, moreover, greatly diversifies the opportunities of the firm in raising money. In the large organization, even the risks associated with the selection of leadership are reduced. Organization replaces individual authority; no individaul is powerful enough to do much damage. Were it otherwise, the stock market would pay close attention to retirements, deaths and replacements in the executive ranks of the large corporations. In fact, it ignores such details in tacit recognition that the organization is independent of any individual.[1]

The massive reduction in risk that is inherent in the development of the modern corporation has been far from fully appreciated. This is partly because the corporation, unlike the worker, farmer or other individual citizen, has been largely able to reduce its insecurity without *overtly* seeking the assistance of government. It has required elaborate organization, but this has been the product of continuous evolution from the original entrepreneurial enterprise. Farmers, workers and other citizens, by contrast, have had openly to seek the assistance of government or (as in the case of the unions) they have had to organize specially for the purpose of reducing insecurity. Consequently, their search for greater security has been notorious. By contrast, the corporate executive, whose concern pioneered the escape from insecurity, has been able to suppose that security is something with which only workers or farmers are preoccupied.

Myth has also played a part in concealing the effort of the modern corporation to minimize insecurity. There is a surviving conviction, even on the part of the executives of the largest business corporations, that they live dangerously. No large industrial corporation in the United States, which is also

1 In the first edition, I noted that "these are matters which I hope to treat in much greater detail in a forthcoming book on the corporation and the corporate personality." This I have now done in *The New Industrial State,* 2nd ed., rev. (Boston: Houghton Mifflin, 1971).

large in its industry, has failed or been seriously in danger of insolvency in many years. Where there has been danger, the government has come to the rescue. The security of tenure of corporation executives is remarkably high. So is their remuneration. Certainly these bear no resemblance to the insecurity of the fortunes of the business entrepreneur of the competitive model. Individual decisions of corporate management may still turn out to have been wrong. But in the large, diversified corporation—in contrast with the small and more specialized firm—such decisions are rarely fatal.

The riskiness of modern corporate life is, in fact, the harmless conceit of the modern corporate executive, and that is why it is vigorously proclaimed. Precisely because he lives a careful life, the executive is moved to identify himself with the dashing entrepreneur of economic literature. For much the same reason, the commander of an armored division, traveling in a trailer and concerning himself with gasoline supplies, sees himself as leading an old-time cavalry charge. Nothing has been more central to the purpose of General Motors or General Electric than to encompass and eliminate the perils to which the onetime entrepreneur was presumed to be subject. Nothing would be more damaging to an executive reputation in General Motors or General Electric than to launch a product without testing the market, to be caught napping by a technological development, to be unprotected on one's raw material supply or to be caught in a foolish price war. These were once the commonplace risks of entrepreneurship.

But the large corporation has been only the leader in the retreat from risk. Nearly everyone else has partcipated to the best of his ability and ingenuity, and in the thirties there was an especially widespread effort to mitigate the economic perils of the average man. The federal government intervened for the first time with relief and welfare funds to protect the individual from economic misfortune. This was followed by social security—unemployment insurance and old age and survivor's pensions. Farmers, through public payments and support prices, were protected from some of the insecurity associated with competitive market prices. The unions developed rapidly during this decade. Along with their redress of bargaining power, they provided the worker with protection against capricious or adventitious firing or demotion and thus increased his security in his job. Pensions, health insurance, supplementary unemployment compensation have added to the protection. Even the smaller businessman, through the Robinson-Patman Act, the Fair Trade laws, legislation against below-cost selling, and through trade associations, won a measure of security from the uncertainties of market competition for which he shared the universal distaste.

The foregoing measures were microeconomic. They protected the individual, firm or group from the specific adversities to which it was subject. But the effective mitigation of insecurity required another and parallel effort of a far more general sort. The position of the worker who is protected against arbitrary firing by a sound seniority system is far from ideal if he receives an entirely nondiscriminatory discharge as the result of an insufficiency of demand for the product he is making. This is especially so if a general shortage of demand keeps him from finding a job elsewhere. While unemployment compensation is better than nothing, a job is better than either. Even with an effective enforcement of the laws preventing price discrimination—roughly the use by a large firm of its size to exact and offer prices which small competitors cannot obtain or quote—the competitive position of the small retailer in a time of depression is not happy. Regardless of the conditions of competition, it is much better when the demand for everyone's product is good. Farm support prices are a useful protection against sudden adverse price movements. But a demand for farm products that holds such prices reliably above support levels will be preferred by every rational farmer.

At a time, as during the thirties, when there was great interest in the microeconomic measures to increase security, it would have been surprising indeed had there been no macroeconomic effort with its greater efficiency to the same end. The two efforts would be in the highest degree complementary. In fact, the reduction of insecurity by macroeconomic measures was central in the economic policy of the time. Efforts to eliminate or mitigate the business cycle and to stabilize the economy at a level where the labor force would be more or less fully employed became a principal goal of public policy. Then, as since, economic stabilization was regarded as an end in itself, but it will now be clear that it was only one part of the broad effort to escape the insecurity which was assumed to be inherent in economic life. The change in attitudes on macroeconomic security during the thirties was remarkable. At the beginning of the decade, it was almost uniformly assumed that cyclical fluctuations with accompanying price and employment uncertainties were inevitable. It was hoped by many that they would not be violent. But there was no general confidence that depressions could be tempered by government action without the risk either of eliminating the self-corrective features of the cycle or simply making things worse. By the end of the decade, under the combined influence of Keynes and the sanguine and experimental mood generated by the New Deal, there was a widespread belief that depressions could be at least partially prevented. The notion that they must be allowed to run their course was virtually extinct.

III

The nineteen-thirties were a remarkable period and the changes to enhance security in this time still call for reflection. They were numerous and massive in their effect, and they were concentrated in the brief span of a few years. (While it is convenient to speak of a decade, most of the drive for increased economic security occurred in the five years from 1933 to 1938.) Conservatives and liberals alike looked at the measures, and at the mass approval they evoked, and concluded that something new and different had been added in economic motivation. Conservatives struggling to reconcile this drive for security with the inherent and seemingly indispensable insecurity of the competitive society were profoundly alarmed. For perhaps the first time in history, they worried not about the turbulent ambitions of the masses but about their yearning for peace and contentment. Liberals, observing the political magic in this desire for security, accepted it and rationalized it. Modern industrial life, they concluded, was a thing of exceptional hazard; the worker lived in constant danger of being torn to pieces by the increasingly complex social machine which he served. Given this image, it was possible to argue that he needed much more elaborate protection than in the simpler economic society assumed by earlier economists. These men could not have foreseen the risks of advanced industrial capitalism. With further advance, ever more protection would be required.

We have since come to see the matter in a clearer light. In this time of change, the average man was simply showing the commonplace reaction to the insecurity of the competitive system. In doing so, he was following a path that had been pioneered by the modern business firm. He was showing, as ever, that insecurity is something that is cherished only for others.

It was inevitable that farmers and workers in general would be the last to concern themselves with security. Before a man will try to protect himself from sudden changes in his economic fortune, he must have some fortune to protect. Businessmen were first to develop a stake in economic society. They were first, as a result, to become concerned with means, explicit or unrecognized, for safeguarding that stake. In the grim world of Ricardo and Malthus, the ordinary citizen could have no interest in social secuirty in the modern sense. If a man's wage is barely sufficient for existence, he does not worry much about the greater suffering of unemployment. Life is a heavy burden in either case. Men who are engaged in a daily struggle for survival do not think of old age, for they do not expect to see it. When the normal expectation of life is very low, sickness and death are normal hazards. A man of eighty does not take out life insurance. He reconciles himself as best he can to the prospect of death. To the landless worker in an Indian village, unemployment is not even a misfortune. It is his normal fortune.

With increasing well-being, all people become aware, sooner or later, that they have something to protect. In the very early stages of the evolution of a business concern, the entrepreneur is not much concerned with security. He has little equity to conserve. Only later do he or his descendants begin to talk about their responsibilities to their stockholders. Henry Ford and James Couzens could gamble on the untested idea of producing in a single model the cheapest possible car for the people. It was a breathtaking step. But they had nothing much to lose. Ford's grandsons would be derelict were they similarly to risk the present assets of the Ford Motor Company. No criticism attaches to the effort of the modern corporation to minimize risk. It would be delinquent in its responsibilities if it failed to do so. It would be gambling where it could be sure.

The development in the labor market is similar. As the real wage of the worker increases and also as employment becomes more certain, unemployment and the absence of income acquires its contrasting horror. With increasing income, it also becomes possible to think of old age; the individual expects to survive, and old age without income is differentiated, as it was not before, by the prospect of discomfort. And as health hazards and the dangers of accident decline, men come to think of them as abnormal rather than normal afflictions. It is not the poor but the well-to-do farmers who find onerous the uncertainties of the market. In the mountain country of Kentucky and Tennessee, a depression is not a grievous hazard. Farmers have little to sell; their property has small value. They are therefore little affected by declining prices and not much concerned about declining property values. In the well-to-do regions, things are different. In the nineteen-thirties, it was comparatively rich farmers of Iowa who threatened with a rope the judges who presided over foreclosure proceedings. From these farms came the demands for farm relief. Unlike those of the Appalachian Plateau, these farmers had something to lose.

Thus the notion, so sanctified by the conventional wisdom, that the modern concern for security is the reaction to the peculiar hazards of modern economic life could scarcely be more in error. Rather, it is the result of improving fortune— of moving from a world where people had little to one where they had much more to protect. In the first world, misfortune and suffering were indemic and unavoidable. In the second, they have become episodic and avoidable. And as they became episodic and avoidable, reasonable men saw the merit of measures to avoid them and the possibilities for so doing.

Increased economic well-being was not the sole cause of the increased interest in economic security. Allowances must be made for differences in national temperament and political development. These may well explain why a comprehensive system of social insurance first appeared in Imperial Germany and why, in the non-communist lands, it has had its greatest development in Scandinavia and the United Kingdom. The Great Depression which struck with especial severity in the United States and Canada brought the interest in economic security in these countries abreast of the European industrial nations.

The Great Depression has, in fact, often been cited as evidence of the growing insecurity of modern industrial life. There was, it is said, no comparable hazard before the Industrial Revolution. This, it will now be clear, is a superficial view. The Great Depression was severe partly because there was so much wealth and income to lose. The hazard was greatest in the United States and Canada where the per capita wealth was greatest. And the depression stimulated concern for economic security in precisely the same way that a conflagration stimulates an interest in fire insurance and a flood in flood control. These also have an effect on individuals which is roughly proportionate to the amount of their property that lies in the path of the flames or the water.

IV

Men of property—the Forsytes of the world—have always known that it is as important to safeguard their wealth as to increase it. But they have never equated the two. Property can be increased without limit; the efforts to safeguard it are subject to sharply diminishing returns. Having insured against fire, theft and high winds, a man has removed the major hazards to his possessions. Protection against earthquakes and falling airplanes may also be worthwhile, but it is not of equal urgency and it does not bring an equivalent increase in peace of mind.

The problem of economic security is much the same. There are more serious hazards and less serious ones; as the more serious are covered, there will be a declining sense of urgency about the less serious ones and indeed, also, about the entire problem of economic security. For the worker, in the past, the greatest hazard was the loss of his job and income. Thereafter, the uncertainties of old age, sickness, accident and death may be assumed to have ranked next in importance. As and when these risks were mitigated, although others remained, none was of comparable importance. For the farmer, protection against a severe decline in his prices was (and remains) of paramount urgency. Such a decline threatens both his income and his assets. After that, depending on the region, comes the danger of drought and crop failure. There are no other hazards of similar importance. For the business man, the situation is much the same. The overwhelming uncertainty concerns product prices and markets. This accounts for the attention it has received from economists, indeed why, in the theory of market behavior, efforts to remove this dimension of risk have been regarded as more or less unique and also, not infrequently, as uniquely reprehensible. There are further hazards—those of cost movements, raw material supplies, labor relations—which it is desirable to eliminate, but their potential for damage is less devastating. Other sources of uncertainty are of still less importance.

The meaning of this is that elimination of insecurity in economic life can be a finished business. Nothing is more completely accepted in the conventional wisdom than the cliché that economic life is endlessly and inherently uncertain. In fact, the major uncertainties of economic life (subject to some marked caution concerning the control of depression and inflation) have already been eliminated. The ones that remain are of much reduced urgency.

The corollary is that parties and governments cannot, as the conventional wisdom so devoutly assumes, go on "inventing" new kinds of security. This would be possible were it merely a matter of invention or were the hazards of modern economic life increasing. But the hazards are finite in number; they increase only in the sense that people have more to lose. This is not to say that no economic insecurity remains. For the average individual of working age in the United States, sickness—which may mean large expenditures at a time when there is no income—is a hazard. Smaller business and agriculture are still insecure vocations. Nonetheless, subject always to the major qualification that depression and severe inflation are to be prevented, the preoccupation with new forms of economic security is over. No hazards remain that are comparable in importance with those that have been covered. And protection once achieved is quickly taken for granted. It ceases to be a matter for discussion or even of thought. Henceforth, in pursuing the goal of greater economic security, we will be completing and perfecting a structure that in all its major features now exists.

One cannot stress too strongly, however, that if economic security is to be considered finished business, or largely finished business, depression and inflation must be prevented. A depression could always break down the micromeasures that have so laboriously been erected by (or for) businessmen, workers, farmers and other citizens for their protection. Business arrangements for modifying and controlling competition in the interests of market stability then turn into cutthroat competition. Unemployment insurance becomes not a transitional protection for the worker who is changing jobs, but an inadequate livelihood. Farm price supports become low maximum rather than high minimum prices. By the same token, inflation reduces the purchasing power of pensions, undermines other steps by which people have insured their future income or had it insured. Prevention of depression and inflation remains a *sine qua non* for economic security.

V

The desire for economic security was long considered the great enemy of increased production. This attitude was firmly grounded in the belief that the insecurity of the competitive model was essential for efficiency. Along with the carrot of pecuniary reward must go the stick of personal economic disaster. Both were essential. To remove the stick, which must be the consequence of increasing economic security, would be to remove half the incentives by which men were inspired.

Plainly, however, the notion that economic insecurity is essential for efficiency and economic advance was a major miscalculation—one of the greatest in the history of economic ideas. It was the common miscalculation of both Marxian and orthodox economists. Marx and his followers were deeply persuaded that capitalism would be crippled by efforts to civilize it. Unemployment compensation, for example, would ruin the operation of the industrial reserve army in regulating wages. In fact, the years of increasing concern for economic security have been ones of unparalleled advance in productivity. Those spokesmen who have been most alarmed over the debilitating effects of the search for security have often remarked most breathlessly on the improvements in productivity which have occurred at the same time.

The data on what has happened to output in the age of security could scarcely be more impressive. In the twenty years prior to the nineteen-thirties, the decades when the problem of security first became a source of conventional concern, labor productivity—national income produced per man-hour—increased from 89.6 cents in 1900 to 113.3 cents in 1929. This was a total of 23.7 cents or at a rate of about 1.2 cents a year. In the ten years following the thirties, the total increase was from 131.5 cents to 179.2 cents or by 47.7 cents. This was by an average of 4.8 cents a year or four times the amount of the earlier period. The increases continued in subsequent decades. Plainly the increased concern for security, so far from being in conflict with increased productivity, was consistent with a greatly accelerated rate of advance.[2] The most impressive increases in output in the history of both the United States and other western countries have occurred since men began to concern themselves with reducing the risks of the competitive system.

However, in the conventional wisdom such empirical evidence is not necessarily decisive. The consequences truly depicted by the conventional wisdom are, it is held, lurking just out of sight. To respect the evidence is only to evince an unsubtle mind. Yet in this instance the reality is somewhat difficult to evade. The increase in economic security and the increase in economic product are accomplished facts. The conflict between security and progress, once billed as the social conflict of the century, doesn't exist.

VI

Not only is there no inconsistency between the mitigation of insecurity and the increase of production, but the two are indissolubly linked. A high level of economic security is essential for maximum production. And a high level of production

2 Estimates are in 1950 prices. They are from *America's Needs and Resources, A New Survey,* by J. Frederic Dewhurst and Associates (New York: Twentieth Century Fund, 1955), p. 40.

is indispensable for economic security. We must carry a step further our examination of this reciprocal relation between production and economic security.

The major threat to production in our day is not, as the more nostalgic exponents of the conventional wisdom still so fondly imagine, the lazy and malingering workman or the unenterprising boss. These wastrels unquestionably exist. Payments designed to bridge periods of involuntary unemployment do provide modestly for some wholly voluntary idleness in Florida. There are featherbedding unions and goldbricking workmen and slothful supernumeraries everywhere. Indeed, it is possible that the ancient art of evading work has been carried in our time to its highest level of sophistication, not to say elegance. One should not suppose that it is an accomplishment of any particular class, occupation or profession. Apart from the universities where its practice has the standing of a scholarly rite, the art of genteel and elaborately concealed idleness may well reach its highest development in the upper executive reaches of the modern corporation.

The loss of production from this conventional and cherished shirking is small as compared with what can be lost from the involuntary idleness of workers and the far more ruthless frustration of entrepreneurial initiative as the result of depression. For the same reason, the potential gain in production from eliminating such involuntary idleness, and from widening entrepreneurial opportunity by expanding markets, is far greater than anything that could be hoped for from the most sweeping strenthening of individual incentives resulting in the most radical increase in the willingness of individuals to work or expend executive energy.

Between 1929 and 1932, the Gross National Product, roughly the total production of the nation, expressed in constant (1958) dollars, dropped by $55 billion from $197.1 billion to $143.0 billion.[8] No diminution in the energy or initiative of workmen or their employers could have an effect comparable with this massive increase in forced idleness by individuals who would have much preferred to work. (Be-

8 U.S. Department of Commerce, *Historical Statistics of the United States* (Washington: U.S. Government Printing Office, 1961), p. 139.

tween 1929 and 1932, unemployment increased from 1.55 million to 12.1 million; nonagricultural employment decreased from 35.1 million to 28.8 million.)[4] This was a demonstration of historic magnitude of the inefficiency of depression. But there have been more modest if still striking demonstrations. In late 1953 and 1954, there was a mild depression and in the latter year, output was slightly below the previous year. ($360.5 billion as compared with $364.5 billion. Prices were the same.) Unemployment increased from 1.6 million in 1953 to 3.2 million in 1954. If instead of this slight decline there had been the commonplace increase of immediately preceding years, and which the labor force could have sustained, production would have been about $20 billion greater. That was equal to nearly a third of the outlays of the federal government at the time and approached the total of all state and local outlays. This production was not missed and, indeed, its loss was little remarked. In the recession years of the mid-seventies, this experience was repeated with a similar absence of grief. We shall see later that there were very good reasons for such equanimity—the goods so sacrificed were not, in fact, of high urgency. But the figures do show the inefficiency of even the mildest depression.

The immediate although not the ultimate cause of depression is a fall in the aggregate demand—meaning in the purchasing power available and being used—for buying the output of the economy. Unemployment insurance means that a man's purchasing power is partially protected when he loses his job. It falls, but no longer to zero. Thus, a measure designed to reduce the insecurity associated with unemployment also acts to counteract the loss of output—the economic inefficiency—of depression. And, to the confusion of the conventional wisdom, it acts on a central cause of inefficiency, one that is far more important than isolated malingering which unemployment insurance might conceivably have encouraged.

This effect, of course, is not peculiar to unemployment insurance. Farm support prices, which force compensatory public outlays when farm prices, income and purchasing

---

[4] *Economic Indicators*, Historical and Descriptive Supplement, 1955. Joint Committee on the Economic Report.

power fall, have the same effect. So do public welfare payments. Old age and survivor's insurance ensure a modest but steady flow of purchasing power from those who are no longer able to work. This flow is unaffected by an ebb in economic activity and thus acts as a stabilizing influence. In the aggregate, these measures to minimize insecurity comprise a considearable part of what economists call the "built-in stabilizers" of the economy. Thus, measures thought by the conventional wisdom to be hostile to productivity all support it at the most crucial point.

But the reciporcal effect is equally clear and the pressures back of it are much more demanding. As noted above, a high level of production is essential for the economic security of workers, farmers and businessmen. With it, there is a tolerable level of security for all. Without a high level of output, the microeconomic measures, in their present form at least, are only a second best. Moreover, although it has been a point in favor of unemployment compensation, old age pensions and other measures for microeconomic security that they enhance economic stability, this has never been their central purpose. They have been centrally designed with the individual recipient in mind.

By contrast, to a very large degree in recent times, increased output has been sought not for the goods involved but for the effect on economic security. Whether we need or even wish the goods that are produced, their assured production means assured income for those who produce them. This serves the goal of economic security. Nothing else serves it so well. To falter on prodcution, even though that production serves the most unimportant of requirements, is to expose some individuals somewhere to loss of employment and income. This cannot be allowed.

The facts here are a matter of common observation. In the political life of western countries—the United States, the United Kingdom, the older British Commonwealths, western Europe—nothing counts so heavily against a government as allowing unnecessary unemployment. It is not the lost production that is mentioned. It is always the unemployment. The remedy is, of course, more employment and higher production. Thus, the effort to enhance economic security becomes the driving force behind production.

The reader scarcely needs to be reminded of the point at which this essay has arrived. The ancient preoccupations of economic life—with equality, security and productivity—have now narrowed down to a preoccupation with productivity and production. Production has become the solvent of the tensions once associated with inequality, and it has become the indispensable remedy for the discomforts, anxieties and privations associated with economic insecurity. Here we have the explanation, or more precisely the beginning of the explanation, of a modern paradox: Why is it that as production has increased in modern times concern for production seems also to have increased? Production has become the center of a concern that had hitherto been shared with equality and security. For these reasons, and supported, we shall see, by an elaborately synthetic reinforcement, it has managed at least superficially to retain the prestige which inevitably it had in the poor world of Ricardo. The nature of the present preoccupation with production, and the devices by which this preoccupation is sustained, are the next order of business.

CHAPTER IX

The Paramount Position
of Production

Some years ago, American statesmen, defending their stewardship under heavy opposition attack, were moved to protest that the current year was the second best in history. It was not, in all respects, a happy defense. Many promptly said that second best was not good enough—certainly not for Americans. But no person in either party showed the slightest disposition to challenge the standard by which it was decided that one year was better than another. Nor was it felt that any explanation was required. No one would be so eccentric as to suppose that second best meant second best in the progress of the arts and the sciences. No one would assume that it referred to health, education or the battle against juvenile delinquency or even violent crime. There was no suggestion that a better or poorer year was one in which the chances for survival amidst the radioactive furniture of the world had increased or diminished. Despite a marked and somewhat ostensible preoccupation with religious observances at the time, no one was moved to suppose that the year in question was the second best as measured by the number of people who had found enduring spiritual solace.

Second best could mean only one thing—that the production of goods was the second highest in history. There had been a year in which production was higher and which hence was better. This measure of achievement was acceptable to all. It is a relief on occasion to find a conclusion that is above faction, indeed above debate. On the importance of production as a test of performance, there is no difference between Republicans and Democrats, right and left, white and minimally prosperous black, Catholic and Protestant. It is common ground for the General Secretary of the Communist Party, the Chairman of Americans for Democratic Action, the President of the United States Chamber of Commerce and the President of the National Association of Manufacturers.

We are, to be sure, regularly told that production is not everything. We set no small store by reminders that there is a spiritual side to life; those who remind are assured a respectful though not necessarily attentive hearing. But it is significant that these are always reminders; they bring to mind what is usually forgotten. No one doubts that in the general course of life one must be sensible and practical. Indeed, it is an index of the prestige of production in our national attitudes that it is identified with the sensible and practical. No greater compliment can be paid to the forthright intelligence of any businessman than to say that he understands production. Scientists are not without prestige in our day, but to be really useful, we still assume that they should be under the direction of a production man. "Any device or regulation which interferes, or can be conceived as interfering, with [the] supply of more and better things is resisted with unreasoning horror, as the religious resist blasphemy, or the warlike pacifism."[1]

The importance of production transcends our boundaries. We are regularly told—in the conventional wisdom it is the most frequent justification of our civilization, even our existence—that the American standard of living is "the marvel of the world." To a very considerable extent, it is.

II

As Tawney observed, we are rarely conscious of the quality of the air we breathe. But in Los Angeles, where it is barely sufficient for its freight, we take it seriously. Similarly, those who reside on a recently reclaimed desert see in the water in the canals the evidence of their unnatural triumph over nature. And the Chicagoan in Sarasota sees in his tanned belly the proof of his intelligence in escaping his dark and frozen habitat. But where sun and rain are abundant, though

[1] Geoffrey Gorer, *The Americans* (London: Cresset Press, 1948), p. 121.

they are no less important, they are taken for granted. In the world of Ricardo, goods were scarce. They were also closely related, if not to the survival, at least to the elemental comforts of man. They fed him, covered him when he was out of doors and kept him warm when he was within. It is not surprising that the production by which these goods were obtained was central to men's thoughts.

Now goods are comparatively abundant. Although there is much malnutrition in the world, more die in the United States of too much food than of too little. No one seriously suggests that all the steel going into the larger of our automobiles is of prime urgency. Their size, in fact, is now deplored. For many women and some men, clothing has ceased to be related to protection from exposure and has become, like plumage, almost exclusively erotic. Yet production remains central to our thoughts. There is no tendency to take it, like sun and water, for granted; on the contrary, it continues to measure the quality and progress of our civilization.

Our preoccupation with production is, in fact, the culminating consequence of powerful historical and psychological forces—forces which only by an act of will we can hope to escape. Productivity, as we have seen, has enabled us to avoid or finesse the tensions anciently associated with inequality and its inconvenient remedies. It has become central to our strivings to reduce insecurity. And as we shall observe in the next chapters, its importance is buttressed by a highly dubious but widely accepted and strenuously defended theory of consumer wants and by powerful vested interest. So all-embracing, indeed, is our sense of the importance of production as a goal that the first reaction to any questioning of this attitude will be, "What else is there?" So large does production bulk in our thoughts that we can only suppose that a vacuum must remain if it should be relegated to a smaller role. Happily, as we shall see in the concluding chapters, there are other things. But first we must examine more closely our present preoccupation with production. For nothing better suggests the extent to which it is founded on tradition and social myth than the highly stylized attitudes with which we approach it and, in particular, the traditional and highly irrational emphasis we accord to the different methods of expanding economic product.

III

Production—the output of the economic system—can, in principle, be increased in five different ways. These are worth listing formally and are as follows:

(1) The productive resources that are available, in particular the labor and capital (including available raw materials), can be more fully employed. In other words, idleness can be eliminated.

(2) Given the technical state of the arts, these resources can be more efficiently employed. Labor and capital can be used in the most advantageous combination, one with the other, and the two can be distributed to the greatest advantage, consumer tastes considered, between the production of various things and the rendering of various services.

(3) The supply of labor can be increased.

(4) The supply of capital, which also serves as a substitute for labor, can be increased.

(5) The state of the arts can be improved by technological innovation. As a result, more output can be obtained from a given supply of labor and capital and the capital will be of better quality.

On purely *a priori* grounds, there is no reason for supposing that any one of these methods of increasing production is more effective than any other.[2] A serious effort to increase

---

2 Study of the comparative effect of these five paths to change does not produce unambiguous results. Changes are closely interrelated. An early study, that of the period between 1869–73 and 1944–53, shows that net national output increased at an average annual rate of 3.5 percent of which about half (1.7 percent) can be attributed to the increase in capital and labor supply. The remainder can reasonably be imputed to technological improvement in capital and the parallel improvement in the people who devise the better capital equipment and operate it. In recent times, a growing share of the increase is attributable to such technological advance and a declining share to mere increases in capital and labor supply. Cf. Moses Abramovtz, *Resources and Output Trends in the United States Since 1870,* and John W. Kendrick, *Productivity Trends: Capital and Labor,* Occasional papers 52 and 53 of the National Bureau of Economic Research, New York, 1956.

output would emphasize all five. Yet it is the truly remarkable fact that we concern ourselves formally in economics with only one of these methods of increasing output and give, at the very most, only passing attention to another two or three.

Thus, even in the conventional wisdom, no one questions the importance of technological advance for increasing the production (and also multiplying the products) from the available resources. These gains are regularly viewed with great and even extravagant pride. Improvements in technology do not come by accident. They are the result of investment in highly organized scientific and engineering knowledge and skills. Yet we do very little of a systematic sort to increase the volume of this investment, except where some objective of military urgency provides the excuse. Rather, we accept whatever investment in technology is currently being made and applaud the outcome.

The investment almost certainly could be much greater and far more rational. Even on the most superficial view, the scientific and engineering resources by which modern technology is advanced are most unevenly distributed between industries. In industries where firms are few and comparatievly large—oil, metallurgy, automobiles, chemicals, rubber, heavy engineering—the investment in technological advance is considerable. The research and developmental work on which this advance depends is well financed and comprehensive. But in many industries where the firms are numerous and small—home construction, clothing manufacture, the natural-fiber textile industry, the service industries—the investment in innovation is negligible. No firm is large enough to afford it on an appreciable scale; there is real question as to whether it is worthwhile for such firms.[8] Unlike agriculture, where innovation is extensively supported by the federal and state governments, there is little or no publicly financed research and development. Yet the absence of investment in innovation in these industries, much though we value its fruits in other in-

8 I have discussed this point in some detail in my *American Capitalism: The Concept of Countervailing Power* (Boston: Houghton Mifflin, 1952, 1956), pp. 84–94.

dustries in which it occurs, excites not the slightest attention. We attach profound importance to the fact that some industries advance. We attach almost no importance to the fact that others do not.

It is easy to overlook the absence of appreciable advance in an industry. Inventions that are not made, like babies that are not born, are rarely missed. In the absence of new developments, old ones may seem very impressive for quite a long while. Until the combine appeared, the self-binder had been the mechanical marvel of the farm machinery industry for forty years. But if we were serious about increased output, we would be much more searching in these matters. Certainly we would regard the absence of investment in innovation in an industry as intolerable. But, in fact, large numbers of industries make little or no such investment, have little or none made on their behalf, and we are quite untroubled.

IV

In everyday economic discourse, nothing is more frequently taken as an index of economic growth than the volume of capital formation. This is the product of saving from current consumption and companion investment. As with technological advance, we content ourselves with whatever volume of capital formation we are getting. An occasional scholar may observe that we are not investing enough—possibly that the proportion of current income invested by the Soviets or the Japanese is much greater. We have routine preachments on the virtues of thrift. But none of this is assumed to call for any practical action. On the contrary, there is a more general conviction that the current volume of investment in the American economy is never less than adequate and is rarely less than remarkable.

As with capital so with the labor force. Once princes and feudal lords who wished to increase the productive wealth of their domains imported craftsmen as a matter of course. So far as there is a single current limitation on the rate of growth in the American economy, it is the size and skill composition of the labor force. (Substitution of capital for labor is ordinarily possible with slight effect on cost over a considerable range of output, but some time is required.) The world contains a great many potential recruits for our labor force. But nothing would be viewed with more suspicion than this method of expanding output. Even to suggest that efforts be made to expand the labor force by increasing the domestic birth rate would seem slightly artful. The resistance arises partly from the belief, not wholly justified, that an increase in population might increase total but not per capita production. No nice philosophical point has ever been so decisively resolved as this: that those who are not conceived do not miss the pleasure of consuming the goods they do not get born to enjoy. But whatever the effect of increasing population on standards of living, it is clear that we are not sufficiently interested in increased output, or sufficiently rational about the means of getting it, to seek it by increasing the labor supply.

Even the production that is lost during a depression—and, as noted in the last chapter, the loss from even a mild setback can be considerable—though it is the subject of a certain amount of erudite regret by economists is not a matter of any general concern. The menace of depressions is not the production that is sacrificed but the jobs and income that are lost—in short, the threat to economic security.

On the other hand, we do take very seriously loss of production which is the result of the deliberate holding of labor or capital out of production or which is the result of any inefficiency in their combination and use. We deplore the malingering workman. We become deeply aroused by the featherbedding union. A monopoly leads, in theory, to a less than optimum employment of labor and capital in a particular industry and therefore a higher than necessary price for the product. The resources not employed in the monopolized industry are employed in larger quantity and to less advantage in other industries, which means that their distribution is less than ideal. No slight enthusiasm can still be aroused for measures that increase output by eliminating monopoly. Economists have never been loath to give their leadership to the effort.[4] There is equal antipathy to and similar popular concern about inefficient use of resources resulting from tariffs and excessive investment in inherently costly industries; about subsidies to favored but inefficient industries or firms; and about the forms of industrial organization which lead to heavy advertising or sales costs or similar seeming waste. Although, curiously, there is no special concern about the industry that does no research and makes little technological progress from one year to the next, nothing inspires indignation like a firm which, having made an invention, holds it out of use.

None of this is here to decry concern for monopoly, tariffs, subsidies or organized and unrepentant idleness. Also, although productive efficiency is the central, it is not the sole issue where these matters are concerned. Rather, my purpose is to show how partial and indeed eccentric is our concern for increased production. Nor are its roots very difficult to uncover. A hundred and twenty-five years ago in mid-nineteenth-century Britain, an economist surveying the possibilities for increasing the production on his islands would have found one important and two or three much less important things to recommend. Most obviously and most importantly, he could urge that by attacking monopolies, lowering tariffs and promoting competition and the free and unhampered movement of labor and capital, the efficiency with which labor and capital were employed would be increased. Much less importantly, he could urge that people be thrifty and save so that the rate of capital formation might be increased. He could always urge workers to be diligent. He could condemn anything that might involve restrictions on their effort or impairment of their incentives.

Few of the modern possibilities for raising production were relevant. In a world that was still under the shadow of Malthus, he could hardly propose adding more people. There were presumed to be as many as the food supply could sus-

---

4 Although there have been competent expressions of doubt as to the losses from monopoly. Cf. in particular "Monopoly and Resource Allocation," by Arnold C. Harberger, *American Economic Review*, Proceedings, Vol. XLIV, No. 2 (May 1954), and "The Social Cost of Corporate Monopoly Profits," by Henry H. Villard, *Political Science Quarterly*, Vol. LXXII, No. 3 (September 1957).

tain. This was well before the age of the large industrial corporation. Only with the arrival of the latter were investment decisions removed from the hands of numerous independent entrepreneurs, responding individually to market incentives, and made subject to a measure of corporate administration. And until this happened, it was not really possible to think of the rate of investment and the consequent rate of growth as anything that might be within range of social interest and decision.

The nineteenth-century scholar could scarcely have been occupied with the volume of research and development in an industry. This is a modern phenomenon and also related to the growth of modern corporate enterprise. In his day, invention was a largely adventitious matter save as it might be encouraged by the patent office. (The patent office, appropriately, was taken very seriously.) The loss of production during depressions was not an issue in a world which lacked good unemployment and output statistics and in which depressions, in any case, were regarded as inevitable.

The lesson will be evident. Our operative concern for increasing production is confined to the measures—for getting greater resource-use efficiency and promoting thrift and diligence—which were relevant a century ago. The newer dimensions along which there might be progress attract our specific and operative attention scarcely at all. The shortcomings and opportunities here are undoubtedly great. But they are outside the formal and stylized concern of the conventional wisdom for the problem of production.

There is an interesting proof of the point in the increase in production which, in the past, we have regularly achieved during war or under the threat of war. Under the stress of circumstance, the conventional wisdom is rejected. We set about expanding output along all the relevant dimensions. Serious efforts are made to expand the labor force. It becomes permissible to import toilers with swarthy skins who speak unintelligible languages. The drive for increased saving becomes serious. Where investment is inadequate, more is made. There is no involuntary idleness. As in the case of alloy steels, synthetic rubber manufacture, and ship construction in World War II, technology is brought purposefully to play to permit of expanded output with available resources. It is at least amusing (though not too much store should be set by the point) that during both World Wars the enforcement of the antitrust laws, the traditional design for ensuring greater resource-use efficiency, was suspended. Because of a rational concern for production, war has brought an astonishing expansion in output, and this despite the withdrawals from the labor force for military purpose.

Though we have been astonished, we should not have been. Our peacetime concern for production, central though it is to our thoughts, is selective and traditional. As a result, at any given time both our total output and its rate of increase are only a small part of what they might be, perhaps indeed only a minor fraction. Nor would the necessary measures to expand the labor force, expand the rate of capital formation, and, perhaps most important, to bring technology to bear on presently backward industries require any very revolutionary change in our economic and political system. It would only require that production have the priority in all public policy which it now has in the traditional areas of resource use and combination.

V

There is another respect in which our concern for production is traditional and irrational. We are curiously unreasonable in the distinctions we make between different kinds of goods and services. We view the production of some of the most frivolous goods with pride. We regard the production of some of the most significant and civilizing services with regret.

Economists in calculating the total output of the economy—in arriving at the now familiar Gross National Product—add together the value of all goods and all services of whatever sort and by whomsoever produced. No distinction is made between public and privately produced services. An increased supply of educational services has a standing in the total not different in kind from an increased output of television receivers. Nothing, however, could be more in conflict with traditional attitudes, and indeed it is rather surprising that economists have not been reproached by the rather considerable number of individuals who, if they fully understood the nature of the calculation, would regard the inclusion of government spending as subversive.

In the general view, it is privately produced production that is important, and that nearly alone. This adds to national well-being. Its increase measures the increase in national wealth. Public services, by comparison, are an incubus. They are necessary, and they may be necessary in considerable volume. But they are a burden which must, in effect, be carried by the private production. If that burden is too great, private production will stagger and fall.

At best, public services are a necessary evil; at worst, they are a malign tendency against which an alert community must exercise eternal vigilance. Even when they serve the most important ends, such services are sterile. "Government is powerless to create anything in the sense in which business produces wealth . . ."[5] Such attitudes lead to some interesting contradictions. We welcome expansion of telephone services as improving the general well-being but accept curtailment of postal services as signifying necessary economy. We set great store by the increase in private wealth but regret the added outlays for the police force by which it is protected. Vacuum cleaners to ensure clean houses are praiseworthy and essential in our standard of living. Street cleaners to ensure clean streets are an unfortunate expense. Partly as a result, our houses are generally clean and our streets generally filthy. In the more sophisticated of the conventional wisdom, this distinction between public and private services is much less sharp and, as I have observed, it does not figure in the calculation of Gross National Product. However, it never quite disappears. Even among economists and political philosophers, public services rarely lose their connotation of burden. Although they may be defended, their volume is almost certainly never a source of pride.

VI

There are a number of reasons for these attitudes, but again tradition plays a dominant role. In the world into which

[5] Francis X. Sutton, Seymour E. Harris, Carl Kaysen, and James Tobin, *The American Business Creed* (Cambridge, Mass.: Harvard University Press, 1956), p. 195.

economics was born, the four most urgent requirements of man were food, clothing and shelter, and an orderly environment in which the first three might be provided. The first three lent themselves to private production for the market; given good order, this production has ordinarily gone forward with tolerable efficiency. But order which was the gift of government was nearly always supplied with notable unreliability. With rare exceptions, it was also inordinately expensive. And the pretext of providing order not infrequently afforded the occasion for rapacious appropriation of the means of sustenance of the people.

Not surprisingly, modern economic ideas incorporated a strong suspicion of government. The goal of nineteenth-century economic liberalism was a state which did provide order reliably and inexpensively and which did as little as possible else. Even Marx intended that the state should wither away. These attitudes have persisted in the conventional wisdom. And again events have dealt them a series of merciless blows. Once a society has provided itself with food, clothing and shelter, all of which so fortuitously lend themselves to private production, purchase and sale, its members begin to desire other things. And a remarkable number of these things do not lend themselves to such production, purchase and sale. They must be provided for everyone if they are to be provided for anyone, and they must be paid for collectively or they cannot be had at all. Such is the case with clean streets and police and the general advantages of mass literacy and sanitation, the control of epidemics, and the common defense. There is a strong possibility that the services which must be rendered collectively, although they enter the general scheme of wants after the immediate physical necessities, increase in urgency more than proportionately with increasing wealth. This is more likely if increasing wealth is matched by increasing population and increasing density of population. Nonetheless, these services, although they reflect increasingly urgent desires, remain under the obloquy of the unreliability, incompetence, cost and pretentious interference of princes. Alcohol, comic books and mouthwash all bask under the superior reputation of the market. Schools, judges, patrolmen, and municipal swimming pools lie under the evil reputation of bad kings.

Moreover, bad kings in a poorer world showed themselves to be quite capable, in their rapacity, of destroying or damaging the production of private goods by destroying the people and the capital that produced them. Economies are no longer so vulnerable. Governments are not so undiscriminating. In western countries, in modern times, economic growth and expanding public activity have, with rare exceptions, gone together. Each has served the other, as indeed they must. Yet the conventional wisdom is far from surrendering on the point. Any growth in public services is a manifestation of an intrinsically evil trend. If the vigor of the race is not in danger, personal liberty is. The structure of the economy may also be at stake. In one branch of the conventional wisdom, the American economy is never far removed from socialism, and the movement toward socialism may be measured by the rise in public spending. Thus, even the most commonplace of public services, for one part of the population, fall under the considerable handicap of being identified with social revolution.

Finally—also a closely related point—the payment for publicly produced services has long been linked to the problem of inequality. By having the rich pay more, the services were provided and at the same time the goal of greater equality was advanced. This community of objectives has never appealed to those being equalized. Not unnaturally, some part of their opposition has been directed to the public services themselves. By attacking these, they could attack the leveling tendencies of taxation. This has helped to keep alive the notion that the public services for which they pay are inherently inferior to privately produced goods.

While public services have been subject to these negitave attitudes, private goods have had no such attention. On the contrary, their virtues have been extolled by the massed drums of modern advertising. They have been pictured as the ultimate wealth of the community. Clearly the competition between public and private services, apart from any question of the satisfactions they render, is an unequal one. The social consequences of this discrimination—this tendency to accord a superior prestige to private goods and an inferior role to public production—are considerable and even grave.

VII

By way of summary, then, while production has come to have a goal of pre-eminent importance in our life, it is not a goal which we pursue either comprehensively or even very thoughtfully. We take production as the measure of our achievement, but we do not strive very deliberately to achieve. Our efforts to increase production are stylized. We stress the evils of idleness and bad resource allocation which were relevant to efforts to increase output a century ago. We do little or nothing in peacetime to increase the rate of capital formation or the rate of technological progress in background industries despite the clear indication that these are the dimensions along which large increases in output are to be expected. We would not deplore the production we lost in depression. We are protected from this loss far more by the threat of depression to economic security. Last of all, on ancient and traditional grounds, we relegate one important class of production, that of public goods, to a second-class citizenship.

The predictable reaction of many readers will be that we should by all means address ourselves to the measures for increasing output that we now ignore. However, a closer look is called for. We need to understand the reasons for our passivity in this matter. In the past, under conditions of emergency, we have addressed ourselves seriously to the measures by which output is seriously increased. Perhaps we fail to do so in present circumstances less because of ignorance or inertia than because the additional production is not of sufficient urgency to justify the effort. Our preoccupation with production, in other words, may be a preoccupation with a problem of rather low urgency. We are not sufficiently concerned about it to have recourse to the measures by which production could be efficiently increased. We are content with what we get, which comes close to saying that we are deeply concerned with production only so far as the problem solves itself. We set great store by doing what, in a manner of speaking, comes naturally.

None of this would be possible if the goods we produced were of great and urgent importance. Then we would be searching vigorously for ways of increasing the supply instead, as at present, of regarding with approval the increases we obtain. All this becomes intelligible, and in degree even obvious, when we contemplate the elaborate myth with which we surround the demand for goods. This has enabled us to become persuaded of the dire importance of the goods we have without our being in the slightest degree concerned about those we do not have. For we have wants at the margin only so far as they are synthesized. We do not manufacture wants for goods we do not produce.

CHAPTER X

The Imperatives
of Consumer Demand

In an economy, such as that of the United
States of America, where leisure is barely
moral, the problem of creating sufficient
wants . . . to absorb productive capacity may
become chronic in the not too distant future.
In such a situation the economist begins to
lead a furtive existence.
                                    —W. Beckerman[1]

Both the ancient preoccupation with production and the
pervasive modern search for security have culminated in our
time in a concern for production. Increased real income
provides us with an admirable detour around the rancor anciently associated with efforts to redistribute weatlh. A high
level of production has become the keystone of effective
economic security. There remains, however, the task of justi-
fying the resulting flow of goods. Production cannot be an incidental to the mitigation of inequality or the provision of
jobs. It must have a raison d'être of its own. At this point,
economists and economic theory have entered the game. So,
more marginally, has the competitive prestige that goes with
expanding national product. The result has been an elaborate
and ingenious defense of the importance of production as
such. It is a defense which makes the urgency of production
largely indepedent of the volume of production. In this way,
economic theory has managed to transfer the sense of ur-

[1] "The Economist as a Modern Missionary," *The Economic Journal*,
March 1956.

gency in meeting consumer need that once was felt in a world where more production meant more food for the hungry, more clothing for the cold, and more houses for the homeless to a world where increased output satisfies the craving for more elegant automobiles, more exotic food, more erotic clothing, more elaborate entertainment—indeed, for the entire modern range of sensuous, edifying and lethal desires.

Although the economic theory which defends these desires and hence the production that supplies them has an impeccable (and to an astonishing degree even unchallenged) position in the conventional wisdom, it is illogical and meretricious and, in degree, even dangerous.

II

The rationalization begins with the peculiar urgency of production not to society but to economic science. There will be occasion later for considering the vested interest in production, but it may be noted here that the interest of the economist is unique. The importance of production is central to his scheme of economic calculation. All existing pedagogy and nearly all research depend on it. Any action which increases production from given resources is good and implicitly important; anything which inhibits or reduces output is, *pro tanto*, wrong. In the choice between two taxes, there is a nearly overriding case for the one that least damages efficiency, meaning the output from a given stock of labor and capital. If a company seems to be restricting production to enhance returns, or for any other reason, it can safely be condemned as antisocial. This is at least equally so with a trade union. The test of effect on productive efficiency is all but universal.

To assess the effect of a given action or measure, say a new union rule, on production is not always easy. There may be a complicated chain of cause and effect on which opinions will differ. The effect on the short run may be different from that on the long. And where it is necessary to assess the effect on a variety of products, or on the total output of the economy, there are numerous difficulties. The latter must be valued, and the prices at which individual items are valued will reflect the existing income distribution (the prices of mink pelts reflect the demand of an opulent minority), or, in some cases, the more or less arbitrary decision of the firms that administer the prices. Hence, to trace and compare the effect of different policies on the output of the economy can be endlessly intricate. But all this provides much of the interest of economics as well as a good deal of its employment. And underlying all is the bedrock agreement on the goal and on the importance of that goal. Anything that increases the product from given resources increases welfare. It is important that it be done. Here is the anchor. To cast doubt on the importance of production is thus to bring into question the foundation of the entire edifice. Action must then be tested by new criteria—criteria which are necessarily difficult and subjective. Nothing could be less welcome. At least in social disciplines, obsolescence and irrelevance are a small price to pay for the privilege of remaining comfortably, even if archaically, with the familiar, the settled and the safe.

And the profession of economics is not lacking in the instinct of self-preservation. The mother bear sees in the threat to her cubs the ultimate threat to the survival of her kind. She reacts with angry venom. Nothing is more likely to produce a similar reaction from defenders of the conventional economic wisdom than an attack on the edifice which now rationalizes the importance of production and the urgency of consumer need.

The parallel with maternal instinct is important, for the defense of the present value system as it relates to production is largely intuitive. Few economists in recent years can have escaped some uneasinss over the kinds of goods which their value system is insisting they must maximize. They have wondered about the urgency of numerous products of great frivolity. They have been uneasy about the lengths to which it has been necessary to go with advertising and salesmanship to synthesize the desire for such goods. That uneasiness has reflected the crucial weakness of the literature on this point.

The weakness, as well as the ultimate defense, lies with the theory of consumer demand. This is a formidable structure; it has already demonstrated its effectiveness in defending the urgency of production. In a world where affluence is rendering the old ideas obsolete, it will continue to be the bastion against the misery of new ones.

III

The theory of consumer demand, as is now widely accepted, is based on two broad propositions, neither of them quite explicit but both extremely important for the present value system of economists. The first is that the urgency of wants does not diminish appreciably as more of them are satisfied or, to put the matter more precisely, to the extent that this happens, it is not demonstrable and not a matter of any interest to economists or for economic policy. When man has satisfied his physical needs, then psychologically grounded desires take over. These can never be satisfied or, in any case, no progress can be proved. The concept of satiation has very little standing in economics. It is held to be neither useful nor scientific to speculate on the comparative cravings of the stomach and the mind.

The second proposition is that wants originate in the personality of the consumer or, in any case, that they are given data for the economist. The latter's task is merely to seek their satisfaction. He has no need to inquire how these wants are formed. His function is sufficiently fulfilled by maximizing the goods that supply the wants.

The examination of these two conclusions must now be pressed. The explanation of consumer behavior has its ancestry in a much older problem, indeed the oldest problem of economics, that of price determination.[2] Nothing originally proved more troublesome in the explanation of prices, i.e., exchange values, than the indigestible fact that some of the most useful things had the least value in exchange and some of the least useful had the most. As Adam Smith observed: "Nothing is more useful than water; but it will purchase scarce anything; scarce anything can be had in exchange for it. A diamond, on the contrary, has scarce any value in use:

[2] The provenance of the theory of consumer behavior is sketched in I.D.M. Little's interesting article, "A Reformulation of Consumer Behavior," *Oxford Economic Papers*, New Series, Vol. 1, No. 1 (January 1949), p. 99.

but a very great quantity of other goods may frequently be had in exchange for it."[8]

In explaining value, Smith thought it well to distinguish between "value in exchange" and "value in use" and sought thus to reconcile the paradox of high utility and low exchangeablity. This distinction begged questions rather than solved them, and for another hundred years, economists sought for a satisfactory formulation. Finally, toward the end of the last century—though it is now recognized that their work had been extensively anticipated—the three economists of marginal utility (Karl Menger, an Austrian; William Stanley Jevons, an Englishman; and John Bates Clark, an American) produced more or less simultaneously the explanation which, in broad substance, still serves. The urgency of desire is a function of the quantity of goods which the individual has available to satisfy that desire. The larger the stock, the less the satisfactions from an increment. And the less, also, the willingness to pay. Since diamonds for most people are in comparatively meager supply, the satisfaction from an additional one is great, and the potential willingness to pay is likewise high. The case of water is just the reverse. It also follows that where the supply of a good can be readily increased at low cost, its value in exchange will reflect that ease of reproduction and the low urgency of the marginal desires it thus comes to satisfy. This will be so no matter how difficult it may be (as with water) to dispense entirely with the item in question.

The doctrine of diminishing marginal utility, as it was enshrined in the economics textbooks, seemed to put economic ideas squarely on the side of the diminishing importance of production under conditions of increasing affluence. With increasing per capita real income, men are able to satisfy additional wants. These are of a lower order of urgency. This being so, the production that provides the goods that satisfy these less urgent wants must also be of smaller (and declining) importance. In Ricardo's England, the supply of bread for many was meager. The satisfaction resulting from an increment in the bread supply—from a higher money income,

[8] *Wealth of Nations.* Smith did not foresee the industrial diamond.

bread prices being the same, or the same money income, bread prices being lower—was great. Hunger was lessened; life itself might be extended. Certainly any measure to increase the bread supply merited the deep and serious interest of the public-spirited citizen.

In the contemporary United States, the supply of bread remains plentiful. The yield of satisfactions from a marginal increment in the supply is small. Measures to increase the supply of bread or wheat have not, therefore, been a socially urgent preoccupation of publicly concerned citizens.[4] Having extended their bread consumption to the point where its marginal utility is very low, people in the industrial countries have gone on to spend their income on other things. Since these other goods entered their consumption pattern after bread, there is a presumption that they are not very urgent either—that *their* consumption has been carried, as with wheat, to the point where marginal utility is small or even negligible. So it must be assumed that the importance of marginal increments of all production is low and declining. The effect of increasing affluence is to minimize the importance of economic goals. Production and productivity become less and less important.

The concept of diminishing marginal utility was, and remains, one of the indispensable ideas of economics. Since it conceded so much to the notion of diminishing urgency of wants, and hence of production, it was remarkable indeed that the situation was retrieved. This was done—and brilliantly. The diminishing urgency of wants was not admitted. In part, this was accomplished in the name of refined scientific method which, as so often at the higher levels of sophistication, proved a formidable bulwark of the conventional wisdom. Obvious but inconvenient evidence was rejected on the grounds that it could not be scientifically assimilated. But even beyond this, it has been necessary at times simply to close one's eyes to phenomena which could not be reconciled with convenience.

4 Earlier editions, with more foresight than I've always manifested, warned that "some possible circumstances of world shortage" could increase this preoccupation. As regards world needs, they have.

IV

The first step, as noted earlier, was to divorce economics from any judgment on the goods with which it was concerned. Any notion of necessary versus unnecessary or important as against unimportant goods was rigorously excluded from the subject. Alfred Marshall, who on this, as on so many other things, laid down the rules to which economists have since adhered, noted that "the economist studies mental states rather through their manifestations than in themselves; and if he finds they afford evenly balanced incentives to action he treats them prima facie as for his purposes equal."[5] He almost immediately added that this simplification, which indeed has rendered profound scientific service to economics, was only a "starting-point." But economists ever since have been content to stay with his starting point and to make it a mark of scholarly restraint and scientific virtue to do so. Nothing is so thoroughly drilled into the minds of the young as the need for this restraint. Nothing in economics so quickly marks an individual as incompetently trained as a disposition to remark on the legitimacy of the desire for more food and the frivolity of the desire for a more expensive automobile.

Next, economics took general cognizance of the fact that an almost infinite variety of goods await the consumer's attention. At the more elementary (and also the more subjective) levels of economic analysis, it is assumed that, while the marginal utility of the individual good declines in accordance with the indubitable law, the utility or satisfaction from a new and different good is not lower than from the initial units of those preceding. So long as the consumer adds new products—seeks variety rather than quantity—he may, like a museum, accumulate without diminishing the urgency of his wants. Since even in Texas the average consumer owns only a fraction of the different kinds of goods he might conceivably possess, there is all but unlimited opportunity for adding such products. The rewards to the possessors are more or less proportional to the supply. The production that supplies these

5 *Principles of Economics*, 8th ed. (London: Macmillan, 1927), p. 16.

goods and services, since it renders undiminished utility, remains of undiminished importance.

This position ignores the obvious fact that some things are acquired before others and that, presumably, the more important things come first. This, as observed previously, implies a declining urgency of need. However, in the slightly more sophisticated theory, this conclusion is rejected. The rejection centers on the denial that anything very useful can be said of the comparative states of mind and satisfaction of the consumer at different periods of time. Few students of economics, even in the elementary course, now escape without a warning against the error of intertemporal comparisons of the utility from given acts of consumption. Yesterday the man with a minimal but increasing real income was reaping the satisfactions which came from a decent diet and a roof that no longer leaked water on his face. Today, after a large increase in his income, he has extended his consumption to include color television and eccentric loafers. But to say that his satisfactions from these latter amenities and recreations are less than from the additional calories and the freedom from rain is wholly improper. Things have changed; he is a different man; there is no real standard for comparison. That, as of a given time, an individual will derive lesser satisfactions from the marginal increments to a given stock of goods, and accordingly cannot be induced to pay as much for them, is conceded. But this tells us nothing of the satisfactions from such additional goods, and more particularly from different goods, when they are acquired at a later time. The conclusion follows. One cannot be sure that the satisfaction from these temporally later increases in the individual's stock of goods diminishes. Hence, one cannot suggest that the production which supplies it is of diminishing urgency.

A moment's reflection on what has been accomplished will be worthwhile. The notion of diminishing utility still serves its indispensable purpose of relating urgency of desire and consequent willingness to pay to quantity. At any given time the more the individual might have, the less would be the satisfaction he would derive from additions to his stock and the less he would be willing to pay. The reactions of the community will be the aggregate of the reactions of the individuals it comprises. Hence, the greater the supply the less the willingness to pay for marginal increments and hence, the demand curve familiar to all who have made even the most modest venture into economic theory. But, at the same time, the question of the diminishing urgency of consumption is elided. For, while the question of willingness to pay for additional quantities is based on a hypothesis as to behavior in face of these quantities at a given point of time, an increase in stock of consumer's goods, as the result of an increase in real income, can occur only over time. On the yield of satisfactions from this the economist has nothing to say. In the name of good scientific method, he is prevented from saying anything.[6] There is room, however, for the broad assumption—given the large and ever-growing variety of goods awaiting the consumer's attention—that wants have a sustained urgency. In any case, it can safely be concluded that more goods will satisfy more wants than fewer goods. And the as-

---

[6] In the yet more technical analysis of consumer demand, attention has been further diverted from the diminishing urgency of product by the shift from cardinal to ordinal utility as an instrument of analysis. Ordinal analysis treats the consumer's desires strictly in terms of the preferences of one good as against the other. This does not mean either that the notion of diminishing marginal utility of a good or the diminishing urgency of additional products disappears. In the indifference map or surface, diminishing marginal utility is what makes the consumer willing, with an increasing stock, to surrender more and more of one product to have a given quantity of another. Recreation will not enter the consumer's preference system except in combination with some minimum quantity of food. Food can be present without recreation.

However, these considerations are not obtrusive in the analysis or its pedagogy. The much more evident fact is that food, gasoline and pinball all exchange for one another at given rates and thus are equated one with the other. The point most stressed in the pedagogy is that the consumer will always find his highest satisfaction on the highest indifference curve that his income allows him to reach. The effect of higher income or of a larger product at lower prices is to put the consumer on a higher curve. This goal is implicit in the analysis. Thus, a line of thought which once might seem to throw doubt on the importance of marginal increments to the stock of goods ends by affirming it. In practice, the analytical apparatus exludes from consideration the possibility that the movement to higher and higher indifference curves is of declining urgency.

The unprofessional reader who wishes to acquaint himself with the essentials of this analysis will find a competent and lucid summary in Paul A. Samuelson's chapter appendix, "Geometrical Analysis of Consumer Equilibrium," *Economics,* 9th ed. (New York: McGraw-Hill, 1973), pp. 441–448.

sumption that goods are an important and even an urgent thing to provide stalks unchallenged behind, for have not goods always been important for relieving the privation of mankind? It will be evident that economics has brilliantly retrieved the dangers to itself and to its goals that were inherent in diminishing marginal utility.

There has been dissent. Keynes observed that the needs of human beings "fall into two classes—those needs which are absolute in the sense that we feel them whatever the situation of our fellow human beings may be, and those which are relative only in that their satisfaction lifts us above, makes us feel superior to, our fellows."[7] However, on this conclusion, Keynes made no headway. In contending with the conventional wisdom, he, no less than others, needed the support of circumstances. And in contrast with his remedy for depressions, this he did not yet have.

[7] J. M. Keynes, *Essays in Persuasion,* "Economic Possibilities for Our Grandchildren" (London: Macmillan, 1931), pp. 365–66. The italics are in the original. Notice that Keynes, as always little bound by the conventional rules, did not hesitate to commit the unpardonable sin of distinguishing between categories of desire.

CHAPTER XI

The Dependence Effect

The notion that wants do not become less urgent the more amply the individual is supplied is broadly repugnant to common sense. It is something to be believed only by those who wish to believe. Yet the conventional wisdom must be tackled on its own terrain. Intertemporal comparisons of an individual's state of mind do rest on technically vulnerable ground. Who can say for sure that the deprivation which afflicts him with hunger is more painful than the deprivation which afflicts him with envy of his neighbor's new car? In the time that has passed since he was poor, his soul may have become subject to a new and deeper searing. And where a society is concerned, comparisons between marginal satisfactions when it is poor and those when it is affluent will involve not only the same individual at different times but different individuals at different times. The scholar who wishes to believe that with increasing affluence there is no reduction in the urgency of desires and goods is not without points for debate. However plausible the case against him, it cannot be proven. In the defense of the conventional wisdom, this amounts almost to invulnerability.

However, there is a flaw in the case. If the individual's wants are to be urgent, they must be original with himself. They cannot be urgent if they must be contrived for him. And above all, they must not be contrived by the process of production by which they are satisfied. For this means that the whole case for the urgency of production, based on the urgency of wants, falls to the ground. One cannot defend production as satisfying wants if that production creates the wants.

Were it so that a man on arising each morning was as

121

sailed by demons which instilled in him a passion sometimes for silk shirts, sometimes for kitchenware, sometimes for chamber pots, and sometimes for orange squash, there would be every reason to applaud the effort to find the goods, however odd, that quenched this flame. But should it be that his passion was the result of his first having cultivated the demons, and should it also be that his effort to allay it stirred the demons to ever greater and greater effort, there would be question as to how rational was his solution. Unless restrained by conventional attitudes, he might wonder if the solution lay with more goods or fewer demons.

So it is that if production creates the wants it seeks to satisfy, or if the wants emerge *pari passu* with the production, then the urgency of the wants can no longer be used to defend the urgency of the production. Production only fills a void that it has itself created.

II

The point is so central that it must be pressed. Consumer wants can have bizarre, frivolous, or even immoral origins, and an admirable case can still be made for a society that seeks to satisfy them. But the case cannot stand if it is the process of satisfying wants that creates the wants. For then the individual who urges the importance of production to satisfy these wants is precisely in the position of the onlooker who applauds the efforts of the squirrel to keep abreast of the wheel that is propelled by his own efforts.

That wants are, in fact, the fruit of production will now be denied by few serious scholars. And a considerable number of economists, though not always in full knowledge of the implications, have conceded the point. In the observation cited at the end of the preceding chapter, Keynes noted that needs of "the second class," i.e., those that are the result of efforts to keep abreast or ahead of one's fellow being, "may indeed be insatiable; for the higher the general level, the higher still are they."[1] And emulation has always played a

1 J. M. Keynes, *Essays in Persuasion*, "Economic Possibilities for Our Grandchildren" (London: Macmillan, 1931), p. 365.

considerable role in the views of other economists of want satisfied is also the process by which wants are created. The creation. One man's consumption becomes his neighbors' wish. This already means that the process by which wants are more wants that are satisfied, the more new ones are born.

However, the argument has been carried farther. A leading modern theorist of consumer behavior, Professor Duesenberry, has stated explicitly that "ours is a society in which one of the principal social goals is a higher standard of living . . . [This] has great significance for the theory of consumption . . . the desire to get superior goods takes on a life of its own. It provides a drive to higher expenditure which may even be stronger than that arising out of the needs which are supposed to be satisfied by that expenditure."[2] The implications of this view are impressive. The notion of independently estabilshed need now sinks into the background. Because the society sets great store by ability to produce a high living standard, it evaluates people by the products they possess. The urge to consume is fathered by the value system which emphasizes the ability of the society to produce. The more that is produced, the more that must be owned in order to maintain the appropriate prestige. The latter is an important point, for, without going as far as Duesenberry in reducing goods to the role of symbols of prestige in the affluent society, it is plain that his argument fully implies that the production of goods creates the wants that the goods are presumed to satisfy. [3]

---

[2] James S. Duesenberry, *Income, Saving and the Theory of Consumer Behavior* (Cambridge, Mass.: Harvard University Press, 1949), p. 28.
[3] A more recent and definitive study of consumer demand has added even more support. Professors Houthakker and Taylor, in a statistical study of the determinants of demand, found that for most products price and income, the accepted determinants, were less important than past consumption of the product. This "psychological stock," as they called it, concedes the weakness of traditional theory; current demand cannot be explained without recourse to past consumption. Such demand nurtures the need for its own increase. H. S. Houthakker and L. D. Taylor, *Consumer Demand in the United States*, 2nd ed., enlarged (Cambrdge, Mass.: Harvard University Press, 1970).

III

The even more direct link between production and wants is provided by the institutions of modern advertising and salesmanship. These cannot be reconciled with the notion of independently dertermined desires, for their central function is to create desires—to bring into being wants that previously did not exist.[4] This is accomplished by the producer of the goods or at his behest. A broad empirical relationship exists between what is spent on production of consumer goods and what is spent in synthesizing the desires for that production. A new consumer product must be introduced with a suitable advertising campaign to arouse an interest in it. The path for an expansion of output must be paved by a suitable expansion in the advertising budget. Outlays for the manufacturing of a product are not more important in the strategy of modern business enterprise than outlays for the manufacturing of demand for the product. None of this is novel. All would be regarded as elementary by the most retarded student in the nation's most primitive school of business administration. The cost of this want formation is formidiable. In 1974, total advertising expenditure—though, as noted, not all of it may be assigned to the synthesis of wants—amounted to approximately twenty-five billion dollars. The increase in previous years was by about a billion dollars a year. Obviously, such outlays must be integrated with the theory of consumer demand. They are too big to be ignored.

But such integration means recognizing that wants are dependent on production. It accords to the producer the function both of making the goods and of making the disires for

---

[4] Advertising is not a simple phenomenon. It is also important in competitive strategy and want creation, is, ordinarily, a complementary result of efforts to shift the demand curve of the individual firm at the expense of others or (less importantly, I think) to change its shape by increasing the degree of product differentiation. Some of the failure of economists to identify advertising with want creation may be attributed to the undue attention that its use in purely competitive strategy has attracted. It should be noted, however, that the competitive manipulation of consumer desire is only possible, at least on any appreciable scale, when such need is not strongly felt.

them. It recognizes that production, not only passively through emulation, but actively through advertising and related activities, creates the wants it seeks to satisfy.

The businessman and the lay reader will be puzzled over the emphasis which I give to a seemingly obvious point. The point is indeed obvious. But it is one which, to a singular degree, economists have resisted. They have sensed, as the layman does not, the damage to established ideas which lurks in these relationships. As a result, incredibly, they have closed their eyes (and ears) to the most obtrusive of all economic phenomena, namely, modern want creation.

This is not to say that the evidence affirming the dependence of wants on advertising has been entirely ignored. It is one reason why advertising has so long been regarded with such uneasiness by economists. Here is something which cannot be accommodated easily to existing theory. More pervious scholars have speculated on the urgency of desires which are so obviously the fruit of such expensively contrived campaigns for popular attention. Is a new breakfast cereal or detergent so much wanted if so much must be spent to compel in the consumer the sense of want? But there has been little tendency to go on to examine the implications of this for the theory of consumer demand and even less for the importance of production and productive efficiency. These have remained sacrosanct. More often, the uneasiness has been manifested in a general disapproval of advertising and advertising men, leading to the occasional suggestion that they shouldn't exist. Such suggestions have usually been ill received in the advertising business.

And so the notion of independently determined wants still survives. In the face of all the forces of modern salesmanship, it still rules, almost undefiled, in the textbooks. And it still remains the economist's mission—and on few matters is the pedagogy so firm—to seek unquestioningly the means for filling these wants. This being so, production remains of prime urgency. We have here, perhaps, the ultimate triumph of the conventional wisdom in its resistance to the evidence of the eyes. To equal it, one must imagine a humanitarian who was long ago persuaded of the grievous shortage of hospital facilities in the town. He continues to importune the passersby for money for more beds and refuses to notice that the town doctor is deftly knocking over pedestrains with his car to keep up the occupancy.

And in unraveling the complex, we should always be careful not to overlook the obvious. The fact that wants can be synthesized by advertising, catalyzed by salesmanship, and shaped by the discreet manipulations of the persuaders shows that they are not very urgent. A man who is hungry need never be told of his need for food. If he is inspired by his appetite, he is immune to the influence of Messrs. Batten, Barton, Durstine & Osborn. The latter are effective only with those who are so far removed from physical want that they do not already know what they want. In this state alone, men are open to persuasion.

IV

The general conclusion of these pages is of such importance for this essay that it had perhaps best be put with some formality. As a society becomes increasingly affluent, wants are increasingly created by the process by which they are satisfied. This may operate passively. Increases in consumption, the counterpart of increases in production, act by suggestion or emulation to create wants. Expectation rises with attainment. Or producers may proceed actively to create wants through advertising and salesmanship. Wants thus come to depend on output. In technical terms, it can no longer be assumed that welfare is greater at an all-round higher level of production than at a lower one. It may be the same. The higher level of production has, merely, a higher level of want creation necessitating a higher level of want satisfaction. There will be frequent occasion to refer to the way wants depend on the process by which they are satisfied. It will be convenient to call it the Dependence Effect.

We may now contemplate briefly the conclusions to which this analysis has brought us.

Plainly, the theory of consumer demand is a peculiarly treacherous friend of the present goals of economics. At first glance, it seems to defend the continuing urgency of production and our preoccupation with it as a goal. The economist does not enter into the dubious moral arguments about the importance or virtue of the wants to be satisfied.

He doesn't pretend to compare mental states of the same or different people at different times and to suggest that one is less urgent than another. The desire is there. That for him is sufficient. He sets about in a workmanlike way to satisfy desire, and accordingly, he sets the proper store by the production that does. Like woman's, his work is never done.

But this rationalization, handsomely though it seems to serve, turns destructively on those who advance it once it is conceded that wants are themselves both passively and deliberately the fruits of the process by which they are satisfied. Then the production of goods satisfies the wants that the consumption of these goods creates or that the producers of goods synthesize. Production induces more wants and the need for more production. So far, in a major tour de force, the implications have been ignored. But this obviously is a perilous solution. It cannot long survive discussion.

Among the many models of the good society, no one has urged the squirrel wheel. Moreover, as we shall see presently, the wheel is not one that revolves with perfect smoothness. Aside from its dubious cultural charm, there are serious structural weaknesses which may one day embarrass us. For the moment, however, it is sufficient to reflect on the difficult terrain which we are traversing. In Chapter VIII, we saw how deeply we were committed to production for reasons of economic security. Not the goods but the employment provided by their production was the thing by which we set ultimate store. Now we find our concern for goods further undermined. It does not arise in spontaneous consumer need. Rather, the dependence effect means that it grows out of the process of production itself. If production is to increase, the wants must be effectively contrived. In the absence of the contrivance, the increase would not occur. This is not true of all goods, but that it is true of a substantial part is sufficient. It means that since the demand for this part would not exist, were it not contrived, its utility or urgency, *ex* contrivance, is zero. If we regard this production as marginal, we may say that the marginal utility of present aggregate output, *ex* advertising and salesmanship, is zero. Clearly the attitudes and values which make production the central achievement of our society have some exceptionally twisted roots.

Perhaps the thing most evident of all is how new and

127

varied become the problems we must ponder when we break the nexus with the work of Ricardo and face the economics of affluence of the world in which we live. It is easy to see why the conventional wisdom resists so stoutly such change. It is far, far better and much safer to have a firm anchor in nonsense than to put out on the troubled seas of thought.

CHAPTER XII

The Vested Interest in Output

The notion of a vested interest has an engaging flexibility in our social usage. In ordinary intercourse, it is an improper advantage enjoyed by a political minority to which the speaker does not himself belong. When the speaker himself enjoys it, it ceases to be a vested interest and becomes a hard-won reward. When a vested interest is enjoyed not by a minority but a majority, it is a human right. These conceptual pitfalls notwithstanding, the time has come for a survey of the vested interests in our present attitudes toward production. Who is most dependent on the present illusion? Who will be most affected when, under the onslaught of ideas, circumstances and time itself, these matters come to appear in a clearer light? As a general makes a reconnaissance of the opposing forces, the author should know who is dug in against him.

Without question, the individual with the greatest stake in the present economic goals is the businessman—more precisely, perhaps, the important business executive. If production is of preoccupying importance, he, as the man with the tradiditional and established right to the title of producer, will be the dominant figure in the social constellation. Society will accord him prestige appropriate to the role he plays; what may well be less important, he will be able, without difficulty or criticism, to command an income that is related to his prestige. As production has increasingly monopolized our economic attitudes, the business executive has grown in esteem. So long as inequality was a matter of serious concern, the tycoon had, at best, an ambiguous position. He performed a function of obvious urgency. But he was also regularly accused of taking far too much for his services. As concern for inequality has declined, this reaction has disappeared. The businessman is no longer subject to a serious challenge of any sort. Although in his hierarchical role in the large corporation he has, perhaps, been more successful than most in eliminating economic insecurity, both personal and institutional, he has even managed to retain a certain cachet as a risk-taker, a man who lives dangerously. No one questions the superior position of the businessman in American society. But no one should doubt that it depends on the continuing preoccupation with production.

The case of water under conditions of plenty and shortage has been mentioned before. Many years ago, the City of New York suffered from a potentially troublesome water shortage. Clouds were watched anxiously and seeded in the hope that they might yield their burden. With fanfare, a program of water conservation was launched. The washing of automobiles, dripping of faucets, sluicing of streets and cooling of air were all prohibited. Presiding over the considerable publicity which these results required was the New York City water commissioner, Mr. Stephen J. Carney. For the time, he was the most important man in the metropolis. His name was on everyone's tongue. Mr. Carney was a public figure. Then the rains came, and the reservoirs filled. Carney was forgotten. One day he was quietly dropped. No one noticed.

The title of producer in our society seems securely honorific. The head of a distillery, a drive-in theater or a dog track is a producer. He is not a basic producer which is better, but a producer nonetheless. As such, he enjoys a position in the community as one of its supports or pillars and the sources of its wealth, which is not necessarily enjoyed by the high school principal or the parish priest. It is as a producer that the President of the United States Steel Corporation calls on the President of the United States. It is thought good, on the whole, for a deparment of the government to be in the hands of a production man. Nothing better can be said of any individual than that he knows production. But the prestige of the producer is only the prestige of production. Should production ever come to be taken for granted, so, in some measure, will the producer. Mr. Carney is a warning.

II

Men fight for what is important to them, and the businessman who senses his self-interest will battle vigorously for a value system which emphasizes the importance of production. Indeed, and perhaps more intuitively than otherwise, he already does. The business liturgy accords an important place to resonant assertions of the vital role of production. "Only the productive can be strong. Only the strong can be free." "Production made America . . ." "Let us stop bickering and produce."

The businessman, with many exceptions, has for long been suspicious of the state—or at least of those activities of the state, the national defense being such an exception, which do not usefully provide him with markets and support to needed research and development. This, it has always been assumed, is because he is an important taxpayer and vulnerable to regulation. But we are too addicted in our social comment to this kind of mechanical economic determinism. Modern government is a major threat to the businessman's prestige. To the extent that problems of conservation, education and social welfare are central to our thoughts, so the administrators, teachers and other professional public servants are the popular heroes. As their prestige, along with that of the men who are associated with the problems and disasters of foreign policy, has increased, businessmen have reacted by pointing out that the government does not produce anything, that it is a barren whore. "Government is powerless to create anything in the sense in which business produces wealth and individuals produce ideas [and] inventions . . ."[1] The case involves some rather strained argument—it makes education unproductive and the manufacturer of school desks productive—but, nonetheless, it has a position of considerable prominence especially in the older business liturgy.

A tension, perhaps ultimately more important, has also long existed between businessmen and the intellectuals. "The emergence of a numerous class of . . . frivolous intellectuals

---

1 Francis X. Sutton, Seymour E. Harris, Carl Kaysen and James Tobin, *The American Business Creed* (Cambridge, Mass.: Harvard University Press, 1956), p. 195.

is one of the least welcome phenomena of the age of modern capitalism. Their obtrusive stir repels discriminating people. They are a nuisance."[2] As in the case of the government, the basis of the tension has long been assumed to be economic. "The men whose research has given rise to new methods of production hate the businessmen who are merely interested in the cash value of their research work. It is very significant that such a large number of American research physicists sympathize with socialism and communism . . . University teachers of economics are also opposed to what they disparagingly call the profit system . . ."[3] However, although the actual or suspected social radicalism of intellectuals may well contribute to hostility between businessmen and intellectuals, there is again another cause. Scientists, writers, professors, artists are also important competitors of the businessmen for public esteem.

This competition is especially noticeable in comment on public affairs—on economic policy, foreign policy, the effect of government measures on popular morals and behavior. Perhaps the most honorific function in our time is that of social prophecy. No one enjoys quite such distinction as the man who, by common consent, is allowed to look ahead and advise as to what we should do to promote or retard a particular occurrence. The intellectual naturally assumes his authority on these matters. He is likely to be gifted well beyond the businessman in erudition and oral capacity. That felicity the businessman counters by stressing his identification with production. He is not a "theorist" but a practical man. His is the forthright approach of the man who knows how to get things done. He has learned about life in the shop; this has provided him with a unique insight into how things are in the country at large or the world. Were anything to happen to the prestige of production, it is plain that the businessman, whose mystique is his identification with production, would suffer severely in his competition with the intellectual for the role of social prophet. If he wishes to defend himself in his

2 Ludwig von Mises, *The Anti-Capitalistic Mentality* (Princeton, N.J.: Van Nostrand, 1956), p. 107.

8 *The Anti-Capitalistic Mentality*, p. 20. The late Professor von Mises, it should be observed in fairness, would be regarded by most present-day businessmen as rather extreme.

present role, he must defend the importance of production. He can almost certainly be expected to do so .

There will be occasion presently for a further word on the competition between the businessman and the intellectual for contemporary esteem.

III

Politics have long been known to make incongruous bedfellows. More rarely, however, have those between the same sheets remained largely unaware of their intimate if odd companionship. This is the strange case with the vested interests in production. Supporting the businessman on the all-importance of the production of goods until comparatively recent times was the American liberal. The prestige which the businessman derives from production was reinforced by the nearly full weight of American liberal comment. The reason for this alliance, though it requires some explanation, was not essentially complex. Men who hold tenaciously to a life raft may expect to be cast upon strange shores among strange companions. So it is with those who hold long enough to an idea amid changing currents and tides. As so often happens, the course of developments in Britain, in broad contour if not in detail, has been the same as in the United States.

Until the decade of the thirties, the liberal, so far as he was concerned with the total output of the economy, addressed himself to the problem of the efficient use of the available resources in capital, manpower and materials. He insisted not without passion that this goal be not defeated by monopoly, tariffs, labor or capital immobility, or other interferences with optimal use. To increase output by increasing the rate of capital formation or by expanding the total labor force or by a serious effort to increase the rate of technological innovation was not part of his concern.[4] Most important of all, the loss of production as the result of depressions was not peculiarly a liberal concern. No one was deeply committed politically on this problem; conservatives had an equal interest with liberals in "smoothing out" the business cycle. During the decade of the twenties, the political leadership in

---

4 See p. 103.

discussion of possible means to mitigate the business cycle was assumed by Herbert Hoover.

The classical program of American liberals, until the decade of the thirties, sought the redistribution of the existing income, greater economic security and the protection of the liberties and immunities of individuals and organizations in face of the highly unequal distribution of economic power. The progressive income tax; the development of government services; the protection of public resources from private appropriation; the extensions of social security; aid to farmers or other especially disadvantaged groups; the strengthening of trade unions; and the regulation of corporations all served these ends. None of these measures was thought much to affect the total output of the economy.

All this changed very much during the decade of the thirties. The Great Depression brought production to a very low level. Between 1929 and 1933, the gross output of the private economy dropped by between a third and a half. The sheer magnitude of this movement focused attention, as never before, on movements in the total output of the economy and on their far-reaching consequences for economic and political fortune. Characteristically, to increase production was less central to men's thoughts than to reduce unemployment. "Our greatest primary task is to put people back to work," Roosevelt said in his first inaugural. But whether directly or as a by-product of the effort to reduce economic insecurity, expanded production began to acquire a growing significance to political liberalism in its American sense.

Then in 1936 came John Maynard Keynes. In the Keynesian system, the notion of an aggregate demand for the output of the economy which determined the total production of the economy was central. Depending on various factors, production might find its equilibrium at a high level or a low one. There was no immutable tendency for it to settle at the particular level where all willing workers had a chance for employment. And by manipulating the level of aggregate demand—the most obvious devices were to add to demand by government spending in excess of taxation, or to subtract from it by taxation in excess of spending—the government could influence the level of production.

The rewards from a successful operation on the level of

output were breathtaking. To increase production was to ameliorate unemployment, agricultural insecurity, the threat of bankruptcy to the small businessman, the risks of investors, the financial troubles of the states and cities, even, somewhat, the overcrowding which results when people cannot afford to own or rent their own homes and must double up. Scarcely a single social problem was left untouched. And within a few years after Keynes, the level of production became the critical factor in war mobilization. It was principally by increased output that we provided for the military requirements of World War II.

As a result, production did more than impress the liberal. It became his program, and it established something akin to a monopoly over his mind. Here was perhaps the nearest thing to alchemy that had even been seen in the field of politics. Increased production solved, or seemed to solve, nearly all of the social problems of the day.

Furthermore, at least for a time, the practical concern for the total output of the economy was a liberal franchise. Conservatives hesitated to abandon the balanced budget, for so long a canon of the conventional wisdom.[5] Yet to do so was essential. To manipulate the level of production also meant that the role of government must be enlarged. This too was unpalatable to conservatives, for it accorded a prestige to government which had previously been accorded exclusively to private production.

Most important of all for its influence on the liberal mind, the promise to raise production and reduce unemployment won elections. From the late thirties to the early fifties, the promise to maintain high production and therewith high employment was the liberal's major claim to votes in the United States, and it was unbeatable. Very nearly the same thing was true of the left in Britain. The promise to "get this country moving again," i.e., to increase production at a faster rate, helped win public office for John F. Kennedy in 1960.

One must notice here another curiosity of the liberal's position. The issue on which he won during the thirties and which continued to bring him victories for another decade

5 Although numerous liberals, including unquestionably Roosevelt himself, were also reluctant. And some chose to become conservatives on the issue.

was the promise of the increased production that eliminated unemployment. This was something of massive importance. But having discovered production, he remained with it. He continued to stress the importance of the increased output in periods when that involved not the elimination of gross unemployment but the increase in output of the already employed. He believed, in brief, that increased production remained the touchstone of political success even when it involved additions to an already opulent supply of goods. Between increases in production that cure widesperad unemployment and increases in production that add to affluence, there is a difference not in degree but in kind. In continuing to emphasize production, liberals, who once had a great issue, came without realizing it to possess a much smaller one. Yet this is not surprising. No less than any others, liberals accepted the elaborate rationalization by which we persuade ourselves of the continued urgency of additions to our stock of consumers' goods.

However, this is a digression. For present purposes, we need only observe that Keynes concentrated the eyes of liberals on production, and their political successes gave them a vested interest in it. Keynesian attitudes became, as ever, the new conventional wisdom.[6]

IV

Or such was the unchallenged wisdom until recent times. Browning observed that "Jove strikes the Titans down, not when they set about their mountain-piling but when another rock would crown their work." So with production. At the moment when its position seemed invulnerable, when it was supported by the deeply vested interest of conservative executives and liberal intellectuals, cracks were appearing in the façade. In these last years, they have widened. That the preoccupation with production *qua* production is still formidable, of that there can be no doubt. It has inherited the concern once felt for equality and the poor. It is still powerfully reinforced by the service it renders to economic security. It is still rationalized by an elaborate and traditional, even if

---

6 In time, it should be observed, even for a Republican president. In 1969, President Nixon proclaimed his conversion to Keynes.

meretricious, theory of consumer demand. But, for businessmen, production no longer means secure prestige. For liberal
politicians, it is no longer a certain formula for public office.

The prestige of production depends on the perstige of
goods. In the more censorious social levels of American society, there has long been a fashionable aversion to gadgetry.
(The word gadget is itself a pejorative term for durable
goods.) In such circles, shiny rumpus rooms, imaginative bar-
becue pits, expansive television screens and magnificent automobiles no longer win acclaim. They may even invite mild
social obloquy. A degree of shabbiness in personal attire is
now sought, and all but universally among the young.
Against more output and more jobs is now set the effect on
the environment. On occasion, that effect is controlling. We
have here a yet small but still significant revolt against goods,
and a refusal to allow competitive emulation to be the source
of wants.

Even more suggestive is the belief of the businessman that
his position in the community is slipping.[7] Business ranks
near the bottom of desired careers for college graduates. The
rise of the public relations industry, which draws its clientele
overwhelmingly from among business executives, shows that
business achievement is no longer of itself a source of acclaim. At a minimum, the achievement must be advertised.
But the first task of the public relations man, on taking over
a business client, is to "re-engineer" his image to include
something beside the production of goods. His subject must
be a statesman, a patron of education, or a civic force. Increasingly, some artistic or intellectual facet of his personality
must be found or invented. A businessman who reads
Business Week is lost to fame. One who reads Proust is
marked for greatness.

These added requirements for esteem are unquestionably
related to changing attitudes toward goods. In the early years
of the automobile age, it was sufficient for Henry Ford or R.
E. Olds that they were makers of cars. What indeed could be

[7] Also, he is no longer boss in the old sense. Rather, he is chairman of
what I have elsewhere called the technostructure. This makes the significant decisions. The name of the current head of Exxon or U.S.Steel
is unknown outside the industry. All the world knew of Rockefeller
and Carnegie.

a source of more acclaim? Now the automobile has become commonplace. And in the more recherché attitudes, it is even big, ungainly and unfunctional in its shape and decoration. It is easy to see why the modern car manufacturer does not enjoy the eminence of a Ford or an Olds.

As noted, the intellectual, along with the public official and politician, is the natural competitor of the businessman for what may be called the solemn acclaim of the community.[8] (Neither competes with Hollywood, football, television commentators or jet society for what both agree is the frivolous applause of the community.) In fact, the position of the intellectual is now far more secure than that of the businessman. It would hardly occur to a successful poet or scientist to hire a public relations man, just as it would scarcely seem wise for a successful corporation president to do without one. Although the businessman must, increasingly, show that he is at home with ideas, it does not occur to the philosopher or artist that he should show that he is a good businessman. Perhaps most suggestive of all, American intellectuals long ago created what amounts to a second-class citizenship for the intellectual efforts of the business executive. They listen to his speeches, review his books and receive his ideas with respectful attention. But they do not judge them to be good or bad in themselves. They are good (or on occasion bad) for a businessman. It is well understood that this is a much lower standard.

Finally, the modern liberal no longer identifies production with all political success. A satisfactory increase in Gross National Product remains the first test of accomplishment. No one should doubt the convenience of a simple arithmetical measure of success in a world in which so many things are subjective. But it is no longer unusual to inquire about the quality of life as opposed to the quantity of production. And a younger generation has become concerned with questions of racial equality, the quality of the environment, the role of the great public and private bureaucracies in our lives and in shaping our beliefs and our prospects for survival, and there

8 For a roughly similar conclusion, see Russell Lynes, *A Surfeit of Honey* (New York: Harper, 1957).

has been a simmering of interest in the honesty of artistic and intellectual expression.

None of this is yet decisive. The purpose of the society is still to produce. This is still its serious business. To be a producer is still to be the truly useful man. Economic success is still the test of whether one is fully to be trusted in Washington—or on the governing body of a university. If the vested position of production is no longer completely secure, one can still marvel at the way it has survived the enormous increase in the output of goods in modern times. Men, in this world, share little in common with the meager and starved existence of the days of Ricardo. But their belief as to what is important is the same. It is a remarkable tribute to man's capacity to protect the beliefs that are important for him. In doubting the supreme power of production, we are still challenging a myth of heroic power.

CHAPTER XIII

The Bill Collector Cometh

The situation is this. Production for the sake of the goods produced is no longer very urgent. The significance of marginal increments (or decrements) in the supply of most goods is slight for most people.[1] We sustain a sense of urgency only because of attitudes that trace to the world not of today but to that into which economics was born. These are reinforced by an untenable theory of consumer demand and by a system of vested interests which marries both liberals and conservatives to the importance of production.

At the same time, production does remain important and urgent for its effect on economic security. When men are unemployed, society does not miss the goods they do not produce. The loss here is marginal. But the men who are without work *do* miss the income they no longer earn. Here the effect is not marginal. It involves all or a large share of the men's earnings and hence all or a large share of what they are able to buy. And, we note, high and stable production is the broad foundation of the economic security of virtually every other group—of farmers, white collar workers and both large businessmen and small. A recession in demand and production remains the major uncovered risk of the modern large corporation.[2] It is for reasons of economic security that we must produce at capacity.

These simple conclusions are not well regarded by the

1 The reference to most goods and most people should perhaps be emphasized. Were income so redistributed as to eliminate the present class stratification in comsumption and bring everyone up to a high minimum, the increased claim on productive resources for supplying the resulting demand would be large. This is a point that might have been more adequately emphasized in earlier editions.

2 The large corporation, as I argue presently, has a far easier time accommodating to inflation.

conventional wisdom. To urge the importance of production because of its bearing on economic security, and to suggest that the product is in any way incidental, is disturbing. It brings the economic society to the brink of the dubious world of make-work and boondoggling. One of the escapes from this world is to make all wants urgent, and no doubt we have here another reason for the obscurantist rationalization of consumer demand. It still seems more satisfactory to say that we need the goods than to stress the real point, which is that social well-being and contentment require that we have enough production to provide income to the willing labor force. But if anyone has surviving doubts as to where the real priorities lie, let him apply a simple test. Let him assume that a President, or other candidate for reelection to major public office, has the opportunity of defending a large increase in man-hour productivity which has been divided equally between greatly increased total output and greatly increased unemployment. And let it be assumed that as an alternative he might choose unchanged productivity which has left everyone employed. That full employment is more desirable than increased production combined with unemployment would be clear alike to the most sophisticated and the most primitive politician.

The foregoing provides the basic rule of procedure for the remainder of this essay. It shows that, in the absence of a genuine grading up of lower incomes, we need not be much concerned with the supply of goods for their own sake. The urgencies here are founded not on substance but on myth. And, indeed, our ultimate purpose is to see the opportunities that emerge as this myth is dispelled. But in all this we must be exceedingly conscious of the importance of production for its bearing on the economic security of individuals. As a source of income for people, its importance remains undiminished. This function of production must be carefully safeguarded.

But myth is rarely benign. And the system of illusions which causes us to attach such importance to production for its own sake is itself damaging or dangerous. And the way that present attitudes cause us to emphasize the supply of private as distinct from all goods and services is the source of deeper social dangers. To these problems, beginning with those inherent in the present methods of manufacturing wants, the essay now turns.

II

One danger in the way wants are now created lies in the related process of debt creation. Consumer demand thus comes to depend more and more on the ability and willingness of consumers to incur debt.

An increase in consumer debt is all but implicit in the process by which wants are now synthesized. Advertising and emulation, the two dependent sources of desire, work across the society. They operate on those who can afford and those who cannot. With those who lack the current means, it is a brief and obvious step from stimulating their desire by advertising to making it effective in the market with a loan. The relation of emulation to indebtedness is even more direct. Every community contains individuals with wide differences in their ability to pay. The example of those who can pay bears immediately on those who cannot. They must incur debt if they are to keep abreast. The great increase in consumer indebtedness in our time has been widely viewed as reflecting some original or unique change in popular attitudes or behavior. People have changed their view of debt. Thus, there has been an inexplicable but very real retreat from the Puritan canon that required an individual to save first and enjoy later. In fact, as always, the pieces of economic life are parts of a whole. It would be surprising indeed if a society that is prepared to spend thousands of millions to persuade people of their wants were to fail to take the further step of financing these wants, and were it not then to go on to persuade people of the ease and desirability of incurring debt to make these wants effective. This has happened. The process of persuading people to incur debt, and the arrangements for them to do so, are as much a part of modern production as the making of the goods and the nurturing of the wants. The Puritan ethos was not abandoned. It was merely overwhelmed by the massive power of modern merchandising.

Viewing this process as a whole, we should expect that every increase in consumption will bring a further increase—possibly a more than proportional one—in consumer debt.

Our march to higher living standards will be paced, as a matter of necessity, by an ever deeper plunge into debt. The evidence is already impressive. The increase in living standards in the twenties was accompanied by a relatively much greater increase in consumer borrowing. The same was true during the years of recovery in the thirties. It has been most spectacularly the case since World War II. From 1952 to 1956, total consumer debt (not including real estate loans) increased from $27.4 billion to $42.5 billion or by 55 percent. Installment credit increased by 63 percent and that for automobiles by nearly 100 percent. Although these were prosperous years, disposable income of individuals increased by only about 21 percent. From 1956 to 1967, consumer debt increased from $42.5 billion to $99.1 billion or by a further 133 percent. Installment credit increased from $31.7 billion to $77.9 billion or by 146 percent and automobile paper from $14.4 billion to $31.2 billion or by 117 percent. During these same twelve years, disposable personal income increased from $293.2 billion to $544.6 billion or by 86 percent.[8] These trends continued into the nineteen-seventies. By 1974, total consumer debt was over $190 billion, of which $156 billion was installment credit, $52 billion of this in automobile paper. Disposable personal income was 80 percent higher at $980 billion; total credit, however, had grown by 92 percent, installment credit by 100 percent. Automobile paper, affected by gasoline prices and shortage, had increased 64 percent.

One wonders, inevitably, about the tensions associated with debt creation on such a massive scale. The legacy of wants, which are themselves inspired, are the bills which descend like the winter snow on those who are buying on the installment plan. By millions of hearths throughout the land, it is known that when these harbingers arrive, the repossession man cannot be far behind. Can the bill collector by the central figure in the good society?

In 1955, the median income of the American family before

---

[8] *Economic Indicators*, Washington: U.S. Government Printing Office, June 1957. And *Consumer Credit*, Supplement to Banking and Monetary Statistics, Board of Governors of the Federal Reserve System, September 1965. And *Statistical Abstract*, 1968. And *Survey of Current Business*, April 1975.

taxes was $3960. Of all families within the income range from $3000 to $4000, 48 percent had installment payments to meet. For nearly a third of those, the payments commanded more than a fifth of the family income before taxes. Among families in the next lower bracket—with incomes from $2000 to $3000—42 percent had payments to make. Of these in turn, 42 percent had committed at least a fifth of their income for installment payments, and one family in nine surrendered 40 percent or more of its income to the bill collector.[4] Between 1960 and 1964, at least one family in ten in the United States had installment payments that consumed a fifth or more of its income.[5] On the desirability of this, each must decide according to his own values. But there are associated economic dangers which are less subjective.

III

In a society where virtuosity in persuasion must keep pace with virtuosity in production, one is tempted to wonder whether the first can forever keep ahead of the second. For while production does not clearly contain within itself the seeds of its own disintegration, persuasion may. On some not distant day, the voice of each individual seller may well be lost in the collective roar of all together. Like injunctions to virtue and warnings of socialism, advertising will beat helplessly on ears that have been conditioned by previous assault to utter immunity. Diminishing returns will have operated to the point where the marginal effect of outlays for every kind of commerical persuasion will have brought the average effect to zero. It will be worth no one's while to speak, for since all speak, none can hear. Silence, interrupted perhaps by brief, demoniacal outbursts of salesmanship, will ensue.

Were this heroic eventuality to occur, there would, unquestionably, be some interesting problems of economic readjustment. There would be a counterpart increase in consumer

[4] These data are all from *Consumer Instalment Credit*, Pt. I. Vol. I, *Growth and Import*, Board of Governors of the Federal Reserve System, Washington, D.C., 1957.
[5] Board of Governors of the Federal Reserve System based on data from Survey Research Center, University of Michigan.

saving as the unpersuaded allowed their bank balances to grow and repaid their debts. Unless these increased savings were speedily offset by increased outlays elsewhere—and the day on which the massed voices of the advertisers bring total cancellation of effect will not be one of supreme business confidence and burgeoning investment spending—the result would be a decline in total spending and, therewith, in the total output of the economy. The further and more painful consequence would be an increase in unemployment and a reduction in other incomes—in brief, a serious curtailment of the social security of which production has become the servant.[6]

The less imaginative dangers arise in connection with consumer borrowing. Here trouble is already foreseeable. Indeed, it has already been accorded a degree of recognition in the conventional wisdom which has taken the usual form of assurances that there are no grounds for concern.

As we expand debt in the process of want creation we come necessarily to depend on this expansion. An interruption in the increase in debt means an actual reduction in demand for goods. Debt, in turn, can be expanded by measures which, in the nature of the case, cannot be indefinitely continued. Periods for payment can be lengthened, although eventually there comes a point when they exceed the life of the asset which serves as the collateral. Down payments can be reduced, but eventually there comes a point when the borrower's equity is so small that he finds it more convenient to allow repossession than to pay a burdensome debt. Poorer and poorer credit risks can be accommodated, but at last it becomes necessary to exclude the borrower who, as a matter of principle, does not choose to pay.

No one can speak with confidence on the extent of the re-

---

6 In the conventional wisdom, just as there has been hesitation in stressing the role of advertising and salesmanship in want creation so there has been little tendency to explore our dependence on such persuasion. An exception is Paul Mazur whose book, *The Standards We Raise* (New York: Harper, 1953) has a forthright Philistinism that, while it doubtless cost him scholarly attention, brought him refreshingly close to the modern role of advertising and related activities. I have dealt in more detail with the functional role of want creation and management in *The New Industrial State*, 2nd ed., rev. (Boston: Houghton Mifflin, 1971).

sulting danger. However, few things are more satisfactorily established in economics than that debt creation, whether by producers or consumers, is a major source of uncertainty in economic behavior. It has long been recognized that times of high income and employment and a generally sanguine outlook are encouraging to both borrowers and lenders. The spending that results from these transactions adds to the general total of purchasing power when, in effect, it is least needed. Under less sanguine circumstances, loans are advanced more cautiously. Instead of spending from new loans, there is repayment of old ones and this, as perversely as in prosperity, occurs at the least propitious time.

Borrowing, in the past, has been mainly by business firms for investment. For this reason, business spending was regarded as the most mercurial of the three major categories of spending. Outlays by consumers and by government were, by contrast, regarded as comparatively reliable. "There is . . . general agreement that [general fluctuations in employment] show themselves predominantly in swings in the demand for labour for investment—chiefly for investment in works of construction."[7] ". . . movements in income, output, and employment are mainly characterized by fluctuations in the rate of real investment. Moreover, consumption rises or falls, in large part, in response to real investment."[8] The effect of the expansion of consumer credit is to add an uncertainty, paralleling that which business borrowing brings to business spending, to the hitherto more reliable consumer spending. The instability may be greater, for the terms of consumer credit will be eased—down payments reduced and repayment periods lengthened—as an aspect of competitive merchandising techniques. In the case of business investment, this may be less likely to occur.

In any case, consumers will add the most spending from borrowed funds to their spending from current income during the period when it is least needed. This will exaggerate infla-

---

7 A. C. Pigou, *Income* (London: Macmillan, 1946), pp. 89–90.
8 Alvin H. Hansen, *Business Cycles and National Income* (New York: Norton, 1951), p. 17. Professor Hansen goes on to observe that consumers' durables, including automobiles, can be an original source of fluctuation. These are the consumer products principally associated with debt creation.

tionary pressures. And it is plain that a family that has committed 40 or even 20 percent of its income to installment payments will have to cut its current spending appreciably if one or more of its income earners lose their job and it does not wish to resort to bankruptcy. Thus, an increase in unemployment, accompanied by the fear that it might get worse, could induce a general effort to avoid new debt and reduce the old. The further effect on consumer spending, thereafter on employment, and thence once again in reducing borrowing and magnifying efforts to meet debts, could be considerable and disagreeable.

IV

By virtue of position, certain individuals in our society are accorded the privilege of stating as fact what, in the nature of things, is unknowable. The tycoon and college president have well-recognized rights along these lines. Any candidate for public office may distinguish with clarity between actions which will lead to unlimited prosperity and those which will lead to utter ruin. Secretaries of State may tell us by which actions our lives and liberties will be preserved to near eternity and by which they and we will be destroyed. In all instances, those privileged as prophets are permitted to identify salvation with the action which at the moment they find most expedient. To a remarkable extent, considering their much more humble status, economists are allowed to tell what present trends in society will culminate in deep trouble and distress. In consequence, it would be entirely permissible to forsee the gravest results from the way consumer demand is now sustained by the relentless increase in consumer debt.

In the course of its study of consumer credit in 1956, the Board of Governors of the Federal Reserve System concluded that while "relatively little is known about the safety margins in the finances of consumers who borrow on a short-term and intermediate-term instalment basis . . . the evidence of a trend over past decades toward more liberal terms suggest that these margins are less than in earlier years." Then, without throwing caution to the winds, it warned that "the possibility of an episode of drastic and spiraling liquidation [of this credit] should not be dismissed." Thereafter, for purpose of practical action, it did dismiss it.

In fact, we do not really know the extent of the danger. A tendency to liquidation of consumer debt, with accompanying contraction in current spending, could be offset by prompt and vigorous government action to cut taxes, increase public outlays and so compensate with spending from other sources. On the other hand, such measures are subject to both psychological and procedural delays. Nothing in our economic policy is so deeply ingrained, and so little reckoned with by economists, as our tendency to wait and see if things do not improve by themselves. In a time of receding income, the income tax reduces itself automatically. Social security, farm and other payments have a similarly automatic tendency to expand. But taxation and expenditure beyond the range of these automatic stabilizers require Executive and Congressional action. Such decision and action could be in a radically slower tempo from that of debt liquidation and the consequent slump in spending.

A possibility of trouble is not a prediction of trouble. Not many, if told twenty-five years ago of the vast expansion in consumer debt that lay ahead, would have thought it safe. But we have so far survived it. Perhaps the expansion can continue and possibly it will one day taper off in benign fashion. But we would do well to keep an alarm signal flying over the consumer-debt creation into which the process of want creation impels us. In a society in which the production and sale of goods seem sacrosanct, there will be extreme hesitation over measures which will seem to restrain the financing of consumers' goods and hence their sale. Measures to prevent the competitive liberalization of consumer credit will encounter the heaviest resistance. When regarded in relation to the underlying interest in stability and economic security, such precautionary measures have a much stronger claim for attention. They promise to help keep the process of synthesizing demand and the purchasing power to make it effective from damaging the continuity of production and employment.

Though such regulation is a commonplace in the United Kingdom and has been used in the past in the United States in wartime, it is unlikely to be authorized in the future except in the aftermath of disaster. Interference with the process of want creation *cum* debt creation will be thought wrong.

V

There is a deeper social aspect to the economy of consumer credit and the bill collector. Not all goods and services are readily subject to sale on the installment plan and to the all but automatic creation of debt that goes therewith. Automobiles, vacuum cleaners, television sets and wall-to-wall carpeting are; the services of schools, hospitals, libraries, museums, police and street-cleaning equipment and rapid transit lines are not. If the capital cost of these last is beyond the convenient reach of current income, there is no equally easy way of going into debt. On the contrary, the controls on this kind of borrowing—debt limitations, provision for voter approval of bond issues—are Draconian. The encouragement to indebtedness which the society accords to the man who wants to buy an automobile or even take a trip is matched by the stern mistrust with which it views the local government that might want to borrow for a school. The individual has an instinct for good living that should be encouraged; the government for prodigality against which all must be protected.

It follows that there is a remarkable discrimination between different classes of goods and services in the ease with which they can be financed. For some, and by any abstract test not the most important, debt is greatly encouraged. For others, and not the least important, it is closely controlled and penuriously viewed. Here, as also in pages to come, we see the most singular feature of the affluent society taking form. It is the great and comprehensive contrast between the care and encouragement which it lavishes on the production of private goods and the severe restraint which it imposes on those that must emerge from the public sector.

CHAPTER XIV

Inflation

Through most of man's history, the counterpart of war, civil disorder, famine or other cosmic disaster has been inflation. In recent times, inflation has acquired new habits; it persists in periods of peace, in periods of decline and stagnation and in periods of high and rising prosperity. This tendency has been strongly manifest in the United States. Except for a few years in the early sixties and, more debatably, in the early seventies inflation has been a continuing feature of American life since World War II. The later experience, that of the mid-seventies in particular, made the earlier inflation seem mild.

The public response to this recurrent inflation has been interesting. It has been widely deplored and condemned. Politicians of both parties have taken a strong position against it. Conservatives, anciently the self-designated custodians of the "honest dollar," have continued to stress this tenet of their faith. Businessmen, bankers, insurance executives and nearly every type of professional public spokesman at one time or another have warned of the dangers of continued inflation. Meanwhile, liberals have deplored failure to take effective action while often proposing none themselves. Next only to the virtues of competition, there is nothing on which the conventional wisdom is more completely agreed than on the importance of stable prices. Yet this conviction leads to remarkably little effort and, indeed, to remarkably few suggestions for specific action. Where inflation is concerned, nearly everyone finds it convenient to confine himself to conversation. All branches of the conventional wisdom are equally agreed on the undesirability of any remedies that are effective.

II

There are several reasons for this barren position. First, to be sure, some reap material benefit from inflation. They too oppose it, for reasons of respectability, but their opposition is less than impassioned. Of importance also is the influence of inaction—or postponement—as a policy. This does not reflect mere negativism, as is often supposed and even more frequently charged. As earlier noted, in the nineteenth-century model of the competitive society, a rhythmic sequence of expansion and contraction in economic activity was assumed. The expansion was accompanied by rising prices; in the contracting phase, these gave way to falling prices. The movements in either direction were thought to be self-limiting. Thus, if prices were rising, one had only to wait. Presently they would reverse themselves and begin to fall.

In the course of time, confidence in the self-limiting character of these movements was seriously weakened. This was especially true as regards the period of contraction or depression, and the Great Depression dealt a decisive blow. Although as late as the early thirties it was a tenet of the conventional wisdom that in depressions the appropriate course of action was a severe "hands-off" policy, government intervention against depression came eventually to be regarded as inevitable.

However, there was never any equally dramatic assault on the older confidence that rising prices and inflation would cure themselves. Keynes led the attack on the conviction that depressions were self-correcting by picturing the possibility, indeed the probability, that the economy would find its equilibrium with an unspecified amount of unemployment. Dozens seized his point and sought to persuade the politicians and the public. The notion that, in peacetime, prices might as a normal thing rise continuously and persistently has had no Keynes.

Thus the conviction, or more precisely the hope, has remained that peacetime inflation might somehow be self-correcting. This is not a hope in which even conservatives repose very great confidence. But in combination with the belief, so common in recent years, that the behavior of the economic system is bound to be favorable if only earnest and God-fearing men are in command of its destinies, it provides a strong reason for always waiting to see if prices won't turn down by themselves. Even liberals, who are required to advocate although not to specify action to prevent inflation, are in practice tempted to wait and see.

This disposition to inaction is reinforced by the belief, powerful ever since the thirties, that the most grievous threat to the American economy is a depression. If this danger lurks, however obscurely, around the corner, then there is all the less reason to act to control inflation. For inflation may any day come to an end in the thunder of economic collapse or the lesser misery of a few million unemployed. These eventualities are much more grave than rising prices. We are especially hesitant, knowingly at least, to invoke measures which might precipitate them. Some inflation remedies might do so or, at any rate, be blamed.

However, the forces which act to make inflation a peculiarly unmanageable problem in our time are imbedded much more deeply in the fabric of our social life. We are impelled, for reasons of economic security, to operate the economy at a level of output where it is not stable—where persistent advances in prices are not only probable but normal. The remedies that would be effective collide with the urgencies of production for purposes of economic security. Or they are in conflict with attitudes which emphasize the importance of economic growth and of unhampered markets for the efficient use of resources. This conflict has been further complicated by what is in part a belief, in part a hope, and in part a faith that the conflict can be evaded. A principal means to this evasion is the manipulation of the monetary supply—what economists have come to call monetary policy.

We shall look first at the nature of inflation and its consequences and then, in the next chapter, at the hope, never so strong as in recent times, that the conflicts which it presents might somehow be elided by monetary policy. Then we shall examine the unresolved conflict between the other remedies and the store we set by economic security and also by economic growth and unhampered markets.

III

Understanding of the problem of the modern inflation[1] begins with a basic distinction between two parts of the economy and the differences in price behavior therein. In that part of the economy where, as with agriculture, there are many producers and an approach to what economists term pure competition, no individual seller controls or influences prices. There prices will move up automatically in response to increased demand. In the typical industrial market—steel, machinery, oil, automobiles, most nonferrous metals, chemicals—a relatively small number of large firms enjoy, in one way or another, a considerable discretion in setting prices. In these markets—the ones characterized by what economists call oligopoly—as capacity operation is approached, it becomes possible to mark up prices. The word approached is emphasized. The possibility exists before capacity operation is reached. The fact that all firms are nearing capacity is assurance that no firm, by holding back, will capture an increased share of the market. It cannot sup-

[1] I have written a good deal on various aspects of the inflation problem, and I am concerned to avoid repeating myself unnecessarily here. I first dealt comprehensively with inflation in the general context of big firms and unions in the final chapters of *American Capitalism: The Concept of Countervailing Power* (Boston: Houghton Mifflin, 1952, 1956). The theoretical implications of the coexistence of competitive and oligopolistic market structures and the absence of full short-run maximization by the latter were then developed in "Market Structure and Stabilization Policy," *Review of Economics and Statistics* (Vol. XXXIX, No. 2. May 1957), and summarized in nontechnical form in a statement prepared for the Subcommittee on Antitrust and Monopoly, Committee on the Judiciary, of the United States Senate (*Hearings*, July 11, 1957). My most recent effort, as this edition goes to press, is *Money: Whence It Came, Where It Went* (Boston: Houghton Mifflin, 1975). My views on the inflation problem have changed (and I trust developed) over the years. In particular, I regard the ensuing statement of the causes of inflation, though similar in broad contour, to be somewhat more precise than that first adumerated in *American Capitalism*. The point of departure, that inflation is the central problem of the economy of countervailing power, is of course the same. The years since 1952, when that book was first published, have, I think, provided a good deal of dismal verification of the point.

ply it. Nor, under these circumstances, is there danger that there will be extra stocks lurking around at a lower price.

At this point, it is necessary to foreclose on what is perhaps the commonest error in contemporary attitudes toward inflation, although the point is well understood by economists. This is the almost inevitable temptation to regard increased production as a remedy for inflation. It is the most natural of errors; the first thoughts on the matter are wonderfully simple and forthright. If inflation is caused by output pressing generally on capacity, then one need only get more capacity and more output and thus ensure that this tension no longer exists. But as just a moment's further thought will suggest, additional all-round production, even when it can be readily obtained from existing capacity, will pay out, in wages and other costs, the income by which it is bought. We have seen, moreover, that wants do not have an origin that is independent of production. They are nurtured by the same process by which production is increased. Accordingly, the effect of increased production from existing plant capacity is to increase also the purchasing power to buy that production and the desires which ensure that the purchasing power will be used.

But there is worse to come. If production is nearing capacity, a considerably increased output will require an increase in capacity. The increased investment that this implies will, in the form of wages, payments for materials, returns to capital and profits, add to purchasing power and the current demand for goods. It does so before the added capacity resulting from the investment is in place to meet the demand. Thus the effort to increase production adds to the pressure on current capacity—and to the prospect for inflationary price increases.

A cat chasing its own tail may, by an extraordinary act of feline dexterity, succeed on occasion in catching it. To overcome inflation by increasing production, while superficially similar, will not so often be successful.

IV

The response of the economy, when it is operating near capacity, to an increase in demand will not be uniform for all industries. As just observed, in the competitive industries, i.e., those where prices are set impersonally by the market, any increase in demand when supply can no longer be readily expanded will, predictably, raise prices. Similarly, a reduction in demand will reduce prices. However, in the characteristic industrial market—those of oligopoly and administered prices—the effect of the increase in demand must be implemented by a specific decision by the firm to change its price. This decision may, on occasion, be delayed and for a variety of reasons: Inertia; the need to establish a consensus on the extent of the increase under circumstances where the antitrust laws forbid formal communication between firms; the fear of a durably adverse public reaction to the advance; the fear that, over a longer span of time, the price increases will be damaging to the competitive position of the firm or industry; and the possibility of attracting the attention of the union and stimulating wage demands all may lead to delay. (It is worth repeating that this kind of price behavior can occur only in that part of the economy where producers are sufficiently few and are otherwise so situated as to have power over their own prices. Such behavior is not vouchsafed to the farmer or to the business man who is one of many in the market.) For many of the same reasons, price increases, when they occur, will not bring prices to the point where they maximize the short-run or current returns of the company. It is the long-run that the corporation likes. If the prices that maximize profits at the moment will bring wage demands that will threaten the cost position of the company over time; or if there promises to be long-run damage to the competitive position of the company; or if the public reputation will be hurt, then short-run maximization of return does not accord with self-interest even when this is defined in the narrowest of pecuniary terms.[2] The firm will not proceed to maximize its current return unless something happens—an important

---

[2] It seems likely that many economists have been reluctant to concede the possibility of such "restraint" in pricing because it seemed to be in conflict with self-interest. In fact, no such forbearance need be involved. As I seek to show in *The New Industrial State*, 2nd ed., rev. (Boston: Houghton Mifflin, 1971), maximization of growth and of the needs of the technostructure also lead to such "restraint." This latter book contains my mature views.

point—to make this possible without damaging the longer-run interest.

Two things follow. In a period of high and rising demand, short-run possibilities for increasing prices are likely to run ahead of the long-run assessment of where prices should be. Therefore, firms in the typical industrial market are likely to have what amounts to a reserve of unliquidated gains from unmade price advances. Unlike the farmer or other competitive producer, who is effectively isolated from any such opportunity, firms in these markets could exact higher prices than they do. They will do so if circumstances so change as to make short-run maximization more nearly consistent with the firm's view of its long-run interest.

As a result, price increases in these industries are not tied tightly to capacity operations or, as in competitive industries, to rising demand. Demand in, say, the steel industry may fall to something less than capacity levels, but if there is an unliquidated gain, and something alters the relation between short- and long-run maximization so as to make the former more feasible, prices will still be increased. As just stated, this can happen when demand is falling. Indeed, falling profits may make price increases inevitable. In the competitive industries, output being given, prices will never go up except by reason of an increase in demand. When demand falls, prices predictably will fall.[8]

While prices in the administered-price industries may rise in face of some excess capacity and fall in face of falling demand, the scope for such movements should not be exaggerated. Excess capacity, if it is considerable, will increase the danger that some firm will fail to go along or, at a later date, resort to surreptitious price-cutting. These dangers will act to enhance the doubts about the wisdom of raising prices to

---

[8] These movements will be affected, also, by differential movements in demand and also differences in the rate at which different industries adapt their plant to changes in demand. To stress the role of unliquidated gains—in the absence of which one cannot satisfactorily explain the ability of industrial firms to respond as they do to wage increase—is not to exclude these commonplace effects. Cf. the article by Robert Solomon, "Galbraith on Market Structure and Economic Stabilization Policy," and my comment, *Review of Economics and Statistics*, Vol. XL, No. 2 (May 1958).

maximize short-run gains and increase the reluctance to do so. There will be similar and perhaps stronger fear of the longer-run consequences of such price increases when demand is falling. The action may have to be reversed. Perhaps meanwhile wages will have moved up partly because of the price increase. The important point is only that in industries characterized by oligopoly, the relation between demand, capacity and price has a degree of play. Prices are not restricted immediately when demand is curbed or excess capacity appears.

V

In the inflation drama, it remains only to introduce Hamlet. That, by common consent, is the union. It is the instigator presumptive of that most familiar of economic phenomena, the wage-price spiral.

The role of wages in relation to inflation has long been a troublesome matter for economists. Obviously wages, through marginal cost effects, have something to do with price increases. Yet a firm that advances its prices after a wage increase could have done so before. At the previous lower costs and the higher prices, it would have made more money. The wage increase did nothing to enable it to get the higher price. An advance in steel wages adds only infinitesimally to the demand for steel mill products and only after a time. In any event, this is not something which steel firms take into consideration in their typically prompt response to a wage increase.[4]

The explanation lies in the existence of the margin of unliquidated gain and in the further fact that the wage advance, of itself, promptly increases the opportunity for short-run maximization in relation to long-run maximization. This is most obviously the case when the firm has been unwilling to advance its prices because of fear that it would attract the attention of the union which would press for wage increases. Now the union's attention has manifestly been attracted, and

---

[4] It is, of course, a part of the progressive expansion of money incomes which sustains the inflationary movement. But it is still true that the price increase precedes and does not follow the expansion in income.

there need no longer be any reluctance on this score. The danger of an adverse public reaction is also least at such times. The public will ordinarily attribute the advance in prices to the union. In steel and other industries, there is now a well-established policy of making the occasion of a wage increase the opportunity for a rather larger increase in prices and company revenues.

This is the core of the relation of wages to prices but not quite all of it. It would be wrong to suggest that the initiative to the whole movement lies with the wage demand of the unions. Living costs rise, eroding the last wage gains and stimulating efforts to recoup. And when demand and responding production are at capacity levels, profits will ordinarily be good. These in turn act as the lodestone to union demands. In the appropriate industries, the unexploited opportunity for price increases can now be seized. So it goes. One cannot single out a particular spoke in a wheel, paint it black (or red) and say that it shoves all the others. However, this does not prevent the effort. Its futility as a subject of social controversy notwithstanding, few subjects are more debated than the relative responsibility of workers and employers for the price advances which inflation comprises.

VI

As stated, the wage, price and profit spiral originates in the part of the economy where firms with a strong (or oligopolistic) market position bargain with strong unions. These price movements work themselves through the economy with a highly diverse effect on different groups. Where firms are strong in their markets and unions are effective, no one is much hurt, if at all, by inflation. Concern over the problem will be marked by the fortitude with which we all are able to contemplate the sorrows of others. Elsewhere, the effect will be highly mixed. Those individuals and groups will suffer most which have least control oevr their prices or wages and hence the least capacity to protect themselves by increasing their own return. Or if such control, as in the case of agriculture, is slight, then the effect will depend on whether the income elasticity of the demand for the particular product— roughly the effect of increased incomes on the demand for the product—is small or great. And something will depend also on whether the particular producer's costs are affected promptly or belatedly by the increase in prices.

Thus, by way of illustration, farmers have little or no control over the prices at which they sell their products. Inflation reaches them by way of impersonal market movements. For the wheat or potato farmer, the income elasticity is very low—as wage incomes rise, individuals spend no more for bread or potatoes and, on occasion, spend less. Meanwhile, the farmer's costs of fuel, fertilizer and other factors from the oligopolistic sector of the economy will have risen. For the beef-cattle producer, by contrast, income elasticity is rather higher. He is the beneficiary of the well-known and statistically quite demonstrable tendency of people who have an increase in pay to celebrate with red meat. Other things equal, and in the cattle business they frequently are not, his position will be happier than that of the producer of bread grains or potatoes.

Such discrimination is pervasive. The individual or firm which, either in line of business or as the result of speculative acumen, holds large unhedged inventories, benefits from the increased demand for these and from the consequent increase in price.

At the other extreme are those who experience the rising costs but whose own prices remain largely unaffected because they are fixed by law or custom or, at a minimum, by someone else. This is the position, during inflation, of the teacher, preacher and other of the white-collar community and of those who are reaping the reward of past services to society in the form of pensions or other such payments. The result of rising costs and comparatively fixed returns for all of these groups is much too familiar to require exegesis. Those on pensions suffer severely. Those who depend for their pay on the public treasury, especially of state and local governments, are also likely to suffer during inflation. Like all others, they experience the increase in prices. Their income is likely to lag. This lag is of considerable social consequence, and it is something to which this essay will return.

Not all venders of professional services do suffer. Occasional groups have discretion over their prices and are able to take prompt advantage of the general increase in money wages and demand, to raise their own charges and revenues. Lawyers and doctors normally fall in such a category. There have been others. In the early days of World War II, a grateful and very anxious citizenry rewarded its soldiers, sailors and airmen with a substantial increase in pay. In the teeming city of Honolulu, in prompt response to this advance in wage income, the prostitutes raised the prices of their services. This was at a time when, if anything, increased volume was causing a reduction in their average unit costs. However, in this instance, the high military authorities, deeply angered by what they deemed improper, immoral and indecent profiteering, ordered a return to the previous scale.[5]

In a free market, in an age of endemic inflation, it is unquestionably more rewarding, in purely pecuniary terms, to be a speculator or a prostitute than a teacher, preacher or policeman. Such is what conventional wisdom calls the structure of incentives.

VII

In basic outline, the requirements for inflation control will now be clear. When the economy is at or near capacity, firms in the concentrated sector can advance their prices and will have inducement from advancing wages to do so. Such price increases, with their further effects, will be prevented only if there is slack in the economy. Then various restraints begin to operate on the price advances, on the firms in granting wage advances, and on unions in asking for them. But, since firms may have unliquidated gains when operating at rather less than capacity, this slack in the absence of other measures may have to be considerable. In recent years, prices have continued to rise in much of the oligopolistic sector of the economy (where strong unions bargain with strong firms) right through recessions.

[5] The example earns its mention here only because it was accomplished under authority delegated to the military authorities by the Office of Price Administration (or, more precisely, its predecessor) in which I held the responsible authority. The step, for which I assumed I would be held to account, greatly worried me. Uniquely among acts of public insanity with which I have been associated, it never became a matter of public knowledge.

Were it possible to prevent wages from reacting on prices, and vice versa, then it would be possible to have price stability with production a good deal closer to current capacity and full employment. Wage movements would not then serve as a reason for raising prices and as a justification, or cover, for adding to profits. The derived effect of these increases on other sectors would be eliminated. It would thus be possible to have higher output and employment without inflation.

In the past, there has been much argument whether, in the strategy of inflation control, one should seek to come to grips with the level of demand (in relation to the capacity of the economy and the labor force) or whether one should seek to deal with the wage-price spiral. Economists have generally emphasized the importance of the level of demand; to the layman, the wage-price spiral has always seemed the phenomenon that most obviously required attention. The proper answer, it will be seen, is that both are important. Inflation can be controlled by a sufficiently heavy reduction in the level of demand. It can be controlled with a less drastic reduction if something could be done to arrest the interaction of wages and prices or, to speak more precisely, of wages, profits and prices.

The conflicts here will be evident. The introduction of slack, especially if it must be considerable, is in conflict with the imperatives of economic security. And the use of controls is in conflict with the ancient conviction that resources must be allocated efficiently among their various employments and that the free market is the most efficient and possibly even the only satisfactory instrument of such allocation. Setting the store that we do by the production of goods, we have here a seemingly decisive argument against the use of controls.

We shall have occasion to examine this conflict more closely chapter after next. But first it is necessary to look at the effort to avoid the conflict entirely by use of monetary policy.

CHAPTER XV

The Monetary Illusion

In Britain throughout the nineteenth century, the Bank of England was able through the increase or decrease of the bank rate—in principle, the rate of interest at which it stood ready to lend money to those who in turn were in the business of lending money—to have a measure of influence on the British banking and business life. The circumstances were undoubtedly favorable. The world was mostly at peace. There were no restraints on the international movement of capital funds; these were free to move anywhere in pursuit of a higher return. An increase in the rate would bring funds from abroad to take advantage of the higher earnings. A reduction would bring borrowers instead. Thus the volume of bank reserves could be influenced with some precision. The British economy in the last half of the century was exposed by free trade to the competition of the rest of the world. One can assume, as a result, that it was fairly sensitive to higher interest costs, which meant higher carrying charges for new investment, or to lower interest costs, which bespoke a favorable opportunity for expansion. There is much room for debate on the extent of the effect of the bank rate on the British economy—how much investment was encouraged or discouraged and to what extent prices were inflated or deflated. Perhaps the bank rate was credited with much that would have happened anyway. Perhaps it derived prestige from its position as a Victorian conversation piece. But perhaps it was of consequence.

What is not in question is that the possibility of exercising control over the economy by such means came to have a compelling charm for all who were in any way identified with it. This was especially true of the banking community. For it meant that bankers, through the central bank, stood at the apex of economic influence. Their power, moreover, was not won by the crude, uncouth and uncertain process of soliciting votes. It was the direct reward of financial achievement and wealth. Not only did monetary policy belong to the banking community, but specific steps were taken to safeguard the exercise of this authority from the intervention or intercession of politicians. The central bank was kept "independent" of the government and in degree above it. Such was the case for two centuries with the Bank of England. It is still so, nominally, of the Federal Reserve System. This independence, though extensively celebrated in the conventional wisdom, would not long sustain determined opposition in the United States to the wishes of the Executive and the Congress. But it reflects, in at least vestigial form, the belief that monetary policy is the highly professional prerogative of the financial community. As such, it must be protected from the crude pressures of democratic government.

The management of the economy by monetary methods involved the exercise of subtle, as distinct from naked, power. No businessman, or indeed no citizen, was told what to do. Instead, they were guided by forces of which they were themselves not wholly aware. If the economy must be given guidance, how gratifying that it be done in this discreet and seemly way.

Moreover, to most people money and credit, the way they are conceived and extinguished, and the fact that pieces of paper of little intrinsic worth can be so valuable, remain a great reservoir of mystery. Decisions on monetary policy had always been taken *in camera* and communicated to the public only by actions—movements in the interest rate or increases or decreases in central-bank portfolios. A learned literature developed which was privy to the mystery and which speculated on the motives behind various moves. Its authors came to have a stake in the policy they interpreted. They belonged to a select few who understood. Outshining them, only, were those who were privy and really knew. Such was the charm of this policy that this affection was easily translated into claims for its effectiveness which, in fact, did invade the supernatural. Monetary policy was graced by effects not only mysterious but magical.

This has not invariably been so. In the nineteen-thirties, the prestige of monetary policy was, for a time, very low. The Federal Reserve System, deeply uncertain in its purpose, had failed to arrest the speculative boom of the late twenties; low interest rates and easy money were equally ineffective in dealing with the Great Depression. Bankers, in these years, as a result of error, unhappy accident and the enthusiastic denigration of left-wing critics, had suffered a severe decline in popular esteem. Down with them went the faith in monetary policy. Keynes argued that the rate of interest was a roundabout way of influencing economic activity and of small practical utility.

From this nadir, in the years following World War II, monetary policy had a great revival. Banks and bankers recovered their prestige and so did the instrument with which they were so intimately identified. Faith in monetary policy became a badge of resistance to the heresies of Keynes and proof that the individual had no part in the radicalism which sought to defame decent and respectable men because they were in the business of holding and lending money.

More important, something had to be done about inflation. The other measures for contending with this ineluctable phenomenon were under the handicap of being unpalatable, impractical or even, like price controls, incipiently un-American. This was the consequence of their being in conflict with other economic goals. Yet something had to be done. Monetary policy remained the only hope. To the affection which the policy elicited and the faith on which it was grounded was added a large element of wishful thinking. There was nothing else, so it had to work. Monetary policy became a form of economic escapism. Without it, the realities would indeed be hard.

Unhappily, faith or urgent need is not an assurance of practical performance. Even if, as bankers have anciently suspected, doubts about monetary policy have on occasion been the invidious reflection of doubts about bankers, this still does not ensure that monetary policy will work. As Chapter II has shown, the ultimate enemy of the conventional wisdom is circumstance. It is never in such peril as when enthusiastic exponents put it to a practical test. Monetary policy, despite its unparalleled position in the conventional wisdom, makes only secondary contact with the problem of inflation. And it has had the misfortune to be subject to extended experiment.

II

First of all, monetary policy suffers from the unfortunate absence of any occult effect. It has long been clear that economic management, especially in the United States, would be greatly facilitated if resort could occasionally be had to witchcraft. Monetary policy, by far the most promising possibility, involves none. This every good citizen must regret.

More somberly, the policy makes no direct contact with the wage-price interaction. This not even its prophets suggest. Accordingly, it must work, if at all, by reducing the aggregate demand for goods. Its handle for accomplishing this is a higher interest rate and a diminished supply of funds for lending. By thus discouraging lending by banks and borrowing by consumers and producers, the policy is presumed to restrict or restrain what the latter have to spend. The reduction in this spending, if it occurs, will then have secondary (or multiplier) effects on the spending of others. The ultimate consequence is to reduce the demand for goods as a whole or to restrain the rate of increase in demand.[1] By thus keeping demand from pressing on capacity and on the labor force, prices are kept stable. Or such must be the hope.

That is the only avenue of effect.[2] An alternative form of exposition emphasizes the effect of this policy on the supply of money. But so far as this argument does not escape into

[1] This will serve the same purposes as an absolute reduction if the plant capacity and labor force of the economy are also increasing. It is convenient in any discussion to speak in terms of absolute magnitudes—whether an increase in interest rates does or does not reduce total spending. But while this is a convenient simplification of language, and one that leads to no important error, the question in a growing economy will ordinarily be whether the rate of increase in demand is reduced relative to the rate of increase in capacity. The difference in these rates will be the source of the slack on which price stability depends.

[2] Theoretically, the rise in the interest rate could encourage consumer saving from current income and by the same act reduce spending from current income. The possibility of such an effect, though once suggested, is no longer seriously urged even by the most convinced supporters of monetary policy.

mysticism, it comes to the same thing. The money supply increases or decreases as the result of increases or decreases in commercial bank lending. An increase in the money supply affects prices by way of the increased spending of borrowers from borrowed funds as well as through the multiplier by those from whom they buy. When one restricts the money supply, one restricts the spending associated with the lending and borrowing of funds. The measures are the same: the supply of funds available for lending is reduced, and the interest rate is raised to discourage borrowing. No matter how the cake is sliced, the policy, if it is to work, must restrain borrowing. And thereby it becomes effective by reducing or restraining the total volume of spending. So far, there is little disagreement among economists.

As just noted, direct spending from borrowed funds is of two kinds—by consumers for consumer goods and by businessmen for investment. The advantage of looking at economic policy in the full context of economic attitudes and behavior will now be evident. To restrict consumer borrowing by increasing the interest cost on installment and other loans collides abruptly with the process of consumer-demand creation. If consumer wants were independently determined, an increase in interest charges could, conceivably, operate through the consumer's demand schedule to reduce borrowing and spending. It seems unlikely that the elasticity of the response would be great, but the possibility exists. But as matters now stand, any step to discourage borrowing and buying will be automatically opposed by the machinery for consumer-demand creation. A shrinkage in consumer borrowing will be merely a warning to those concerned with the synthesis of consumer demand to increase their efforts. Or they can take steps to annul the effect of the increased interest charge.

This is a matter of minimum difficulty. Consumer credit is ordinarily repaid in installments, and one of the mathematical tricks of this type of repayment is that a very large increase in interest rates brings a very small increase in the monthly payment. Thus a man who signs a note for $3800 on the purchase of a new car (after trade-in) to be repaid over twenty-four months, and who agrees to an "add-on" of 9 percent of this amount as interest, will have a total interest bill of $684 and monthly payments of $187. If the interest charge is increased by one-third to an add-on of 12 percent, his total interest obligation becomes $912, but the increase in monthly payments is only $9. The one-third increase in interest brings but a one-twentieth increase in the payment. This increase can easily be offset by a lengthening of the term of repayment, a common practice in the high-interest-rate period of the late nineteen-sixties and early seventies. In practice, it is submerged by a variety of additional inspection, insurance and other charges. Since the customer, in contemplating the purchases, is less aware of the interest rate than of the monthly charge, it will be seen how readily a very large increase in interest charges can, in practice, be offset. During periods of active monetary policy, increased finance charges have regularly been followed by large increases in consumer loans. Want creation, and the process of financing it, were still acting to exaggerate rather than to restrain the inflationary effect of consumer spending.

There is no chance that monetary policy can have even a minimal effect on consumer spending while its conflict with the machinery of consumer-want creation remains unresolved and, in degree, even unrecognized, and while we concede the paramount importance of the latter. And though the reasons have not been fully seen, there is, in fact, considerable agreement that monetary policy does not make any effective contact with consumer borrowing and spending.

III

That the restriction of business investment by monetary policy involves a similar conflict with a prior goal will now be apparent to everyone. We set primary store by production. Monetary policy seeks to prevent price increases by cutting down on the investment by which productive growth is made possible and is sustained. It would be hard to imagine a more abrupt collision with the dominant position of production. Oddly enough, those who set the greatest store by monetary policy—bankers and businessmen—are often those who are most inclined to emphasize the importance of production and to view increases in output with the most satisfaction.

In practice, the conflict between monetary policy and

production is not so severe. This is partly because of a surviving belief that monetary policy somehow makes contact with the price level without affecting the volume of investment. It is not unknown for men of sound faith to call for a high and rising volume of business investment and incentives, including tax revision, to encourage it. At the same time, they strongly endorse a policy of monetary restraint designed to prevent inflation. These remarkably contradictory positions can be reconciled only if there is faith that, by essentially occult means, monetary policy will stabilize prices without affecting the volume of producer borrowing, investment and spending.

The conflict between production and a monetary policy designed to decrease business investment is also eased by our tendency, described in Chapter IX, to accept and even to applaud whatever rate of economic growth we are currently enjoying. Concern for such growth is rhetorical rather than real. Hence, we are not notably disturbed by a policy which, by reducing the volume of new investment, seeks to lower the rate of economic growth so long as serious unemployment does not appear.

However, if individual firms were prevented by the policy from making the investment which seemed to them wise and profitable, there would, of course, be objection. And this brings us to the final reason why the conflict rarely reaches the acute stage.

IV

In times of high or near-capacity production, the context in which inflation becomes acute, profits and profits prospects are certain to be favorable. Because production is near capacity, investment in expansion will seem to the individual firm both advantageous and singularly logical from the point of view of the community. (The firm will be much more impressed by the visible service it renders in increasing the supply of its product than by the invisible effect of its investment in adding to total spending and thus to inflationary pressure.) For all of these reasons, most investment will be extremely unresponsive to moderate increases in the interest rate, which is the way in which monetary policy presents itself to the ordinary business firm.

If the policy is applied severely, some firms will be squeezed by the higher rates. And in practice, since interest rates are comparatively sticky, some rationing of credit will occur. Some firms which would like to borrow will be unable to do so. If the policy is pressed far enough, investment spending will be curtailed. In the end, the slack required for price stability would appear. So would the conflict with our attitudes on the importance of production. There would be an equally urgent conflict between this policy and the employment and associated economic security which is the counterpart of high production. But before this point is reached, another problem of even greater import arises. That is the effect of monetary policy on different kinds and sizes of firms.

As we have seen, when demand has been growing and the economy is at or near capacity, firms in the oligopolistic sector are likely to have a reserve of unliquidated gains.[8] This enables them to pass higher interest charges along to the consumer. (If they can pass along wage increases, they can obviously do the same with interest.) And by raising prices and income, they can resort to unliquidated gains for investment purposes. The need to price for returns sufficient to cover a considerable share of investment requirements has been a stock defense of industrial price increases for many years. Thus, industries which have unliquidated gains are able, in effect, to contract out from the effect of monetary policy. The attractiveness of the large firm as a bank customer and its ability to go directly to the market for funds also help exempt it from the effects of the policy. In the rationing that follows, it is the small firm that finds itself unable to borrow.

Firms in competitive markets—those whose prices and

[8] In *The New Industrial State*, 2nd ed., rev. (Boston: Houghton Mifflin, 1971), as I have earlier observed, I deal more fully with this failure to maximize revenues. As I show there, it derives from the large need to stabilize the parameters within which the planning of the large industrial firm proceeds. And security, growth and technological virtuosity share pride of place with profits as a goal of this planning. In later writing. I might note, I've called the oligopolistic sector the Planning System. See *Economics and the Public Purpose* (Boston: Houghton Mifflin, 1973).

costs are impersonally determined by the market for all—obciously cannot pass higher interest costs ahead to the customer. In the relevant short-run, they cannot raise the prices that they do not control to get investment funds from their customers. As a rule, being small they cannot circumvent the rationing of bank credit by selling securities in the market. Hence, for competitive industries—farmers, small builders, small retailers, service industries, dealers—monetary policy is effective. And it will be effective for these firms much before it affects the industries in which there is a greater measure of market control.[4]

It will be easy to see why monetary policy is regarded with equanimity and even approval by larger and stronger firms. Unless applied with severity over time, it does not appreciably affect them. But, for the same reason, there must be grievous doubts about the workability of the policy. Before the large-volume investment spending of the larger and more powerful firms is affected, a severe squeeze will ordinarily be placed on the capital requirements of small-scale firms. For such firms, the conflict between monetary policy and productive growth will be highly visible and, indeed, very painful.

V

As noted, the most mercurial source of spending in the economy has long been recognized to be that for business investment. Spending by consumers and by governments have (consumer borrowing apart) substantial elements of reliability. They are related to income being received. They are grounded on customary patterns of behavior. In the case of government outlays, they have a markedly greater constancy than the revenues which support them. Investment spending, by contrast, depends on an estimate of future returns. The singular feature of the future is that it cannot be known. Estimates as to what it holds will change. So, accordingly, will in-

---

4 Events of the nineteen-seventies emphasized these conclusions. A particularly painful manifestation was the severe depression in the housing industry which followed from the efforts to arrest the inflation of the mid-seventies with monetary policy.

vestment outlays. And the changes in these latter, by changing prospective earnings, change the future itself.

If monetary restraint is exercised over a period of time, it may eventually affect the investment of larger firms. This may come about in a variety of ways but most obviously because the curtailment of the borrowing and investment of weaker firms and industries will, in the end, affect demand and investment prospects for the more concentrated sector of the economy. When this happens, there will be a revision of investment plans, and this may be large.

Monetary policy thus operates on the most mercurial dimension of economic activity. This is the final source of inutility and it may, indeed, be a source of considerable danger. If, the conflict with production notwithstanding, it is applied with rigor and persistence to produce the requisite slack, there is danger that it will do too much. Or, to speak more precisely, there is unavoidable uncertainty as to just what it will do. It seeks to influence the most unpredictable element of aggregate demand. The result of this influence is, accordingly, unpredictable. There must always be danger that monetary policy will reduce investment to the point of causing a serious depression. Such a depression would not be incorrectible. But neither would it be desirable. And it can and would indeed occur well before prices were stabilized.[5]

VI

The thrust of this chapter, it will be evident, is highly negative. There is no magic in the monetary system, however brilliantly or esoterically administered, which can reconcile price stability with the imperatives of production and employment as they are regarded in the affluent society. On the contrary, monetary policy is a blunt, unreliable, discriminatory and somewhat dangerous instrument of economic control. It survives in esteem partly because so few understand it, including so few of those—builders, smaller businessmen who must finance inventories, farmers—on whom it places the prime burden of its restraint. It survives, also, because an active

[5] As the experience of the mid-seventies has also affirmed.

monetary policy means that, at times, interest rates will be high—a circumstance that is far from disagreeable for those with money to lend.[6]

6 Since the earlier editions of this book, circumstance has forced some increase in understanding of these matters. The Vietnam war, and the delay in raising taxes to offset the increased spending occasioned by that eccentrice enterprise, forced an unparalleled reliance on monetary policy. As this inflationary influence receded, the wage-price spiral took over as a strong inflationary force with abetting effect from fiscal policy and materials shortages. Interest rates were raised to levels unknown for forty years. This was with punishing effect on those who had to pay them. This punishment extended to states and localities which are heavily dependent on borrowed funds. And it added to the problem of social balance to which we shall presently come. While General Motors was not inhibited in its investment, the municipality contemplating a school-bond issue most certainly was. So was the home-builder. And withal, prices continued to rise—inflation was doubtless tempered, but it was not controlled. The lessons of this dismal experience were not lost, at least on the less passionate friends of monetary policy. Yet in economics, as in love, hope dies hard. No other course of action in economics has ever rivaled monetary policy in its capacity to survive failure.

CHAPTER XVI

Production and Price Stability

In the political spectrum of modern economic policy, monetary measures are the instrument of conservatives. The weapon of liberals is fiscal policy. And among economists generally, fiscal policy is regarded as the ultimate economic weapon. The friends of monetary policy aver its effectiveness, perhaps partly to allay their unconscious doubts. The effectiveness of fiscal policy is much more rarely debated. Moreover, it had the implicit blessing of Keynes. As the converse of the public spending which was the Keynesian remedy for unemployment, it has still a slight cachet of rational radicalism.

Fiscal policy is much simpler and more forthright in its operation than monetary policy. The mysticism has been exorcised, and the theoretical chain which links the original action and the ultimate effect, something always to be watched in economics, is far shorter and involves far fewer asseverations as to what *should* happen. The government taxes more than it spends. This difference is not spent. Hence, it is a net reduction in the spending of the country as a whole. If this difference is sufficiently increased, then total spending in the economy will no longer press on the capacity of the economy. Slack will result. If this slack is large enough, firms will hesitate to raise prices—in terms of the present analysis, short-run maximization will seem inconsistent with longer-run return—and wage demands will be resisted. Demand will not pull up prices in the competitive sector. Prices, as a result, will be stable unless, indeed, the process is pressed too far, in which case they will fall.

Business firms feel the impact of monetary policy initially in the form of a change in factor cost or availability—specifically, in the cost or availability of credit for capital. Large firms and those with substantial market power are able, as we have seen, to pass this cost increase along to customers, and in case of a shortage of credit, they can have recourse to alternative sources of supply. Competitive and smaller firms have no similar escape. Fiscal policy works, in the main, by reducing demand. This reduction affects the demand for the products of all firms, large and small, strong and weak. No firm, in the technical idiom, can contract out of the movement in its demand curve. The effect of the policy will not be precisely the same, as between competitive and oligopolistic markets and as between large firms and small, but it is much more nearly equal.[1]

Yet in the years since World War II in the United States, fiscal policy has also revealed itself as a very poor defense against inflation. The reason was not that it failed to work but that not even its principal proponents argued for its vigorous use. It was favored in principle but not in practice. The explanation is simple. Here is another unresolved conflict in economic goals. Once again the advantage of seeing things in full social context will be plain.

II

For reasons that will be explored in detail in the next chapter, civilian government spending is likely at any given time to be near the minimum which the community regards as tolerable. Complaint about waste and inefficiency in performing these services, which is endemic in our political comment and rarely without foundation, should not be allowed to confuse the issue. Very important functions can be performed very wastefully and often are. And waste can rarely be eliminated by reducing expenditure. It is far easier to cut the function than the waste, and this is what occurs. In time of inflation, the economic context of which we are speaking, the situation of the public services is certain to be even more tenuous because of the inevitable tendency for public budgets to lag behind the general increase in prices.

[1] Where there are unliquidated gains, prices will fall less promptly and earnings will be less promptly reduced than in a competitive industry where there are no such gains.

This means that a positive fiscal policy to counter inflation will almost always require an increase in taxes. The importance of cutting or postponing expenditures, however much it may be urged on the more vacuous margins of the conventional wisdom, may on occasion sustain hope. But the actual accomplishment will invariably be negligible. On this point, experience is complete. Whenever inflation is a danger (and now and then when it is not), spokesmen urge the Administration and the Congress, and the latter urge upon themselves, sometimes with seeming seriousness, the importance of cutting expenditures. Nothing is ever accomplished of sufficient magnitude to affect appreciably the total spending of the economy. Quite often nothing is accomplished. And indeed the expectations of nonaccomplishment are such that the Congressional discussion of budget-cutting each winter has now assumed the innocent aspect of a folk rite. It begins as the budget time approaches. It reaches full pitch a few days after the budget is submitted. The gods are appeased by stern denunciations of public profligacy and inspired promises of vast economies. The ceremony is solemnly described to the people by press and television. Thereafter, the seemingly indispensable outlays are voted, and the result is almost invariably to increase the budget.

To raise taxes to reduce demand encounters at the outset a problem of understanding. That, in the event of insufficient demand and depression, taxes should be cut and public outlays increased in order to increase aggregate demand and employment is now widely accepted. There is an inherent logic to the procedure. This is also true of cutting public expenditures to counter inflation—were this only possible. However, the logic of increasing taxes is by no means so evident. The first and obvious effect is to increase the consumer's living costs or reduce his income. This happens at a time when inflation is making it difficult for many people to maintain accustomed living standards. Other taxes add to the producer's costs. Thus to attack inflation by raising taxes seems at first glance a curiously backhanded procedure. It is strongly resisted by the very considerable number of plain men who insist, never without fervor and pride, that subtlety in

economic relationships is an indication of error and that truth
is revealed only to the uncomplicated mind.[2]

III

However, the most serious problem of fiscal policy is the
conflict with other economic goals.

It collides, first of all, with the tacit truce outlined in
Chapter VII on income inequality. Taxes are the device by
which governments have most nakedly sought to influence income distribution. As a result, they have a considerable
practical and an even deeper symbolic importance in relation
to this issue. Hence, a proposal to increase taxes for fiscal
reasons automatically provokes a debate on the question if
inequality. Liberals, who hitherto had been abiding comfortably by the terms of the truce, are required by their
faith to rally to the support of taxes which reduce inequality.
Conservatives rally to oppose them. In wartime, this debate
can to some extent be evaded by invoking the doctrine of
equality of sacrifice—the rich man can be told that his suffer-
ings at the hands of the tax authorities are roughly the
counterpart of those of the soldier under shellfire. Despite
much concentrated thought, no entirely suitable reply has
ever been devised by men of means. Thus, in wartime, it has
been practical to employ the income tax to absorb excess
purchasing power. In peacetime, such use of taxation will at a
minimum be complicated by some argument over the essentially unrelated issue of equality.

Finally, there is the now classic conflict with production.
Fiscal policy becomes effective only as the reduced demand
brings output below the current capacity of plant and the labor force. Having persuaded ourselves that production is of
paramount importance, we must now persuade ourselves to
sacrifice it in return for price stability. Moreover, once again
the sacrifice may have to be considerable. Where concerns
are strongly organized in their markets and deal with strong
unions, i.e., where the likelihood of unliquidated gains is
great, the slack required, as already noted, may have to be

2 The straightforward, uncomplicated, free-enterprise mind is enjoying a
special vogue in the years preceding this edition.

quite large. Even though, in fact, the output is not of high urgency, the income to those whom the slack makes unemployed is of utmost interest and importance.

Unlike monetary policy, fiscal policy makes its initial contact with the economy not by reducing investment expenditure but by reducing (in the main) consumer expenditure. In not attacking investment, it is thus, at first glance, less inimical to economic expansion or growth. However, too much should not be made of this distinction. Firms are encouraged to invest at least partly because production is pressing on capacity. When it ceases to do so—when there is slack—they can be expected to cut back on investment. Just as demand will have an acceleration effect on investment, to use the term familiar to economists, as production approaches capacity and the latter is enlarged, so it will have a decelerating effect as production drops away from capacity levels. So magnified, the movement in investment and therewith in total demand would appear offhand to reinforce the effect of fiscal policy. It gives a leverage to the change in spending that is brought about by government action. But it also means that once the economy ceases to be at capacity, there is a substantial sacrifice in investment for growth. Or, to put the matter differently, growth will be at a maximum only when the economic system is under that pressure to use the capacity which helps produce inflation.

Were the economy given to occasional bouts of stimulation with excessive investment and rising prices—the business cycle of the central economic tradition—then countercyclical repression of demand might involve no serious problem. Some who have seen no conflict between fiscal policy and growth have, without doubt, viewed it in such a context. But if full employment and full use of capacity is taken as the norm of economic policy, as in modern times it is, then the rate of investment associated with full use of capacity is also normal. A policy which holds production below capacity in the interest of price stability inescapably sacrifices economic growth.

However, the much more serious conflict is between fiscal policy and the unemployment which stability requires in modern markets. Insufficient production and growth can be tolerated but this unemployment cannot be. And to induce it deliberately is a politically unalluring policy. In addition, even though the unemployment necessary for price stability is not, as a national total, very great, it will never be uniformly distributed. Black and unskilled workers, often the same, lose their jobs first. Those industries and communities that are stationary or in which demand is increasing more slowly will feel curtailment first. Here there will be pockets of unemployment and distress. The policy strikes with especial force not only on particular people but also on particular politicians.

Conservatives will always prefer inflation to its remedies. And faced with a choice between unemployment and price increases, the liberal politician unhesitatingly condemns both.

The politics of an anti-inflationary fiscal policy could scarcely be less promising.

IV

So long as the use of fiscal policy is in unresolved conflict with other and prior economic goals, it will not be used with effective vigor, at least in peacetime. This conflict and the resulting inutility of fiscal measures are not yet widely conceded by economists. The textbooks still elucidate the use of fiscal measures as a device for ensuring price stability. They concede that we must settle for something less than completely full employment and that this will offer difficulties. But they assume that, given inflation, taxes can be increased. The only difficulty is that the policy never looks practical at any particular moment. While the conflict with other goals persists, it never will.

One last possibility remains. That is to combine fiscal policy with control over prices and wages. As a result, prices and wages are unable to respond to the price-increasing influences that develop as production approaches capacity. The controls rather than the slack serve to prevent price increases at capacity operations. Thus they reconcile capacity output (and also related growth) with price stability. It would not be necessary to enforce any substantial amount of idle capacity and unemployment.

There is a general view that price and wage controls accomplish nothing of themselves—that they deal with symptoms rather than with causes. To use them is to juggle with the thermometer, not the furnace. If current demand is far in excess of the capacity of the economy, there is an important element of truth in this contention. The only recourse is to bring demand into balance with supply. Anything else is an escape. But if, by fiscal or other measures, the aggregate of demand is kept about equal to the current capacity of the economy, then any such view of wage and price controls is a gross oversimplification. Wages act on prices and prices on wages as capacity is approached. Controls prevent this interplay. In doing so, they allow the economy to function closer to capacity without price increases.

Some economists have conceded this function explicitly;[8] more have concurred implicitly by agreeing that such controls are necessary in a wartime emergency, i.e., when there is no escape from the need to reconcile full use of capacity with the greatest possible degree of price stability. But, on balance, the conventional wisdom still asserts the unwisdom of direct controls in peacetime. Nothing better establishes the good sense and soundness of an economist than a suitably solemn condemnation of such controls.

The objections to controls are numerous. To be effective, it is assumed that they must apply comprehensively to all prices and all wages. This means that the administrative problems are indubitably grave and become more serious with passage of time. The specter of such control invokes the ancient resistance to the intrusions of government. This intrusion is indeed considerable, for the power to set prices is not insignificant in economic decision-making. To the extent that Social Darwinists and the utilitarian philosophers have successfully identified vitality and liberty with the free market, controls will be regarded as an even more far-reaching menace.

Finally, and perhaps most important, such controls are sharply in conflict with stylized attitudes toward production. As Chapter IX has shown, we set great store by the efficient

---

[8] On the whole, there has been movement in this direction since the first edition of this book, although the use of controls by the Nixon Administration—controls that were mismanaged by individuals who did not believe in their use—was without doubt a setback. I have dealt with this matter in detail in *Money: Whence It Came, Where It Went* (Boston: Houghton Mifflin, 1975).

allocation of resources as the device for maximizing production. That was the accepted formula for economic efficiency in the last century. Social nostalgia still accords it a central role. This allocation is accomplished in the capitalist society by the market—by the pull and push of market prices and market wages bringing labor, capital and materials to the firms and industries of most efficient use. Obviously one cannot have both controls and a free market which performs this function.

None of the foregoing objections holds. In the war years, controls were consistent with a very large increase in output. That was because production was expanded along less stylized but far more effective dimensions than those related to improved resource allocation. Nor is it certain that the controls which would serve to arrest the wage-price spiral would have to be comprehensive. It is possible that very limited restraints will serve to reconcile capacity output and price stability. This is an important point to which this essay will return. The prices fixed by controls are already fixed by monopoly or oligopoly power. Here nothing decisive is changed. However, for the moment it is sufficient to note that price and wage control, as a way of reconciling price stability, maximum product and minimum unemployment, is in conflict, no less important if it is ostensible rather than real, with historic attitudes toward production.[4]

V

A word of summary is now in order. We are impelled by present attitudes and goals to seek to operate the economy at capacity where, we have seen, inflation must be regarded not as an obnormal but as a normal prospect. The same attitudes which lead us to set store by capacity use of plant and labor force largely deny us the use of measures for preventing inflation. Monetary Policy collides with the process of

4 The hold of these ideas is sufficiently strong so that many would prefer the minor effect on output that would come from efficient resource allocation by the market in a context of price stability and some unemployment to the much greater effect on production which would come from (a) using the unemployed resources and (b) having the incentive to increased output which may be expected when demand presses on capacity.

consumer-demand creation and, since it works on business investment, is in conflict with our emphasis on growth. It is also ineffectual, discriminatory and, possibly, dangerous. Fiscal policy is sharply at odds with the commitment to a level of output that ensures full employment and the accompanying economic security. Direct controls, which in theory might reconcile high employment with price stability, are under a heavy ideological cloud. We assume that we must have them in unworkable mass or not at all. They are in ostensible conflict with the goal of efficient production, for that has anciently been identified with market allocation of resources.

These conflicts are partly obscured. The conservative disguises the conflict between monetary policy and production by his faith that his policy has occult or other transcendental effects not visible to the naked eye. The liberal, including the Keynesian economist, conceals the conflict between fiscal policy and production at full employment not so much by resort to mysticism as by a systematic refusal to face issues. This he accomplishes by keeping his advocacy of fiscal measures in general terms while being specifically critical of unemployment and underuse of plant. He commonly surrenders the opportunity for reconciling the conflict by agreeing that direct controls are unsound.

Thus the way is open to recurrent inflation. This, as Chapter XIV has shown, has a highly discriminatory impact on different groups. And we shall see in the next chapter that there are deeper social consequences. Inflation strikes the economy at the point where it is most vulnerable to damage. We may put it down—after the process of consumer-demand creation and its financing—as the second of the unsolved problems of the affluent society.

CHAPTER XVII

The Theory of Social Balance

> It is not till it is discovered that high individual incomes will not purchase the mass of mankind immunity from cholera, typhus, and ignorance, still less secure them the positive advantages of educational opportunity and economic security, that slowly and reluctantly, amid prophecies of moral degeneration and economic disaster, society begins to make collective provision for needs no ordinary individual, even if he works overtime all his life, can provide himself.
>
> —R. H. Tawney[1]

The final problem of the productive society is what it produces. This manifests itself in an implacable tendency to provide an opulent supply of some things and a niggardly yield of others. This disparity carries to the point where it is a cause of social discomfort and social unhealth. The line which divides our area of wealth from our area of poverty is roughly that which divides privately produced and marketed goods and services from publicly rendered services. Our wealth in the first is not only in startling contrast with the meagerness of the latter, but our wealth in privately produced goods is, to a marked degree, the cause of crisis in the supply of public services. For we have failed to see the importance, indeed the urgent need, of maintaining a balance between the two.

This disparity between our flow of private and public

---

1 *Equality*, 4th ed., rev. (London: Allen & Unwin, 1952), pp. 134–135.

goods and services is no matter of subjective judgment. On the contrary, it is the source of the most extensive comment which only stops short of the direct contrast being made here. In recent years, the papers of any major city—those of New York are an excellent example—tell daily of the shortages and shortcomings in the elementary municipal and metropolitan services. The schools are old and overcrowded. The police force is under strength. The parks and playgrounds are insufficient. Streets and empty lots are filthy, and the sanitation staff is underequipped and in need of men. Access to the city by those who work there is uncertain and painful and becoming more so. Internal transportation is overcrowded, unhealthful and dirty. So is the air. Parking on the streets should be prohibited, but there is no space elsewhere. These deficiencies are not in new and novel services but in old and established ones. Cities have long swept their streets, helped their people move around, educated them, kept order, and provided horse rails for equipages which sought to pause. That their residents should have a nontoxic supply of air suggests no revolutionary dalliance with socialism. Only one major change has occurred in the years following World War II: By virtue of the exercise of union power, municipal workers, at least in many of the larger cities, are no longer underpaid.

In most of the last thirty years, the discussion of this public poverty was matched by the stories of ever-increasing opulence in privately produced goods. The Gross National Product was rising. So were retail sales. So was personal income. Labor productivity also advanced. The automobiles that could not be parked were being produced at an expanded rate. The children, though subject in the playgrounds to the affectionate interest of adults with odd tastes, and disposed to increasingly imaginative forms of delinquency, were admirably equipped with television sets. The care and refreshment of the mind was principally in the public domain. Schools, in consequence, were often severely overcrowded and usually underprovided, and the same was even more often true of the mental hospitals.

The contrast was and remains evident not alone to those who read. The family which takes its mauve and cerise, air-conditioned, power-steered and power-braked automobile out for a tour passes through cities that are badly paved, made hideous by litter, blighted buildings, billboards and posts for wires that should long since have been put underground. They pass on into a counrtyside that has been rendered largely invisible by commercial art. (The goods which the latter advertise have an absolute priority in our value system. Such aesthetic considerations as a view of the countryside accordingly come second. On such matters, we are consistent.) They picnic on exquisitely packaged food from a portable icebox by a polluted stream and go on to spend the night at a park which is a menace to public health and morals. Just before dozing off on an air mattress, beneath a nylon tent, amid the stench of decaying refuse, they may reflect vaguely on the curious unevenness of their blessings. Is this, indeed, the American genius?

II

In the production of goods within the private economy, it has long been recognized that a tolerably close relationship must be maintained between the production of various kinds of products. The output of steel and oil and machine tools is related to the production of automobiles. Investment in transportation must keep abreast of the output of goods to be transported. The supply of power must be abreast of the growth of industries requiring it. The existence of these relationships—coefficients to the economist—has made possible the construction of the input-output table which shows how changes in the production in one industry will increase or diminish the demands on other industries. To this table, and more especially to its ingenious author, Professor Wassily Leontief, the world is indebted for one of its most important of modern insights into economic relationships. If expansion in one part of the economy were not matched by the requisite expansion in other parts—were the need for balance not respected—then bottlenecks and shortages, speculative hoarding of scarce supplies and sharply increasing costs would ensue. Fortunately in peacetime the market system, combined with considerable planning, serves to maintain this balance, and this, together with the existence of stocks and some flexibility in the coefficients as a result of substitution, ensures that no serious difficulties will arise. We are reminded of the problem only by noticing how serious it is for those countries which seek to solve it by a more inflexible planning and with a much smaller supply of resources.

Just as there must be balance in what a community produces, so there must also be balance in what the community consumes. An increase in the use of one product creates, ineluctably, a requirement for others. If we are to consume more automobiles, we must have more gasoline. There must be more insurance as well as more space on which to operate them. Beyond a certain point, more and better food appears to mean increased need for medical services. This is the certain result of the increased consumption of tobacco and alcohol. More vacations require more hotels and more fishing rods. And so forth.

However, the relationships we are here discussing are not confined to the private economy. They operate comprehensively over the whole span of private and public services. As surely as an increase in the output of automobiles puts new demands on the steel industry so, also, it places new demands on public services. Similarly, every increase in the consumption of private goods will normally mean some facilitating or protective step by the state. In all cases if these services are not forthcoming, the consequences will be in some degree ill. It will be convenient to have a term which suggests a satisfactory relationship between the supply of privately produced goods and services and those of the state, and we may call it social balance.

The problem of social balance is ubiquitous, and frequently it is obtrusive. As noted, an increase in the comsumption of automobiles requires a facilitating supply of streets, highways, traffic control and parking space. The protective services of the police and the highway patrols must also be available, as must those of the hospitals. Although the need for balance here is extraordinarily clear, our use of privately produced vehicles has, on occasion, got far out of line with the supply of the related public services. That result has been hideous road congestion, an annual massacre of impressive proportions and chronic colitis in the cities. As on the ground, so also in the air. Planes are delayed or collide over airports with disquieting consequences for passengers when the public provision for air traffic control fails to keep pace with the private use of the airways.

But the auto and the airplane, versus the space to use them, are merely an exceptionally visible example of a requirement that is pervasive. The more goods people procure, the more packages they discard and the more trash that must be carried away. If the appropriate sanitation services are not provided, the counterpart of increasing opulence will be deepening filth. The greater the wealth, the thicker will be the dirt. This indubitably describes a tendency of our time. As more goods are produced and owned, the greater are the opportunities for fraud and the more property that must be protected. If the provision of public law enforcement services does not keep pace, the counterpart of increased well-being will, we may be certain, be increased crime.

The city of Los Angeles, in modern times, is the near-classic study in the problem of social balance. Magnificently efficient factories and oil refineries, a lavish supply of automobiles, a vast consumption of handsomely packaged products, coupled for many years with the absence of a municipal trash collection service which forced the use of home incinerators, made the air nearly unbreathable for an appreciable part of each year. Air pollution could be controlled only by a complex and highly developed set of public services—by better knowledge of causes stemming from more public research, public requirement of pollution control devices on cars, a municipal trash collection service and possibly the assertion of the priority of clean air over the production of goods. These were long in coming. The agony of a city without usable air was the result.

The issue of social balance can be identified in many other current problems. Thus, an aspect of increasing private production is the appearance of an extraordinary number of things which lay claim to the interest of the young. Motion pictures, television, automobiles and the vast opportunities which go with the mobility, together with such less enchanting merchandise as narcotics, comic books and pornographia, are all included in an advancing Gross National Product. The child of a less opulent as well as a technologically more primitive age had far fewer such diversions. The red schoolhouse is remembered mainly because it had a paramount position in the lives of those who attended it that no modern school can hope to attain.

In a well-run and well-regulated community, with a sound school system, good recreational opportunities and a good police force—in short, a community where public services have kept pace with private production—the diversionary forces operating on the modern juvenile may do no great damage. Television and the violent mores of Hollywood must contend with the intellectual discipline of the school. The social, athletic, dramatic and like attractions of the school also claim the attention of the child. These, together with the other recreational opportunities of the community, minimize the tendency to delinquency. Experiments with violence and immorality are checked by an effective law enforcement system before they become epidemic.

In a community where public services have failed to keep abreast of private consumption, things are very different. Here, in an atmosphere of private opulence and public squalor, the private goods have full sway. Schools do not compete with television and the movies. The dubious heroes of the latter, not Miss Jones, become the idols of the young. Violence replaces the more sedentary recreation for which there are inadequate facilities or provision. Comic books, alcohol, narcotics and switchblade knives are, as noted, part of the increased flow of goods, and there is nothing to dispute their enjoyment. There is an ample supply of private wealth to be appropriated and not much to be feared from the police. An austere community is free from temptation. It can be austere in its public services. Not so a rich one.

Moreover, in a society which sets large store by production, and which has highly effective machinery for synthesizing private wants, there are strong pressures to have as many wage earners in the family as possible. As always, all social behavior is of a piece. If both parents are engaged in private production, the burden on the public services is further increased. Children, in effect, become the charge of the community for an appreciable part of the time. If the services of the community do not keep pace, this will be another source of disorder.

Residential housing also illustrates the problem of the social balance, although in a somewhat complex form. Few would wish to contend that, in the lower or even the middle income brackets, Americans are munificently supplied with housing. A great many families would like better located or merely more houseroom, and no advertising is necessary to persuade them of their wish. And the provision of housing is in the private domain. At first glance at least, the line we draw between private and public seems not to be preventing a satisfactory allocation of resources to housing.

On closer examination, however, the problem turns out to be not greatly different from that of education. It is improbable that the housing industry is greatly more incompetent or inefficient in the United States than in those countries—Scandinavia, Holland, or (for the most part) England—where slums have been largely eliminated and where *minimum* standards of cleanliness and comfort are well above our own. As the experience of these countries shows, and as we have also been learning, the housing industry functions well only in combination with a large, complex and costly array of public services. These include land purchase and clearance for redevelopment; good neighborhood and city planning, and effective and well-enforced zoning; a variety of financing and other aids to the housebuilder and owner; publicly supported research and architectural services for an industry which, by its nature, is equipped to do little on its own; and a considerable amount of direct or assisted public construction for families in the lowest income brackets. The quality of the housing depends not on the industry, which is given, but on what is invested in these supplements and supports.[2]

III

The case for social balance has, so far, been put negatively, Failure to keep public services in minimal relation to private production and use of goods is a cause of social disorder or impairs economic performance. The matter may now be put

[2] In *Economics and the Public Purpose* (Boston: Houghton Mifflin, 1973), I have related the performance of public functions much more closely to the power of the part of the private sector being served. Thus the comparativly ample supply of highways, the more than ample supply of weapons and the poor supply of municipal services and public health care.

affirmatively. By failing to exploit the opportunity to expand public production, we are missing opportunities for enjoyment which otherwise we might have. Presumably a community can be as well rewarded by buying better schools or better parks as by buying bigger automobiles. By concentrating on the latter rather than the former, it is failing to maximize its satisfactions. As with schools in the community, so with public services over the country at large. It is scarcely sensible that we should satisfy our wants in private goods with reckless abundance, while in the case of public goods, on the evidence of the eye, we practice extreme self-denial. So, far from systematically exploiting the opportunities to derive use and pleasure from these services, we do not supply what would keep us out of trouble.

The conventional wisdom holds that the community, large or small, makes a decision as to how much it will devote to its public services. This decision is arrived at by democratic process. Subject to the imperfections and uncertainties of democracy, people decide how much of their private income and goods they will surrender in order to have public services of which they are in greater need. Thus there is a balance, however rough, in the enjoyments to be had from private goods and services and those rendered by public authority.

It will be obvious, however, that this view depends on the notion of independently determined consumer wants. In such a world, one could with some reason defend the doctrine that the consumer, as a voter, makes an independent choice between public and private goods. But given the dependence effect—given that consumer wants are created by the process by which they are satisfied—the consumer makes no such choice. He is subject to the forces of advertising and emulation by which production creates its own demand. Advertising operates exclusively, and emulation mainly, on behalf of privately produced goods and services.[3] Since management of demand and emulative effects operate on behalf of private production, public services will have an inherent tendency to

---

[3] Emulation does operate between communities. A new school in one community does exert pressure on others to remain abreast. However, as compared with the pervasive effects of emulation in extending the demand for privately produced consumers' goods, there will be agreement, I think, that this intercommunity effect is probably small.

lag behind. Automobile demand which is expensively synthesized will inevitably have a much larger claim on income than parks or public health or even roads where no such influence operates. The engines of mass communication, in their highest state of development, assail the eyes and ears of the community on behalf of more beer but not of more schools. Even in the conventional wisdom it will scarcely be contended that this leads to an equal choice between the two.

The competition is especially unequal for new products and services. Every corner of the public psyche is canvassed by some of the nation's most talented citizens to see if the desire for some merchantable product can be cultivated. No similar process operates on behalf of the nonmerchantable services of the state. Indeed, while we take the cultivation of new private wants for granted, we would be measurably shocked to see it applied to public services. The scientist or engineer or advertising man who devotes himself to developing a new carburetor, cleanser or depilatory for which the public recognizes no need and will feel none until an advertising campaign arouses it, is one of the valued members of our society. A politician or a public servant who dreams up a new public service is a wastrel. Few public offenses are more reprehensible.

So much for the influences which operate on the decision between public and private production. The calm decision between public and private consumption pictured by the conventional wisdom is, in fact, a remarkable example of the error which arises from viewing social behavior out of context. The inherent tendency will always be for public services to fall behind private production. We have here the first of the causes of social imbalance.

IV

Social balance is also the victim of two further features of our society—the truce on inequality and the tendency to inflation. Since these are now part of our context, their effect comes quickly into view.

With rare exceptions such as the postal service, public services do not carry a price ticket to be paid for by the individual user. By their nature, they must, ordinarily, be available to all. As a result, when they are improved or new services are initiated, there is the ancient and troublesome question of who is to pay. This, in turn, provokes to life the collateral but irrelevant debate over inequality. As with the use of taxation as an instrument of fiscal policy, the truce on inequality is broken. Liberals are obliged to argue that the services be paid for by progressive taxation which will reduce inequality. Committed as they are to the urgency of goods (and also, as we shall see in a later chapter, to a somewhat mechanical view of the way in which the level of output can be kept most secure), they must oppose sales and excise taxes. Conservatives rally to the defense of inequality—although without ever quite committing themselves in such uncouth terms—and oppose the use of income taxes. They, in effect, oppose the expenditure not on the merits of the service but on the demerits of the tax system. Since the debate over inequality cannot be resolved, the money is frequently not appropriated and the service not performed. It is a casualty of the economic goals of both liberals and conservatives for both of whom the questions of social balance are subordinate to those of production and, when it is evoked, of inequality.

In practice, matters are better as well as worse than this description of the basic forces suggests. Given the tax structure, the revenues of all levels of government grow with the growth of the economy. Services can be maintained and sometimes even improved out of this automatic accretion.

However, this effect is highly unequal. The revenues of the federal government, because of its heavy reliance on progressive income taxes, increase more than proportionately with private economic growth. In addition, although the conventional wisdom greatly deplores the fact, federal appropriations have only an indirect bearing on taxation. Public services are considered and voted on in accordance with their seeming urgency. Initiation or improvement of a particular service is rarely, except for purposes of oratory, set against the specific effect on taxes. Tax policy, in turn, is decided on the basis of the level of economic activity, the resulting revenues, expediency and other considerations. Among these, the total of the thousands of individually considered appropriations is but one factor. In this process, the ultimate tax consequence of any individual appropriation is *de minimus,* and the tendency to ignore it reflects the simple mathematics of the situation. Thus it is possible for the Congress to make decisions affecting the social balance without invoking the question of inequality.

Things are made worse, however, by the fact that a large proportion of the federal revenues are pre-empted by defense. The increase in defense costs has also tended to absorb a large share of the normal increase in tax revenues. The position of the federal government for improving the social balance has also been weakened since World War II by the strong, although receding, conviction that its taxes are at artificial wartime levels and that a tacit commitment exists to reduce taxes at the earliest opportunity.

In the states and localities, the problem of social balance is much more sever. Here tax revenues—this is especially true of the General Property Tax—increase less than proportionately with increased private production. Budgeting too is far more closely circumscribed than in the case of the federal government—only the monetary authority enjoys the pleasant privilege of underwriting its own loans. Because of this, increased services for states and localities regularly pose the question of more revenues and more taxes. And here, with great regularity, the question of social balance is lost in the debate over equality and social equity.

Thus we currently find by far the most serious social imbalance in the services performed by local governments. The F.B.I. comes much more easily by funds than the city police force. The Department of Agriculture can more easily keep its pest control abreast of expanding agricultural output than the average city health service can keep up with the needs of an expanding industrial population. One consequence is that the federal government remains under constant and highly desirable pressure to use its superior revenue position to help redress the balance at the lower levels of government.

V

Finally, social imbalance is the natural offspring of inflation. In the past, inflation had two major effects on public services. Wages in the public service tended to lag well behind those in private industry. There was thus an incentive to desert public for private employment. More important, in the United States the most urgent problems of social balance involve the services of states and localities and, most of all, those of the larger cities. Increasing population, increasing urbanization and increasing affluence all intensify the public tasks of the metropolis. Meanwhile the revenues of these units of government, in contrast with those of the federal government, are relatively inelastic. In consequence of the heavy dependence on the property tax, when prices rise, the revenues of these units of government lag behind. The problem of financing services thus becomes increasingly acute as inflation proceeds.

In very recent times in the larger cities, stronger union organization among muncipal employees has arrested and in some communities reversed the tendency for wages of public workers to lag. So the competitive position of the public services does not, with inflation, automatically become adverse. But the inelasticity of the revenues remains. And with high labor costs, the constraints on services—cuts, on occasion, instead of urgent expansion—have become more severe.

The deterioration of the public services in the years of inflation has not gone unremarked. However, there has been a strong tendency to regard it as an adventitious misfortune— something like a nasty shower at a picnic. This is a very inadequate view. Discrimination against the public services is an organc feature of inflation. Nothing so weakens government as persistent inflation.

VI

A feature of the years immediately following World War II was a remarkable attack on the notion of expanding and improving public services. During the depression years, such services had been elaborated and improved partly in order to fill some small part of the vacuum left by the shrinkage of private production. During the war years, the role of government was vastly expanded. After that came the reaction. Much of it, unquestionably, was motivated by a desire to rehabilitate the prestige of private production and therewith of producers. No doubt some who joined the attack hoped, at least tacitly, that it might be possible to sidestep the truce on taxation vis-á-vis equality by having less taxation of all kinds. For a time, the notion that our public services had somehow become inflated and excessive was all but axiomatic. Even liberal politicians did not seriously protest. They found it necessary to aver that they were in favor of rigid economy in public spending too.

In this discussion, a certain mystique was attributed to the satisfaction of privately supplied wants. A community decision to have a new school means that the individual surrenders the necessary amount, willy-nilly, in his taxes. But if he is left with that income, he is a free man. He can decide between a better car or a television set. The difficulty is that this argument leaves the community with no way of preferring the school. All private wants, where the individual can choose, are inherently superior to all public desires which must be paid for by taxation and with an inevitable component of compulsion.

The cost of public services was also held to be a desolating burden on private production, although this was at a time when the private production was burgeoning. Urgent warnings were issued of the unfavorable effects of taxation on investment—"I don't know of a surer way of killing off the incentive to invest than by imposing taxes which are regarded by people as punitive."[4] This was at a time when the inflationary effect of a very high level of investment was causing concern. The same individuals who were warning about the inimical effects of taxes were strongly advocating a monetary policy designed to reduce investment. However, an understanding of our economic discourse requires an appreciation of one of its basic rules: Men of high position are allowed, by a special act of grace, to accommodate their reasoning to the answer they need. Logic is only required in those of lesser rank.

Finally, it was argued, with no little vigor, that expanding government posed a grave threat to individual liberties. "Where distinction and rank is achieved almost exclusively by

[4] Arthur F. Burns, Chairman of the President's Council of Economic Advisers, *U.S. News and World Report*, May 6, 1955.

becoming a civil servant of the state . . . it is too much to expect that many will long prefer freedom to security."[5]

With time, this attack on public services has subsided. The disorder associated with social imbalance has become visible even if the need for balance between private and public services is still imperfectly appreciated.

Freedom also seemed to be surviving. Perhaps it was realized that all organized activity requires concessions by the individual to the group. This is true of the policeman who joins the police force, the teacher who gets a job at the high school and the executive who makes his way up in the hierarchy of General Motors. If there are differences between public and private organization, they are of kind rather than of degree. In time, the pendulum swung back—a little. Many if not yet most would now agree that the modern large corporation also exacts its price in discipline, conformity and pressure for convenient thought.

Nonetheless, the postwar onslaught on the public services left a lasting imprint. To suggest that we canvass our public wants to see where happiness can be improved by more and better services has a sharply radical tone. Even public services to avoid disorder must be defended. By contrast, the man who devises a nostrum for a nonexistent need and then successfully promotes both remains one of nature's noblemen.

[5] F. A. von Hayek, *The Road to Serfdom* (London: George Routledge & Sons, 1944), p. 98. As a retrospective reward for this and similar if more technical thought, Professor von Hayek received the Nobel Prize in 1974.

CHAPTER XVIII

The Investment Balance

Social balance relates to the goods and services we consume. There is an allied problem in the way we commit the resources that are available for investment in the economy. The same forces which bring us our plenitude of private goods and leave us poverty-stricken in our public services also act to distort the distribution of investment as between ordinary material capital and what we may denote as the personal capital of the country. This distortion has far-reaching effects. One of them is to impair the production of private goods themselves. The situation will be seen in sharpest focus if we pursue the latter point. It is not, however, the only or, indeed, the most important consequence.

Economic growth—the expansion of economic output—requires an increase in the quantity of the productive plant and equipment of the country or in its quality or, as in the usual case, in both. This is fully agreed. The increase in quantity is capital formation. The increase in quality is technological advance.

In the earliest stages of economic development, from which so many of our economic attitudes are derived, the simple and sufficient way of getting more growth was to have more saving and therefore more material capital. Entrepreneurial talent was needed but, at least in western countries, it was almost invariably, if not invariably, forthcoming. To perform this function required some education. But, as the example of any number of great entrepreneurs from Commodore Vanderbilt to Henry Ford made clear, the education could be exiguous and often was. The existence of an educated and literate body of workers was desirable but by no means essential. Some of the greatest industrial enterprises in the United States in the past were manned principally by men who could write no language, speak no English. Most important, in all the earlier stages of development there was no close and predictable correlation between the supply of educated men and the nature of their training and the rate of technological innovation. Inventions were more often the result of brilliant flashes of insight than the product of long prepared training and development. The Industrial Revolution in England was ushered in by the invention of the flying shuttle by John Kay, the spinning jenny by James Hargreaves, the spinning frame by (presumptively) Richard Arkwright and, of course, by James Watt's steam engine. These represented vast improvements in the capital which was being put to industrial use. But only in the case of Watt could the innovation be related to previous education and preparation. Kay and Hargreaves were simple weavers with a mechanical turn of mind. Arkwright had been apprenticed as a boy as a barber and a wigmaker and was barely literate.

However, with the development of a great and complex industrial plant, and even more with the development of a great and sophisticated body of basic science and of experience in its application, all this has been changed. In addition to the entrepreneurs (and perhaps one should add the accountants and clerks) who were more or less automatically forthcoming, modern economic activity now requires a great number of trained and qualified people. Investment in human beings is, *prima facie*, as important as investment in material capital. The one, in its modern complexity, depends on the other.

What is more important, the *improvement* in capital—technological advance—is now almost wholly dependent on investment in education, training and scientific opportunity for individuals. One branch of the conventional wisdom clings nostalgically to the conviction that brilliant, isolated and intuitive inventions are still a principal instrument of technological progress and can occur anywhere and to anyone. Benjamin Franklin is the sacred archetype of the American genius and nothing may be done to disturb his position. But in the unromantic fact, innovation has become a highly organized enterprise. The extent of the result is predictably related to the quality and quantity of the resources being applied to it. These resources are men and women. Their quality and quantity depends on the extent of the investment in their education, training and opportunity. They are the source of technological change. Without them investment in material capital will still bring growth, but it will be the inefficient growth that is combined with technological stagnation.

II

We come now to the nub of the problem. Investment in material capital is distributed to the various claimant industries by decision within the private sector. If growth prospects are good or earnings are high (at the margin) in the oil industry and low in the textile business, it is in the oil industry that capital will be invested. This allocation system works, it would appear, with tolerable efficiency. Among the recognized crimes of economics, any interference with the "free flow" of capital has a very high standing.[1]

But while this flow operates as between different material claimants on investment funds, it operates only with manifest uncertainty and inefficiency as between material and personal capital. Nearly all of the investment in individuals is in the public domain. It is the state which, through primary and secondary schools, and through the colleges and universities, makes the largest investment in individuals. And where, as in the case of private colleges and universities, the state is not directly involved, the amount of the investment is not directly related to the eventual pay-out in production. Investment in refineries being higher than in textile mills, the refineries will draw investment funds. But engineers to design the refineries may be even more important—in effect, yield a higher return. And the highest return of all may come from the scientist who makes a marked improvement in the refining process. These are not imaginative possibilities but common probabilities. Yet the high return to scientific and technical

1 I have argued in *The New Industrial State*, 2nd ed., rev. (Boston: Houghton Mifflin, 1971) and in *Economics and the Public Purpose* (Boston: Houghton Mifflin, 1973) that it is not a reflection of freely operating market forces responding exclusively to the prospect for profit. It reflects the planning goals of the firm that makes it, and these will include growth, security and even some technological virtuosity for its own sake.

training does not cause the funds to move from material capital to such investment. There is no likely flow from the building of the refineries to the education of the scientists. Here, at the most critical point in the vaunted process of investment resource allocation, is an impediment of towering importance. Characteristically, however, it has received little comment. It is not, like the tariff or monopoly, one of the classic barriers to capital movement. Hence, it did not get a foothold in economics in the last century and, accordingly, under the intellectual grandfather clause which has such sway in the subject, it has no real standing now.

There can be no question of the importance of the impediment. Investment in individuals is in the public domain; this investment has become increasingly essential with the advance of science and technology; and there is no machinery for automatically allocating resources as between material and human investment. But this is not all. As we have seen in earlier chapters, there is active discrimination against the investment in the public domain. The investment in the refinery is an unmitigated good. It adds to our stock of wealth. It is a categorical achievement. But the training of the scientists and engineers who will run the refinery, improve its economic efficiency, and possibly in the end replace it with something better is not a categorical good. The money so invested in education is part of the burden of government. Many still judge the excellence of the achievement by the smallness of this burden. Others will hold the investment, i.e., the burden, in abeyance while arguing over who should pay—in effect reviving the ancient issue of the relation of the tax system to the increase of equality. Some part of the investment must be begged as a grace from the rich—or their foundations. Even the prestige of the word investment itself is not regularly accorded to these outlays. A century ago, when education was not intimately related to production, men sensibly confined the word investment to the increases in capital which brought a later increase in product. Education was correctly regarded as a consumer outlay. The popular usage has never been revised.[2]

[2] Since this was written and under the impact of Soviet scientific achievements, there has been considerable discussion of our lag in *investment* *in* scientific education. However, this is being treated as a

Could it be legally arranged that youngsters were sorted out at an early age, possibly by their test score in mathematics, and the promising then be indentured for life to a particular corporation, the flow of investment into human development might soon be placed on a rough parity with that into material capital. Firms would perceive the need for investing in their scientific and engineering stock much as major league baseball clubs have learned the wisdom of investing in their farm teams. Under ideal arrangements, any surplus talent could be marketed. The cost of unsuccessfully trying to educate the inevitable errors of selection would be either written off or partially retrieved by using the individuals as salesmen. Under such a system, which as noted would unfortunately involve the elimination of the liberty of choice of the individuals in question, investment in human beings would rise and at a rapid rate.

But so long as free choice remains, such investment must remain largely a public function. The individual, since he is only at the beginning of earning power, cannot himself make any appreciable part of the investment. Whether his parents can and will be willing to do so depends heavily on accident. His future employer can hardly be expected to invest in an asset that may materialize in the plant of a competitor or another industry. At most he will, as now, distribute a few scholarships and fellowships along with help-wanted advertising in the hope of ultimately influencing the choice of those in whom the investment is nearly complete. This has no appreciable effect on the total of the investment in people. It is a scalping operation. It does, however, suggest the store which is set by the resulting assets.

---

kind of aberration, and not as a fundamental flaw in our machinery of resource allocation.

(The foregoing footnote was to the first edition. Since then the allocation of resources to human development has increased, as also the tendency to describe it as an investment in human capital. Thus progress. But the basic problem of allocation as between material and personal capital, reflecting their respective locations in the private and public sector, remains. And so does the discrimination in favor of material investment.)

III

Human development, in other words, is what economists have long termed an external economy.[3] Its benefits accrue to all firms; it is not sufficiently specific to any one to be bought and paid for by it.

What is true of human development is also true of one of its principal fruits. That is scientific research. A society which sets for itself the goal of increasing its supply of goods will tend, inevitably, to identify all innovation with additions to, changes in, or increases in its stock of goods. It will assume, accordingly, that most research will be induced and rewarded by the market.

Much will be. Under the proper circumstances—firms must be of adequate size in the industry, and certain other conditions must be met[4]—we may expect the economy to do a superior job of inventing, developing and redesigning consumers' goods and improving their process of manufacture. Nor is there reason to doubt that similar attention will be given, under equally favorable circumstances, to the capital goods industries which support this consumers' goods consumption. Much of this achievement will impress us only so long as we do not inquire how the demand for the products so developed is contrived and sustained. If we do, we are bound to observe that much of the research effort—as in the automobile industry—is devoted to discovering changes that can be advertised. The research program will be built around the need to devise "selling points" and "advertising pegs" or to accelerate "planned obsolescence." All this suggests that the incentive will be to allocate research resources to what, in some sense, are the least important things. The quantity is more impressive than the way it is allocated. Still,

[3] There is a differing view that much of the value of education lies in its role as a filter—as a means, in effect, of legitimatizing discrimination in favor of the talented. On this, see Lester C. Thurow, "Education and Economic Equality," *The Public Interest*, No. 28 (Summer 1972), and Kenneth J. Arrow, "Higher Education as a Filter," *Journal of Public Economics*, Vol. 2, No. 3 (July 1973).

[4] Cf. *American Capitalism*, 2nd ed. (Boston: Houghton Mifflin, 1956), pp. 84–94.

one would not wish to suggest that the American economy is delinquent in the attention it devotes to change and improvement in consumers' goods. Clearly it is not.

These incentives, however, operate over but a small part of total scientific and research activity and, indeed, over but a small part that is potentially applicable to the production of goods. Thus a very large amount of highly useful research cannot be specialized to or be sustained by any marketable product. This is most obviously true of much so-called basic research. But it is also true of a large amount of applied effort. The modern air transport is the stepchild of the military airplane. It would never have sustained the underlying research and development endeavor on its own. The same is true in even greater degree of the nonmilitary uses of nuclear energy. And with the communications satellite and the electronic computer.

It is because military considerations have induced a large allocation of resources to research that this problem is, on the whole, less striking than that of investment in personal resources. Although the research must be in the public domain, military urgency has helped to offset this blight. There is little comfort for man in the circumstances which have induced this allocation of resources or from the resulting weapons. But it has catalyzed a considerable amount of scientific innovation and development. Far more significant research lies back of the effort to exceed the speed of sound than lies back of even the best new soap. It may well be more significant for industry itself. In any event, the rate of technical progress in American industry in recent decades would have been markedly slower had it not been for militarily inspired and for this reason publicly supported research.

IV

As noted, one must, where possible, deal with the conventional wisdom on its own terms. The conventional wisdom stresses the paramount urgency of increased production of goods. To show that even for this purpose its allocation of investment is irrational—that it is tolerable for research only as a by-product of military claims and that for investment in individuals it can make no claim at all to rationality—is impressive. However, it would be barbarous to suggest that the only claim to be made on behalf of education is the increased production of goods. It has its independent and, one must suppose, its higher justification. A horse almost certainly appreciates a comfortable stable, a secure supply of oats, a measure of recreation, and conceivably the pleasure of being esteemed at least as highly as any other horse in the stable. The nontheological quality which most distinguishes men from horses is the desire, in addition to these attributes of material and psychic well-being, to know, understand and reason. One may hope that investment in the things that differentiate man from his animals requires no further justification. If, however, this investment is less than would be justified even for the production of goods, one wonders how very much less than the ideal it must be for the purposes of human satisfaction and fulfillment.

V

A final and rather more speculative issue remains, which is the joint legacy of the problem of social balance in consumption and of balanced investment in material and personal capital.

As Chapter XIII has argued, the process by which wants are now synthesized is a potential source of economic instability. Production and therewith employment and social security are dependent on an inherently unstable process of consumer debt creation. This may one day falter. And a decay in emulative compulsions or in the ability to synthesize demand could bring a fall in consumption, an increase in unemployment and a difficult problem of readjustment.

However great or small these dangers, they will be lessened if our consumption is widely distributed—if productive energies serve uniformly the whole span of man's wants. Since public wants are not contrived,[5] they are not subject to a failure of contrivance. Since they are not sold on the installment plan, they are not subject to curtailment by any of

[5] Some are. Military needs reflect the substantial management of military demand by supplying firms. On this, also see *The New Industrial State,* Chs. XXVI–XXIX.

the factors which may make people unwilling or unable to incur debt. Thus the better the social balance, the more immune the economy to fluctuations in private demand.

There is another and opposite possibility. Simple minds, presumably, are the easiest to manage. Better education, one product of improved social balance, might well be expected to lessen the effectiveness of synthesis and emulation in the manufacture of new wants. Synthesis and emulation are most persuasive in creating desire for simply physical objects of consumption or simple modes of enjoyment which require no previous conditioning of the consumer. Houses, automobiles; the uncomplicated forms of alcohol, food and sexual enjoyment; sports; and movies require little prior preparation of the subject for the highest enjoyment. A mass appeal is thus successful, and hence it is on these things that we find concentrated the main weight of modern want creation. By contrast, more esoteric desires—music and fine arts, literary and scientific interests, and to some extent travel—can normally be synthesized, if at all, only on the basis of a good deal of prior education.

Education, therefore, is a double-edged sword for the affluent society. It is essential, given the technical and scientific requirements of modern industry. But by widening tastes and also inducing more independent and critical attitudes, it undermines the want-creating power which is indispensable to the modern economy. The effect is enhanced as education enables people to see how they are managed in the interest of the mechanism that is assumed to serve them. The ultimate consequence is that the values of the affluent society, its preoccupation with production as a test of performance in particular, are undermined by the education that is required in those that serve it.

Or so it could be. For so stern have been the forces channeling our thoughts in the past that there is little to go on in these fertile valleys of the imagination.

CHAPTER XIX

The Transition

In one sense, the main task of this essay has been accomplished. Its concern has been with the thralldom of a myth—the myth that the production of goods, by its overpowering importance and its ineluctable difficulty, is the central problem of our lives. We have now seen the sources of this myth. And we have seen some of the consequences—the tenuous and maybe dangerous process of consumer-demand creation, recurrent inflation, social imbalance—to which the myth commits us. Emancipation of the mind is a no less worthy enterprise than emancipation of the body. The bondsman, given his freedom and persuaded of its virtues, is ordinarily left to enjoy it. Nor is his emancipator blamed for failing to give him a list of things to do.

A concern for new goals, once the old ones become suspect, is not only the next order of philosophical business but the inevitable one. Social philosophy, far more than nature, abhors a vacuum. Men must see a purpose in their efforts. This purpose can be nonsensical and, as we have seen, if it is elaborately nonsensical, that is all to the good. Men can labor to make sense out of single steps toward the goal without ever pausing to reflect that the goal itself is ludicrous. But they must not question the goal. For to do so is to initiate a search for one that serves better. Thus it is that an essay such as this is far more important for what it destroys—or to speak more accurately, for the destruction which it crystallizes, since the ultimate enemy of myth is circumstance—than for what it creates.

This is sharply at odds with the conventional wisdom. The latter sets great store by what it calls constructive criticism. And it reserves its scorn for what it is likely to term a purely destructive or negative position. In this, as so often, it manifests a sound instinct for self-preservation. The attack on the conventional or accepted thought is dismissed as an inferior and, indeed, a wanton activity and, as such, not something that should be taken seriously. At the same time, "constructive alternatives" are invited. These are a much lower order of danger. The threat to the conventional wisdom is always its own irrelevance, not the appeal of a relevant alternative. In postwar West Germany, in contrast with the Weimar regime, governments have displayed notable stability of tenure. Some credit goes to the constitutional provision for the so-called "constructive veto." This, in effect, requires the parliament to decide on a new administration before it votes out the old one. To settle in advance on such an alternative is difficult or impossible. Thus, parliaments have had no choice but to maintain the status quo. The conventional wisdom finds similar strength in asserting the moral superiority of constructive criticism.

However, as always, it is sound strategy to deal with the conventional wisdom on its own terms. If it inquires how we escape the present preoccupation with production; or how we escape the race to manufacture more wants for more goods and then yet more wants for yet more goods; or what is to fill the seemingly vast vacuum which abandoning this race would leave in our lives; or what are to be the symbols of happiness if goods cease to be so regarded, then it is well that there be answers. The defenses of the conventional wisdom are formidable. One should not concede it any points. What replaces the profound preoccupation with production?

II

In the world of minor lunacy, the behavior of both the utterly rational and the totally insane seems equally odd. The notion that ours, inevitably, is a world in which production is of supreme urgency is an old one. So is the corresponding behavior. The discovery that production is no longer of such urgency—that it is something of which we are reasonably assured and which, paradoxically, is most threatened by our failure to see it in proper perspective[1]—involves a major wrench in our attitudes. What was sound economic behavior before cannot be sound economic behavior now. What were the goals of individuals, organizations and, perhaps more especially, of government before may not be so now. Many who will find it possible to believe that production has lost its pristine urgency will still find the changes in behavior and policy that this suggests rather difficult to swallow. This behavior and these policies will have an air of fecklessness, even of danger. And this, needless to say, will be exploited vigorously by the conventional wisdom.

It was ever so. During the Great Depression, many could agree that the clear and immediate cause of difficulty was a shortage of demand for goods. That the private economy might find its equilibrium not with a demand sufficient to ensure full employment but at a level where substantial millions were left unemployed seemed plausible enough. Yet, having conceded all this, it was still not easy for a long while to agree that the government should supplement the deficient private demand by public borrowing and spending. This seemed vastly reckless. The Keynesian diagnosis was one thing, but the Keynesian remedy was another.

Life and certainly the language would be simpler were we to accept change, and the consequent policies, at their face value. But it would also destroy an engaging, almost Oriental, quality of our political life which leads us to drape the urgencies of the present in the symbols of the past. Though production has receded in importance, we shall doubtless continue to pretend that it isn't so.

III

For the number of questions which we agree to resolve in accordance with whether production is aided or retarded—made more or less important—is enormous. If something seems to contribute to increased production, it is good. If it fails to do so, it is useless. If it damages production, it is evil. If it can be shown that a tax is damaging to incentives and

---

1 Committing us, to repeat, to the tenuous process of private want creation, causing social imbalance, contributing to economic instabilty, and threatening, among other things, the supply of trained manpower.

thus to production, it is *per se* a bad tax; and even if this result cannot be shown, it is still worth alleging. Our oldest and for some still the most beloved topic of controversy is the tariff. Its enemies have always argued that the industries it nurtures are inefficient—that resources could be used more efficiently elsewhere. They have never doubted that efficiency was the decisive consideration. And their opponents, while challenging the defense of the higher efficiency of free trade in various ways, never challenged that criterion as such.

Similarly, the debate over the large corporation has been concerned almost exclusively with its efficiency. Its defenders have justified it by its competence as a producer. Its critics have held that it has exceeded the optimally efficient size.[2] The corporation is a creature of no small political importance. Until very recently this aspect of its existence has been uniformly dismissed as of small account. As with the corporation, so with the trade union. It is defended or condemned in accordance with its effect on the productivity of its members. That it has made work more tolerable; has enhanced the dignity of its members; and, through seniority rules, accorded its members what seem to be the natural rights of advancing age are not decisive. The decisive thing is the effect these have had on productivity.

If a locality is declining—if power, transportation, raw material supplies, consumer taste or the tax laws have given other areas or countries an advantage—then one should encourage the people to leave. Mobility means efficiency. It is true that the ties of family, friends, pastor and priest, countryside and mere inertia may make this a Draconian and even cruel prescription. But it is the efficient course. Until relatively recent times, a large amount of industrial and occupational disease could be justified on the grounds that considerations of cost did not permit of its elimination. Such a contention is no longer acceptable in the conventional wisdom. The latter would not hesitate, however, to point out that

[2] Cf. Hearings before the United States Senate Select Committee on Small Business, June 29, 1967. My case that the size of the large corporation served its planning purposes was strongly attacked on the noncongruent ground that it was larger than necessary for technical efficiency.

the concessions won over the years by the coal miners have speeded the relative decline of this industry in many areas. Given the importance of production, this was most unfortunate.

But if the things produced are not of great urgency, it follows that the efficiency of the process by which they are produced ceases to be an overriding consideration. New and usually much more difficult tests must be applied. It is not unlikely, indeed, that these will already be found playing a considerable but surreptitious role and this now becomes obtrusive.

Thus the argument over the progressive income tax has long been concerned with its effect on efficiency. Some have argued that it impairs incentives to increased efficiency. Others have argued that it does not. But if efficiency is not decisive, then the debate must go forward on other grounds. These may well include the simple and uncouth question of who is to pay how much. It is with this question that many who now talk about efficiency are really concerned.

Moreover, if efficiency is no longer a prime criterion, tariff policy will have to be resolved on the basis of how far we should go in making trade the handmaiden of larger national policy or what part compassion should play in easing the problems of distressed industries or areas. But, in fact, trade policy is already partly subordinate to both international comity and local charity. Efficiency has already partly surrendered to these other and more urgent considerations.

If the modern corporation must manufacture not only goods but the desire for the goods it manufactures, the efficiency of the first part of this activity ceases to be decisive. One could indeed argue that human happiness would be as effectively advanced by inefficiency in want creation as efficiency in production. Under these circumstances, the relation of the modern corporation to the people it comprises—their chance for dignity, individuality and full development of personality—may be at least as important as its efficiency. These may be worth having even at a higher cost of production. Evidently the unions, in seeking to make life tolerable on the job, were being governed by a sound instinct. Why should life be intolerable to make things of small urgency?

Attitudes toward the declining community may need to be revised. The happiness and contentment of the people of an old New England mill town and their preference, remarkable as it may seem, for life in one of these decaying communities, now become a consideration to set against the efficiency with which they are employed. The rational and compassionate society may seek to avoid the heartbreaks of an industrial Diaspora. If the goods have ceased to be urgent, can we sternly command men to leave their homes to produce them with maximum efficiency?

The Benthamite test of public policy was "what serves the greatest happiness of the greatest number," and happiness was more or less implicitly identified with productivity. This is still the official test. In modern times, the test has not been very rigorously applied. We have sensed though we have not recognized the declining importance of goods. Yet, even in its deteriorated form, we cling to this criterion. It is so much simpler than to substitute the other tests—compassion, individual happiness and well-being, the minimization of community or other social tensions—which now become relevant.

IV

Much more than decision on economic policy are involved. A system of morality is at stake. For what we regard as the Puritan inheritance was soundly grounded on economic circumstance. In a country that was being carved from the wilderness, thrift and labor were the obligations of everyone, for they conserved and enlarged the supply of goods which sustained life itself. And the central or classical tradition of economics was more than an analysis of economic behavior and a set of rules for economic polity. It also had a moral code. The world owed no man a living. Unless he worked, he did not eat. The obligation thus imposed required him to labor on his own behalf and therewith on behalf of others. Failure to work, even when it could be afforded, was offensive to what came to be called the Victorian, but could as well have been named the economic, morality. "To live in idleness, even if you have the means, is not only injurious to yourself, but a species of fraud upon the community."[3]

But if the goods have ceased to be urgent, where is the fraud? Are we desperately dependent on the diligence of the worker who applies maroon enamel to the functionless metal of a motorcar? The idle man may still be an enemy of himself. But it is hard to say that the loss of his effort is damaging to society. Yet it is such damage which causes us to condemn idleness.

Again, the fact that a man was damaging society by his failure to produce has been, in the last analysis, the basis for a fair amount of highly convenient indifference and even cruelty in our behavior. The churches have long featured the virtue of loving one's neighbor. But the practical churchman has also recognized the need to reconcile this with basic economic necessities. A good deal of practical heartlessness was what served the social good. Many people have always found it painful to work. To show them compassion might be to damage production. The heartbreaks of migration in pursuit of jobs might be considerable, but how much worse the inefficiency of producing in the wrong place. No tears should be wasted on the farmers who go bankrupt. This is the path to more efficient farm production. In the United States, as in other western countries, we have for long had a respected secular priesthood whose function it has been to rise above questions of religious ethics, kindness and compassion and show how these might have to be sacrificed on the altar of the larger good. That larger good, invariably, was more efficient production. The sacrifice obviously loses some of its point if it is on behalf of the more efficient production of goods for the satisfaction of wants of which people are not yet aware. It is even more tenuous, in its philosophical foundations, if it is to permit the more efficient contriving of wants of which people are not aware. And this latter is no insignificant industry in our time.

At this point, even the most calloused of readers will regard with sympathy the tragic implications for established

---

3 William A. Alcott (a New England moralist and schoolmaster of the last century) quoted by Irving G. Wyllie in *The Self-Made Man in America* (New Brunswick: Rutgers University Press, 1954), p. 41.

211

ideas which the rejection of scarcity and the acceptance of affluence involves. The almost incredibly elaborate efforts of the conventional economic wisdom to protect the present myth become understandable. One has a sense of disloyalty, almost of treachery, in destroying it.

Yet the escape from the thralldom of productive efficiency and unremitting labor is not without its opportunities. However, one final bridge must be built between the world of scarcity and that of affluence. For, in the world of scarcity, the need for goods was, as just noticed, powerfully reinforced by the compulsion to work. The individual who did not work, unless rarely favored by circumstance, was penalized by a total loss of income. That penalty still persists widely even though it now enforces the production of relatively unimportant goods. Obviously we shall not reap the rewards of affluence until we solve this problem.

CHAPTER XX

The Divorce of
Production from Security

We have seen that while our productive energies are used to make things of no great urgency—things for which demand must be synthesized at elaborate cost lest they not be wanted—the process of production continues to be of nearly undiminished urgency as a source of income. The income men derive from producing things of slight consequence is of great consequence to them. The production reflects the low marginal utility of the goods to society. The income reflects the high total utility of a livelihood to a person. For this reason, although there is conventional effort to deny it, income and employment rather than goods have become our basic economic concern. This is revealed in the almost uncontrollable tendency to think of depression or low growth rate not in terms of lost output but in terms of unemployment and of the equally powerful tendency to identify good times with high employment, not high production.

Moreover, the urgency of offering employment to all who seek it is probably increasing. This is a natural consequence of affluence. When the income of the employed worker is high, it is not easy to defend a situation in which a small minority of workers have no employment income at all. Such discrimination seems altogether too flagrant. With increasing affluence, we are thus more firmly committed to finding jobs for everyone. Our situation is that of a factory which must be operated at top speed for three shifts and seven days a week even at some risk of eventual breakdown, not because the product is in demand—on the contrary, much ingenuity is required to clear the shipping platform—but because any lower rate of operation will leave some of the people in town without a livelihood. If that misfortune is the alternative, then the factory may have to be so operated. But the question of freeing the community from such dangerous dependence will unquestionably arise.

In the real world, apart from the danger of breakdown,[1] there is the problem of inflation. So long as we are committed by the imperatives of employment and income to operate at the capacity of plant and labor force and take no other steps, we shall enhance the threat of rising prices. Persistent inflation is not a happy prospect. It is also the long-run enemy of social balance.

The solution, or more precisely part of it, is to have some reasonably satisfactory substitutes for production as a source of income. This would loosen the present nexus between production and income and enable us to take a more relaxed and rational view of output without subjecting individual members of the society to hardship.

II

An obvious device for breaking the nexus between production and income security is at hand—that is the system of unemployment compensation. It provides income apart from production. In the past, unemployment compensation has served two principal purposes. It has eased the hardship of the worker who was making a routine change of jobs such as might be the result of a declining demand for one product and an increasing demand for another. And it has protected the worker from short-run changes in the level of aggregate demand which, on occasion, reduced the requirement for workers below the presently available labor force. Unemployment compensation did not protect him from a continuing failure to employ the full labor force, for the duration of the payments was strictly limited, and useful though they might be as a stopgap, they were far from being a substitute for wage income. In 1974, payments were 38.1 percent of the average weekly wage. This compares with 34.4 percent in 1950. In no state were payments as high as one-half the average wage.[2]

[1] See pp. 144ff.
[2] *Statistical Abstract of the United States,* 1974, p. 292.

The meagerness of the payments is related to attitudes toward production. If production is all-important, then there should be no source of income that is a close substitute. People should be required to work and produce—or else. And, in fact, nothing has so haunted the discussion of social security legislation as the specter of the worker who lives amiably off his unemployment compensation check and contributes nothing to society in return. So payments have been kept at levels relevant to survival rather than to comfort. And the lazy worker has been faced with the fact that, sooner or later, his eligibility would be exhausted and he would have to find a job.

Were unemployment compensation to approach the level of the weekly wage, we should in fact be prepared for some increase in deliberate idleness—in malingering as a way of life. So long as production was accorded priority, any increase in voluntary idleness was *pro tanto* intolerable although, in keeping with the refined illogic with which the conventional wisdom regarded production, involuntary unemployment in depression, and the consequent loss of output, were never especially reprehensible. But in a world where production is no longer urgent, we can obviously view an increase in voluntary idleness with some equanimity. And even if the unemployment compensation were close to the wage, it is not certain that the malingering would be great. Fears in this matter have always been extraordinarily exaggerated. When the system was being devised in the thirties, it was widely assumed that unemployment compensation, even as a badly paid alternative to toil, would be seized upon by a large number of people. In fact, the proportion of the active labor force exercising this option has always been negligible. The aversion to idleness is remarkably strong both in those who view with misgivings those who work and in those who work. The tendency to think of idleness as "a species of fraud upon the community" is not peculiar to the upper income classes. One problem in winning a measure of release from our present commitment to full employment is the stigma which for a long time for all social strata will continue to attach to any kind of unemployment.

III

The answer is to find some way of diminishing the reliance now being placed on production as a source of income. This cannot, given present attitudes, go so far as to sanction unemployment for any considerable number of people who would prefer work. But it can soften the consequence of any failure of production to supply jobs and, therewith, a source of income. And it can supply income to the considerable number of people for whom production, as a source, works badly. And it can prevent these steps from leading to inflation.

The needed action is in three steps. The first is to bring the level of unemployment compensation much closer to the average weekly wage and to extend greatly the period of eligibility. The result, to repeat, will be some increase in malingering but this must be measured against the comparative unimportance of the goods being sacrificed. And the advantage will be in diminishing the pressure to operate the economy at the very highest level of output and employment for purely welfare reasons by diminishing sensibly the discomfort of those who suffer most from a failure to do so. This reform will require greater nationalization of the present state systems of unemployment compensation both in standards and funding. But this is a highly desirable reform in any case.

The next step is to provide alternative sources of income, unrelated to production, to those whom the modern economy employs only with exceptional difficulty or unwisdom. The ancient reference to unemployment as a percentage of the total labor force implies that labor is more or less homogeneous in its employability; the 3 or 4 or 5 percent who are without work differ from the rest principally in the fact that the supply of jobs ran out before they were reached. This is far from being so. Those who are without work lack education, are young or otherwise without previous job experience, are unskilled or untrained and are frequently black. Especially they lack education. While they are unemployed, more qualified workers may be, indeed usually are, in great demand. To use production to bring employment and income to this unfavored part of the working force is to require that the economy operate under exceptional pressure. And even then employment of the kind required may not be forthcoming. In the early nineteen-sixties, there was a strenuous debate among American economists as to whether unemployment was the result of a shortage of demand, and thus curable by an increase in the latter, or whether it was primarily to be explained by the unemployability of some part of the labor force whatever the level of demand. Reputability was strongly on the side of those who argued the crucial role of demand; in consequence, they had the better of the argument. But, on the whole, the facts have favored the structuralists as they were called. A high level of demand is admittedly a condition for a high level of employment. But it is not sufficient for full employment. Beyond a certain point, and given the shortage of qualified workers that will exist, it is impractical to pull the uneducated, the inexperienced and the black workers into the labor force and into jobs.[3] Along with these are a large number of others—women heading households, the physically or mentally infirm—who, if the need for their product is not very great, should not be in the labor market at all.

For those who are unemployable, employable only with difficulty or who should not be working, the immediate solution is a source of income unrelated to production. This has come extensively into discussion under various proposals for a guaranteed income or a negative income tax.[4] The principle common to these proposals is provision of a basic income as a matter of general right and related in amount to family size but not otherwise to need. If the individual cannot find (or does not seek) employment, he has this income on which to survive. With income from employment, part of the payment is withdrawn and above a certain level is converted into a payment *to* the state. (Hence the term negative income tax.) To work is always to have more income.[5] The

---

[3] For a balanced summary of this discussion, see articles by Denis F. Johnston and Charles C. Killingsworth in the *Monthly Labor Review*, September 1968, pp. 1–17.

[4] A discussion that has developed since the earlier editions of this book. I did not then think such ideas within the realm of practical political feasibility.

[5] Which is not necessarily the case under present arrangements. If the head of a family receiving annual welfare payments of $5000 takes a job that earns him that amount, he, in effect, toils for nothing.

minimum income so provided once again reduces the pressure to produce for welfare reasons. And since such production is an ineffective and unreliable source of income to the workers directly concerned, it compensates for the inadequacy of production as an instrument of welfare.

The above two steps will, as noted, diminish the pressure to have production always at the highest possible level. It will not make tolerable the creation of unemployment as a deliberate policy. And in the absence of unemployment, the bargaining power of both unions and unorganized workers will remain relatively strong and there will be opportunity for compensating price increases. In short, the wage-price spiral will continue. Also, if unemployment compensation approaches the weekly wage and if, at the lower levels of skill and compensation, there is the alternative of guaranteed income, the effect of unemployment in lowering the bargaining position of workers will be appreciably diminished.

The third needed step is some form of control over wages and prices to prevent the upward spiral that otherwise occurs as full employment is approached. Such control, active or implicit in wage-bargaining, is now general in the industrial countries. However, to state this publicly is to abandon faith in the free and uninhibited market. The intellectual capital of the economist is extensively invested in the market. To admit of the need for wage and price control to prevent the wage-price spiral is to concede the limitations of the market and the obsolescence of much knowledge, including that in the textbooks in which it is revealed. The present solution is to condemn controls in principle but to urge them in practice. Economists serving with the Council of Economic Advisers, or otherwise in high office, ask for price and wage limitations as they survey the requirements of their policy but condemn wage and price control as they contemplate their eventual return to academic respectability.[6]

The conventional wisdom holds that a system of control must be comprehensive—must cover all wages and prices. It then, perhaps rightly, dismisses this as impractical. In fact, the needed apparatus of control, once a decision is taken to

---

6 I have dealt with these attitudes in detail in *Money: Whence It Came, Where It Went* (Boston: Houghton Mifflin, 1975).

have it, need not be very complex. Only the highly organized sector of the economy—that part where large corporations bargain with strong unions—need be covered. It is here that the wage-price spiral operates. It is not too difficult to restrain by public action those prices and wages that, routinely, are fixed by private action. Although there are pace-setting effects, especially in the wage negotiations in the organized sector of the industrial system, control here does not ensure stability elsewhere. But elsewhere in the world of the small firm, the self-employed, the service trades, the farm, costs are not thrust up by organized labor and the firm does not have plenary power over its prices. In other words, the market still rules. And if demand is not excessive, if it is reasonably related to the capacity of this part of the economy, there will be (bottlenecks apart) a reasonable chance for price stability.

The proper mechanism is some form of public tribunal on which labor, management and the public are represented. Jurisdiction would be limited to the larger unions and employers—to the organized sector. Wage settlements not requiring price increases would not require ratification and could not, thereafter, be the basis for a price increase. Those requiring a price increase, or those in excess of some amount determined to be within the capacity of the industry to absorb, would be subject to approval. And if they could not be absorbed, and were not otherwise inequitable, they would be disapproved, as would, of course, any resulting price increase. Although the scope of the control should be limited, it must be strongly intentioned, seriously administered—and permanent.[7]

Those who find such arrangements unappealing may reflect that they only put in orderly procedural form the pressure, cajolery, threat and blackmail which Presidents and advisers now bring to bear on unions and corporations on behalf of price stability and will continue otherwise to use.

---

[7] All features which were lacking from the shortlived experiment with controls by the Nixon Administration beginning in 1971. That, nonetheless, did serve to combine high employment with stable prices until it was abandoned in 1973.

IV

In one branch of the conventional wisdom, diminishing in power but still influential, unemployment, inflation and controls can all be avoided. Only faith or the right President is required. The strongest condemnation is reserved for those who lack such faith—who say that the irreconcilable cannot be reconciled and accordingly proceed to theologically inconvenient suggestions, including those which accept the irrelevance of the free market as a concept in the organized sector of the economy.

A choice as to the course of action must be made. It is the good fortune of a rich country that, like a rich man, it has the luxury of choice. But it cannot avoid choosing. All things considered, the best choice is a combination of steps to reduce the present reliance on production as a source of income and to combine this with a limited system of controls to prevent inflation. Those who find this intolerable should specify and defend the alternatives—more unemployment, more inflation or, for that matter, more iron-clad controls—which they presumptively prefer.

CHAPTER XXI

The Redress of Balance

Our next task is to find a way of obtaining and then of maintaining a balance in the great flow of goods and services with which our wealth each year rewards us. Specifically we must find a way to remedy the poverty which afflicts us in public services—those in particular that are unrelated to industrial need or power—and which is in such increasingly bizarre contrast with our affluence in private goods. This is necessary to temper and, more hopefully, to eliminate the social disorders which are the counterpart of the present imbalance.

Such balance is a matter of elementary common sense in a country in which need is becoming so exiguous that it must be cherished where it exists and nurtured where it does not. To create the demand for new automobiles, we must contrive elaborate and functionless changes each year and then subject the consumer to ruthless psychological pressures to persuade him of their importance. Were this process to falter or break down, the consequences would be disturbing. In the meantime, there are large ready-made needs for schools, hospitals, slum clearance and urban redevelopment, sanitation, parks, playgrounds, police and a thousand other things. Of these needs, almost no one must be persuaded. They exist because, as public officials of all kinds and ranks explain each day with practiced skill, the money to provide for them is unavailable. So it has come about that we get growth and increased employment along the dimension of private goods only at the price of increasingly frantic persuasion. We exploit but poorly the opportunity along the dimension of public services. The economy is geared to the least urgent set of human values. It would be far more secure if it were based on the whole range of need.

II

The problem will not be settled by a resolve to spend more for schools and streets and other services and to tax accordingly. Such decisions are made every day, and they do not come to grips with the causes of the imbalance. These lie much deeper. The most important difference between private and public goods and services is a technical one. The first lend themselves to being sold to individuals. The second do not. As noted above, in the evolution of economic enterprise, the things which could be produced and sold for a price were taken over by private producers. Those that could not, but which were in the end no less urgent for that reason, remained with the state. Bread and steel went naturally to private enterprise, for they could readily be produced and marketed by individuals to individuals. Police protection, sanitation and sewer systems remained with public authority for, on the whole, they could not. Once the decision was taken to make education universal and compulsory, it ceased to be a marketable commodity. With the rise of the national state, so did national defense. The line between public and private activity, as we view it at any given moment, is the product of many forces; tradition, ideological preference, social urgency and political convenience all play some part. But to a far greater degree than is commonly supposed, functions accrue to the state because, as a purely technical matter, there is no alternative to public management.

The goods and services which are marketable at a price have a position of elementary strategic advantage in the economy. Their price provides the income which commands labor, capital and raw materials for production. This is inherent in the productive process. In the absence of social intervention, private production will monopolize all resources. Only as something is done about it will resources become available for public services. In Anglo-Saxon constitutional history, the requirement of an affirmative act to divert resources from private to public use was the key weapon of parliament in contending for power with the sovereign. The king had no—or, more precisely, but few—recurring revenues. Hence, all taxes for public purposes had to be specifically voted. Gradually it became settled that there must be redress of grievances before supply. Apart from the use of the power of the purse as the protector of popular liberty, there was much else to be said for the practice. In poor and ill-governed societies, private goods meant comfort and life itself. Food, clothing and shelter, all technically subject to private purchase and sale, once had an urgency greater than any public service with the possible exception of the provision of law and order. The burden of proof was on any step that diverted resources from the satisfaction of these simple biological requirements to the (at the time) almost invariably spendthrift services of the state.

Recurring revenues are now commonplace. The control of the purse is still an element in the distribution of power between the legislative and executive authority. But it is only one element in a complex relationship and, unilke England under the Stuarts, the approval of expenditures, not the voting of taxes, is the linchpin of the legislature's power. Yet a good deal remains unchanged. We still seek to synthesize, on behalf of private goods, an urgency that was once provided not by Madison Avenue but by the even more effective importunities of hunger and cold. And for a very large part of our public activity, revenues are relatively static. Although aggregate income increases, many tax systems return a comparatively fixed dollar amount. Hence new public needs, or even the increase in the requirements for old ones incident on increasing population, require affirmative steps to transfer resources to public use. There must first be a finding of need. The burden of proof lies with those who propose the expenditure. Resources do not automatically accrue to public authority for a decision as to how they may best be distributed to schools, roads, police, public housing and other claimant ends. We are startled by the thought. It would lead to waste.

But with increasing income, resources do so accrue to the private individual. Nor when he buys a new automobile out of increased income is he required to prove need. We may assume that many fewer automobiles would be purchased than at present were it necessary to make a positive case for their purchase. Such a case must be made for schools.

III

The solution is a system of taxation which automatically makes a pro rata share of increasing income available to public authority for public purposes. The task of public authority, like that of private individuals, will be to distribute this increase in accordance with relative need. Schools and roads will then no longer be at a disadvantage as compared with automobiles and television sets in having to prove absolute justification.

The practical solution would be much eased were the revenues of the federal government available for the service of social balance. These, to the extent of about four fifths of the total, come from personal and corporation income taxes. Subject to some variations, these taxes rise rather more than proportionately with increases in private income. Unhappily they are presently pre-empted in large measure by the requirements (actual or claimed) of national defense and the competition of arms.

It is worth hoping that the time will come when federal revenues and the normal annual increase will not be pre-empted so extensively for military purposes. Conventional attitudes hold otherwise; on all prospects of mankind, there is a chance for betterment, save those having to do with an eventual end, without war, to the arms race. Here the hard cold voice of realism warns there is no chance. Perhaps things are not so utterly hopeless.

But meanwhile the problem of social balance must be faced. So far as the federal government is concerned, it must be accomplished while relying primarily on the personal and corporate income taxes. As we shall see presently, there are other taxes with a high claim to consideration, but there are other units of government with higher claim to their use. As usual, the solution is implicit in the alternatives. The test is not that high military costs make reductions in other public outlays necessary. Rather, it is whether, given these military outlays, we are more in need of the services that improve social balance or the additional private goods with which we are more affluently supplied than ever before. When the issue is so presented and faced, there can be but one conclusion.[1]

However, even though the higher urgency of federal expenditures for social balance is conceded, there is still the problem of providing the revenue. And since it is income taxes that must here be used, the question of social balance can easily be lost sight of in the reopened argument over equality. The truce will be broken and liberals and conservatives will join battle on this issue and forget about the poverty in the public services that awaits correction and, as we shall see presently, the poverty of people which can only be corrected at increased public cost. All this—schools, hospitals, even the scientific research on which increased production depends—must wait while we debate the ancient and unresolvable question of whether the rich are too rich.

The only hope—and in the nature of things it rests primarily with liberals—is to separate the issue of equality from that of social balance. The second is by far the more important question. The fact that a tacit truce exists on the issue of inequality is proof of its *comparative* lack of social urgency. In the past, the liberal politician has countered the conservative proposal for reduction in top bracket income taxes with the proposal that relief be confined to the lower brackets. And he has insisted that any necessary tax increase be carried more than proportionately by the higher income brackets. The result has been to make him a co-conspirator with the conservative in reducing taxes, whatever the cost in social balance; and his insistence on making taxes an instrument of greater equality has made it difficult or impossible to increase them. Meanwhile, the individuals with whom he sympathizes and whom he seeks to favor are no longer the tax-ridden poor of Bengal or the First Empire but people who would be among the first beneficiaries of the better education, health, housing and other services which would be the fruits of improved social balance, and they would be the

---

[1] This discussion assumes a satisfactory level of employment. When social imbalance is great, it will be clear that there is a strong case for correcting a shortage of demand by increased spending for needed public services rather than by a tax reduction which allows of increased spending for less needed private goods.

long-run beneficiaries of more nearly adequate investment in people.

The rational liberal, in the future, will resist tax reduction, even that which ostensibly favors the poor, if it is at the price of social balance. And, for the same reason, he will not hesitate to accept increases that are neutral as regards the distribution of income. His classical commitment to greater equality can far better be kept by attacking as a separate issue the more egregious of the loopholes in the present tax laws. These loopholes—preferential treatment of capital gains and the special depletion allowances for mineral, including in particular, oil, recovery—are strongly in conflict with traditional liberal attitudes, for this is inequality sanctioned by the state. There is work enough here for any egalitarian crusader.

IV

While there is much that the federal government must do by way of redressing balance, as Chapter XVII has suggested, it is in state and local services that the imbalance is most striking. Here, however, the solution—though it involves another wrench in liberal attitudes—is most clear. It involves much expanded use of the sales tax.[2]

So long as social balance is imperfect, there should be no hesitation in urging high rates. Coverage should be general on consumer products and services. In the affluent society, no sharp distinction can be made between luxuries and necessaries. Food and clothing are as difficult as ever to do without. But they can be and frequently are among the most opulent of expenditures.

The relation of the sales tax to the problem of social balance is admirably direct. The community is affluent in privately produced goods. It is poor in public services. The obvious solution is to tax the former to provide the latter—by making private goods more expensive, public goods are made more abundant. Motion pictures, electronic entertainment

[2] Since the first edition of this book, the use of the sales tax has expanded—and for the reasons here urged. Though the views of authors are not to be trusted on such matters, it seems likely that the argument here offered has had something to do with the result. It has been repeatedly cited in legislative battles over the sales tax.

and cigarettes are made more costly so that schools can be more handsomely supported. We pay more for soap, detergents and vacuum cleaners in order that we may have cleaner cities and less occasion to use them. We have more expensive cars and gasoline so that we may have more agreeable highways and streets on which to drive them. Food being relatively cheap, we tax it in order to have better medical services and better health in which to enjoy it. This forthright solution has the further advantage that sales taxation can be employed with fair efficiency by states and even by cities. It is in the services rendered by these governments that the problem of social balance is especially severe. The yield of the sales tax increases with increasing production. As wants are contrived for private goods, more revenues are provided for public use. The general property tax, the principal alternative to the sales tax, is rigid and inflexible. Since its rates must ordinarily be raised for additional services, including those that are associated with increasing income and product, the burden of proving need is especially heavy. This tax is a poor servant of social balance.

During the present century, the use of sales taxation by states and cities has been growing. Liberals have ordinarily resisted its use. At a minimum, they have viewed it with grave misgiving. This has again made the liberal the effective enemy of social balance. The reasons for this opposition provide an interesting example of how ideas, as they remain stereotyped in face of change, can force those who hold them into roles inconsistent with their own professions. The American liberal has been, all things considered, the opponent of better schools, better communities, better urban communications and indeed even of greater economic stability.

The effect of a sales tax varies greatly as between a poor and an affluent country, and the difference is one not of degree but of kind. Under the *ancien régime* in France, the tax on salt achieved an enduring reputation for its oppressiveness which it retains in parts of India to this day. In the United States, a tax on salt, even one that doubled or trebled its price, would work no perceptible hardship. It is not that salt is more dispensable now than in the day of the *gabelle*. But where it was then a major object of expenditure, it is now an insignificant one. And where the price of salt once affected visibly and directly what remained for other use, it is now too small to have a noticeable effect.

As with salt, so with other things. In a family which can buy only bread and cloth, a tax on bread and clothing means that children will be hungrier and less well clad. In a family which can buy many things, the adjustment comes at the margin in spending for gasoline, installment payments, the races or the quality of the ceremonial steak.

Thus does affluence alter the case against sales taxation. It will be argued that some people are still very poor. The sales tax, unlike the income tax, weighs heavily on the small consumption of such individuals. But if the income tax is unavailable or in service of other ends, the only alternative is to sacrifice social balance. A poor society rightly adjusts its policy to the poor. An affluent society may properly inquire whether, instead, it shouldn't remove the poverty. As we shall see in the next chapter, moreover, improved social balance is one of the first requisites for the elimination of poverty. The modern liberal rallies to protect the poor from the taxes which in the next generation, as the result of a higher investment in their children, would help eliminate poverty.

V

There is another objection to greatly multiplied use of the sales tax which is that, unlike the personal and corporation income taxes, it makes no positive contribution to economic stability. The latter do so in two respects. Falling on the corporations and the well-to-do, they weigh most heavily on income that is on its way to be saved rather than on income that is on its way to be spent for consumer goods. The investment of saved income has long been considered the most mercurial and hence the least certain link between the receipt of income and its return to the spending stream. The income tax thus taps and ensures spending where this is intrinsically the least certain. Income taxes and especially the personal income tax have, in addition, their role as built-in stabilizers of the economy. As incomes fall, the personal tax, through the mechanism of the progressive rates, automatically reduces itself. As a result, and not without reason, it has come to be regarded as central to the strategy of economic management.

However, it is of the essence of the present argument that other goals share in urgency with protection and maximization of total output. One is the social balance that is served by sales taxation. Moreover, the principal purpose of the measures outlined in the last chapter was to make possible the escape from the commitment to maximum production without doing damage to individual economic security.

But social balance also adds to the stability and security of production along another dimension, for we have seen that exploitation of the solid needs of the public sector of the economy, as distinct from the tenuous and expensively synthesized wants for private goods, will almost certainly contribute to stability and orderly economic growth. Production will then be based on the whole range of human wants, not a part. As such, it will be more secure.

Finally, with better social balance, investment in human resources will be kept more nearly abreast of that in material capital. This, we have seen, is the touchstone for technological advance. As such, it is a most important and possibly the most important factor in economic growth. Such are the paradoxes of economic policy.

The much increased use of the sales tax, as here suggested, is obviously not intended as a substitute for the income tax. This has long been the fond dream of conservatives. The present intention, which is to break the deadlock imposed by the extraneous relation of the income tax to equality and divert a much increased share of resources to public need, accords with the conventional wisdom of neither conservatives nor liberals.

Nonetheless, it is the latter who will be most reluctant. Apart from the ancient commitment to equality, the Keynesian system is, pre-eminently, the conventional wisdom of liberals. And here support for the income tax is categorical. Keynes did not foresee that the rapid expansion in output which was implicit in his ideas would soon bring us to the time when not total output but its composition would become the critical matter. Had he survived, he would no doubt have been perturbed by the tendency of his followers to concentrate their policy on the single goal of increased output. He did not lack discrimination. But these followers or some of them will almost certainly continue to protect the Keynesian system, with its concentration on aggregate demand and output, from ideas which Keynes might have been disposed to urge. Such is the fate of anyone who becomes a part of the conventional wisdom.

VI

Given a sufficiency of demand, the responding production of goods in the modern economy is almost completely reliable. We have seen in the early chapters of this essay why men once had reason to regard the economic system as a meager and perilous thing. And we have seen how these ideas have persisted after the problem of production was conquered. There will be some who will still suggest that to divert more resources to public use will be to imperil private production. There is not the slightest ground for this fear, and we have seen, in fact, that the risk lies in another direction— that our reliance on private goods is by methods that threaten the stability of demand, and that social imbalance imperils the prospect for long-run economic growth. Still, the fear will be expressed.

Here is the last advantage of sales taxation as a technique for diverting resources to public use. This tax has been recommended for years by the most impeccable of conservatives. Such august audiences as the National Association of Manufacturers have repeatedly heard and applauded speeches reciting its virtues. It has been made clear that it does not damage incentives or interfere with production. It is true that the sales tax has been given these credentials as an alternative to other taxes. But it has received this blessing from those who speak with the prestige of producers. As a political point, this is not negligible.

VII

One final observation may be made. There will be question as to what is the test of balance—at what point may we conclude that balance has been achieved in the satisfaction of private and public needs. The answer is that no test can be applied, for none exists. The traditional formulation is that the satisfaction returned to the community from a marginal increment of resources devoted to public purposes should be equal to the satisfaction of the same increment in private employment. These are incommensurate, partly because different people are involved, and partly because it makes the cardinal error of comparing satisfaction of wants that are systematically synthesized as part of an organic process with those that are not.

But a precise equilibrium is not very important. For another mark of an affluent society is the existence of a considerable margin for error on such matters. The present imbalance is clear, as are the forces and ideas which give the priority to private as compared with public goods. This being so, the direction in which we move to correct matters is utterly plain. We can also assume, given the power of the forces that have operated to accord a priority to private goods, that the distance to be traversed is considerable. When we arrive, the opulence of our private consumption will no longer be in contrast with the poverty of our schools, the unloveliness and congestion of our cities, our inability to get to work without struggle and the social disorder that is associated with imbalance. But the precise point of balance will never be defined. This will be of comfort only to those who believe that any failure of definition can be made to score decisively against a larger idea.

CHAPTER XXII

The Position of Poverty

"The study of the causes of poverty," Alfred Marshall observed at the turn of the century, "is the study of the causes of the degradation of a large part of mankind." He spoke of contemporary England as well as of the world beyond. A vast number of people both in town and country, he noted, had insufficient food, clothing and houseroom; they were: "Overworked and undertaught, weary and careworn, without quiet and without leisure." The chance of their succor, he concluded, gave to economic studies, "their chief and their highest interest."[1]

No contemporary economist would be likely to make such an observation about the United States. Conventional economic discourse makes obeisance to the continued existence of some poverty. "We must remember that we still have a great many poor people." In the nineteen-sixties, poverty promised, for a time, to become a subject of serious political concern. Then war came and the concern evaporated or was displaced. For economists of conventional mood, the reminders that the poor still exist are a useful way of allaying uneasiness about the relevance of conventional economic goals. For some people, wants must be synthesized. Hence, the importance of the goods to them is not *per se* very high. So much may be conceded. But others are far closer to physical need. And hence we must not be cavalier about the urgency of providing them with the most for the least. The sales tax may have merit for the opulent, but it still bears heavily on the poor. The poor get jobs more easily when the economy is expanding. Thus, poverty survives in economic discourse partly as a buttress to the conventional economic wisdom.

1 *Principles of Economics*, 8th ed. (London: Macmillan, 1927), pp. 2–4.

The privation of which Marshall spoke was, a half century ago, the common lot at least of all who worked without special skill. As a general affliction, it was ended by increased output which, however imperfectly it may have been distributed, nevertheless accrued in substantial amount to those who worked for a living. The result was to reduce poverty from the problem of a majority to that of a minority. It ceased to be a general case and became a special case. It is this which has put the problem of poverty into its peculiar modern form.

II

For poverty does survive. In part, it is a physical matter; those afflicted have such limited and insufficient food, such poor clothing, such crowded, cold and dirty shelter that life is painful as well as comparatively brief. But just as it is far too tempting to say that, in matters of living standards, everything is relative, so it is wrong to rest everything on absolutes. People are poverty-stricken when their income, even if adequate for survival, falls radically behind that of the community. Then they cannot have what the larger community regards as the minimum necessary for decency; and they cannot wholly escape, therefore, the judgment of the larger community that they are indecent. They are degraded for, in the literal sense, they live outside the grades or categories which the community regards as acceptable.

Since the first edition of this book appeared, and one hopes however slightly as a consequence, the character and dimension of this degradation have become better understood. There have also been fulsome promises that poverty would be eliminated. The performance on these promises has been less eloquent.

The degree of privation depends on the size of the family, the place of residence—it will be less with given income in rural areas than in the cities—and will, of course, be affected by changes in living costs. The Department of Health, Education and Welfare has established rough standards, appropriately graded to family size, location and changing prices, to separate the poor from the less poor and the affluent. In 1972, a non-farm family of four was deemed poor if it had an income of $4275; a couple living otherwise than on a farm was called poor if it had less than $2724 and an unattached individual if receiving less than $2109. A farm family of four was poor with less than $3639; of two with less than $2315.[2]

By these modest standards, 24.5 million households, including individuals and families, were poor in 1972 as compared with 13.4 million in 1959. Because of the increase in population, and therewith in the number of households, in these years the reduction in the number of poor households, as a proportion of all households, was rather greater—from 24 percent in 1959 to 12 percent in 1972.[3]

One can usefully think of the foregoing deprivation as falling into two broad categories. First, there is what may be called *case* poverty. This one encounters in every community, rural or urban, however prosperous that community or the times. Case poverty is the poor farm family with the junk-filled yard and the dirty children playing in the bare dirt. Or it is the gray-black hovel beside the railroad tracks. Or it is the basement dwelling in the alley.

Case poverty is commonly and properly related to some characteristic of the individuals so afflicted. Nearly everyone else has mastered his environment; this proves that it is not intractable. But some quality peculiar to the individual or family involved—mental deficiency, bad health, inability to adapt to the discipline of industrial life, uncontrollable procreation, alcohol, discrimination involving a very limited minority, some educational handicap unrelated to community shortcoming, or perhaps a combination of several of these handicaps—has kept these individuals from participating in the general well-being.

Second, there is what may be called *insular* poverty—that which manifests itself as an "island" of poverty. In the island, everyone or nearly everyone is poor. Here, evidently, it is not easy to explain matters by individual inadequacy. We may mark individuals down as intrinsically deficient in social performance; it is not proper or even wise so to characterize an

[2] *Statistical Abstract of the United States*, 1974, p. 389.
[3] *Statistical Abstract*, p. 389.

entire community. The people of the island have been frustrated by some factor common to their environment.

Case poverty exists. It has also been useful to those who have needed a formula for keeping the suffering of others from causing suffering to themselves. Since this poverty is the result of the deficiencies, including the moral shortcomings, of the persons concerned, it is possible to shift the responsibility to those involved. They are worthless and, as a simple manifestation of social justice, they suffer for it. Or, at a somewhat higher level of social perception and compassion, it means that the problem of poverty is sufficiently solved by private and public charity. This rescues those afflicted from the worst consequences of their inadequacy or misfortune; no larger social change or reorganization is suggested. Except as it may be insufficient in its generosity, the society is not at fault.

Insular poverty yields to no such formulas. In earlier times, when agriculture and extractive industries were the dominant sources of livelihood, something could be accomplished by shifting the responsibility for low income to a poor natural endowment and thus, in effect, to God. The soil was thin and stony, other natural resources absent and hence the people were poor. And, since it is the undoubted preference of many to remain in the vicinity of the place of their birth, a homing instinct that operates for people as well as pigeons, the people remained in the poverty which heaven had decreed for them. It is an explanation that is nearly devoid of empirical application. Connecticut is very barren and stony and incomes are very high. Similarly Wyoming. West Virginia is well watered with rich mines and forests and the people are very poor. The South is much favored in soil and climate and similarly poor and the very richest parts of the South, such as the Mississippi-Yazoo Dalta, have long had a well-earned reputation for the greatest deprivation. Yet so strong is the tendency to associate poverty with natural causes that even individuals of some modest intelligence will still be heard, in explanation of insular poverty, to say, "It's basically a poor country." "It's a pretty barren region."

Most modern poverty is insular in character and the islands are the rural and urban slums. From the former, mainly in the South, the southern Appalachians and Puerto

Rico, there has been until recent times a steady flow of migrants, some white but more black, to the latter. Grim as life is in the urban ghetto, it still offers more hope, income and interest than in the rural slum. Largely in consequence of this migration, the number of poor farm families—poor by the standards just mentioned—declined between 1959 and 1973 from 1.8 million to 295,000. The decline in the far larger number of poor non-farm households in these years was only from 6.5 million to 4.5 million.[4]

This is not the place to provide a detailed profile of this poverty. More than half of the poor households are headed by a woman, although in total women head only 9 percent of families. Over 30 percent are black, another 10 percent are of Spanish origin. A very large proportion of all black households (31 percent in 1973 as compared with 8 percent of whites) fall below the poverty line. Especially on the farms, where the young have departed for the cities, a disproportionate number of the poor are old. More often than not, the head of the household is not in the labor force at all.[5]

But the more important characteristic of insular poverty is forces, common to all members of the community, which restrain or prevent participation in economic life at going rates of return. These restraints are several. Race, which acts to locate people by their color rather than by the proximity to employment, is obviously one. So are poor educational facilities. (And this effect is further exaggerated when the poorly educated, endemically a drug on the labor market, are brought together in dense clusters by the common inadequacy of the schools available to blacks and the poor.) So is the disintegration of family life in the slum which leaves households in the hands of women. Family life itself is in some measure a manifestation of affluence. And so, without doubt, is the shared sense of helplessness and rejection and the resulting demoralization which is the product of the common misfortune.

The most certain thing about this poverty is that it is not remedied by a general advance in income. Case poverty is

[4] U.S. Department of Commerce, *Current Population Reports*, "Consumer Income," Series P-60, No. 98 (Washington, D.C.: U.S. Government Printing Office, 1975).
[5] "Consumer Income."

not remedied because the specific individual inadequacy precludes employment and participation in the general advance. Insular poverty is not directly alleviated because the advance does not remove the specific frustrations of environment to which the people of these islands are subject. This is not to say that it is without effect. If there are jobs outside the ghetto or away from the rural slum, those who are qualified, and not otherwise constrained, can take them and escape. If there are no such jobs, none can escape. But it remains that advance cannot improve the position of those who, by virtue of self or environment, cannot participate.

III

With the transition of the very poor from a majority to a comparative minority position, there has been a change in their political position. Any tendency of a politician to identify himself with those of the lowest estate usually brought the reproaches of the well-to-do. Political pandering and demagoguery were naturally suspected. But, for the man so reproached, there was the compensating advantage of alignment with a large majority. Now any politician who speaks for the very poor is speaking for a small and generally inarticulate minority. As a result, the modern liberal politician regularly aligns himself not with the poverty-ridden members of the community but with the far more numerous people who enjoy the far more affluent income of (say) the modern trade union member or the intellectual. Ambrose Bierce, in *The Devil's Dictionary*, called poverty "a file provided for the teeth of the rats of reform." It is so no longer. Reform now concerns itself with the needs of people who are relatively well-to-do—whether the comparison be with their own past or with those who are really at the bottom of the income ladder.

In consequence, a notable feature of efforts to help the very poor is their absence of any very great political appeal.[6] Politicians have found it possible to be indifferent where they

---

[6] This was true of the Office of Economic Opportunity—the so-called poverty program—and was ultimately the reason for its effective demise.

could not be derisory. And very few have been under a strong compulsion to support these efforts.

The concern for inequality and deprivation had vitality only so long as the many suffered while a few had much. It did not survive as a decisive political issue in a time when the many had much even though others had much more. It is our misfortune that when inequality declined as an issue, the slate was not left clean. A residual and in some ways rather more hopeless problem remained.

IV

An affluent society, that is also both compassionate and rational, would, no doubt, secure to all who needed it the minimum income essential for decency and comfort. The corrupting effect on the human spirit of unearned revenue has unquestionably been exaggerated as, indeed, have the character-building values of hunger and privation. To secure to each family a minimum income, as a normal function of the society, would help ensure that the misfortunes of parents, deserved or otherwise, were not visited on their children. It would help ensure that poverty was not self-perpetuating. Most of the reaction, which no doubt would be adverse, is based on obsolete attitudes. When poverty was a majority phenomenon, such action could not be afforded. A poor society, as this essay has previously shown, had to enforce the rule that the person who did not work could not eat. And possibly it was justified in the added cruelty of applying the rule to those who could not work or whose efficiency was far below par. An affluent society has no similar excuse for such rigor. It can use the forthright remedy of providing income for those without. Nothing requires such a society to be compassionate. But it no longer has a high philosophical justification for callousness.

The notion that income is a remedy for indigency has a certain forthright appeal.[7] As elsewhere argued,[8] it would also ease the problems of economic management by reducing

---

[7] As earlier noted, in the first edition, the provision of a guaranteed income was discussed but dismissed as "beyond reasonable hope."
[8] See p. 218.

the reliance on production as a source of income. The provision of such a basic source of income must henceforth be the first and the strategic step in the attack on poverty.

But it is only one step. In the past, we have suffered from the supposition that the only remedy for poverty lies in remedies that allow people to look after themselves—to participate in the economy. Nothing has better served the conscience of people who wished to avoid inconvenient or expensive action than an appeal, on this issue, to Calvinist precept—"The only sound way to solve the problem of poverty is to help people help themselves." But this does not mean that steps to allow participation and to keep poverty from being self-perpetuating are unimportant. On the contrary. It requires that the investment in children from families presently afflicted be as little below normal as possible. If the children of poor families have first-rate schools and school attendance is properly enforced; if the children, though badly fed at home, are well nourished at school; if the community has sound health services, and the physical well-being of the children is vigilantly watched; if there is opportunity for advanced education for those who qualify regardless of means; and if, especially in the case of urban communities, housing is ample and housing standards are enforced, the streets are clean, the laws are kept, and recreation is adequate—then there is a chance that the children of the very poor will come to maturity without inhibiting disadvantage. In the case of insular poverty, this remedy requires that the services of the community be assisted from outside. Poverty is self-perpetuating partly because the poorest communities are poorest in the services which would eliminate it. To eliminate poverty efficiently, we must, indeed, invest more than proportionately in the children of the poor community. It is there that high quality schools, strong health services, special provision for nutrition and recreation are most needed to compensate for the very low investment which families are able to make in their own offspring.

The effect of education and related investment in individuals is to help them overcome the restraints that are imposed by their environment. These need also to be attacked even more directly—by giving the mobility that is associated with plentiful, good and readily available housing, by provision of comfortable, efficient and economical mass transport, by making the environment pleasant and safe, and by eliminating the special health handicaps that afflict the poor.

Nor is case poverty entirely resistant to such remedies. Much can be done to treat those characteristics which cause people to reject or be rejected by the modern industrial society. Educational deficiencies can be overcome. Mental deficiencies can be treated. Physical handicaps can be remedied. The limiting factor is not a lack of knowledge of what can be done. Overwhelmingly, it is a shortage of money.

V

It will be clear that, to a remarkable extent, the remedy for poverty leads to the same requirements as those for social balance. The restraints that confine people to the ghetto are those that result from insufficient investment in the public sector. And the means to escape from these constraints and to break their hold on subsequent generations just mentioned—better nutrition and health, better education, more and better housing, better mass transport, an environment more conducive to effective social participation—all, with rare exceptions, call for massively greater investment in the public sector. In recent years, the problems of the urban ghetto have been greatly discussed but with little resultant effect. To a certain extent, the search for deeper social explanations of its troubles has been motivated by the hope that these (together with more police) might lead to solutions that would somehow elide the problem of cost. It is an idle hope. The modern urban household is an extremely expensive thing. We have not yet taken the measure of the resources that must be allocated to its public tasks if it is to be agreeable or even tolerable. And first among the symptoms of an insufficient allocation is the teeming discontent of the modern ghetto.

A further feature of these remedies is to be observed. Their consequence is to allow of participation in the economic life of the larger community—to make people and the children of people who are now idle productive. This means that they will add to the total output of goods and services. We see once again that even by its own terms the present preoccupation with the private sector of the economy as compared with the whole spectrum of human needs is inefficient. The parallel with investment in the supply of trained and educated manpower discussed above[9] will be apparent.

But increased output of goods is not the main point. Even to the most intellectually reluctant reader, it will now be evident that enhanced productive efficiency is not the motif of this volume. The very fact that increased output offers itself as a by-product of the effort to eliminate poverty is one of the reasons. No one would be called upon to write at such length on a problem so easily solved as that of increasing production. The main point lies elsewhere. Poverty—grim, degrading and ineluctable—is not remarkable in India. For few, the fate is otherwise. But in the United States, the survival of poverty is remarkable. We ignore it because we share with all societies at all times the capacity for not seeing what we do not wish to see. Anciently this has enabled the nobleman to enjoy his dinner while remaining oblivious to the beggars around his door. In our own day, it enables us to travel in comfort by Harlem and into the lush precincts of midtown Manhattan. But while our failure to notice can be explained, it cannot be excused. "Poverty," Pitt exclaimed, "is no disgrace but it is damned annoying." In the contemporary United States, it is not annoying but it is a disgrace.

9 Chapter XVIII.

CHAPTER XXIII

Labor, Leisure and the New Class

In a society of high and increasing affluence, there are three plausible tendencies as regards toil. As the production of goods comes to seem less urgent, and as individuals are less urgently in need of income for the purchase of goods, they will work fewer hours or days in the week. Or they will work less hard. Or, as a final possibility, it may be that fewer people will work all the time.

Since the last century, a drastic decline has occurred in the work week. In 1850, it is estimated to have averaged just under seventy hours, the equivalent of seven ten-hour days a week or roughly six days at from six in the morning to six at night.[1] A century and a quarter later, the normal work week was 40.0 hours or five eight-hour days.[2]

This decline reflects a tacit but unmistakable acceptance of the declining marginal urgency of goods. There is no other explanation. However, such is the hold of production on our minds that this explanation is rarely offered. The importance and rewards of leisure are urged, almost never the unimportance of goods. Or, since production per hour has been increasing as the work week has declined, it is said that we are able to reduce the work because more is produced in less time. No mention is made of the fact that even more would

---

[1] J. Frederic Dewhurst and Associates, *America's Needs and Resources, A New Survey* (New York: Twentieth Century Fund, 1955), p. 1053. These figures are the weighted average of agricultural and nonagricultural workers. The average work week in nonagricultural enterprise in 1950 was estimated to be 38.8 hours.
[2] U.S. Department of Labor, *Monthly Labor Review*, Vol. 98, No. 4 (April 1975), p. 30.

be produced in more time. Or, finally, the decline is related to the feeling that steps must be taken to share the available work as productivity per worker rises. This also implies that the marginal urgency of production is low or negligible, but again the point remains unmade.

A reduction in the work week is an exceedingly plausible reaction to the declining marginal urgency of product. Over the span of man's history, although a phenomenal amount of education, persuasion, indoctrination and incantation have been devoted to the effort, ordinary people have never been quite persuaded that toil is as agreeable as its alternatives. Thus, to take increased well-being partly in the form of more goods and partly in the form of more leisure is unquestionably rational. In addition, the institution of overtime enables the worker to go far to adjust work and income to his own taste and requirements. It breaks with the barbarous uniformity of the weekly wage with its assumption that all families have the same tastes, needs and requirements. Few things enlarge the liberty of the individual more substantially than that which grants him a measure of control over the amount of his income.

Unfortunately, in the conventional wisdom the reduction in hours has emerged as the only legitimate response to increasing affluence. This is at least partly because the issue has never been faced in terms of the increasing unimportance of goods. Accordingly, though we have attributed value to leisure, a ban still lies on other courses which seem to be more directly in conflict with established attitudes on productive efficiency. In a society rationally concerned with its own happiness, these alternatives have a strong claim to consideration.

II

The first of these is that work can be made easier and more pleasant.

The present-day industrial establishment is a great distance removed from that of the last century or even of twenty-five years ago. This improvement has been the result of a variety of forces—government standards and factory inspection; general technological and architectural advance; the fact that productivity could often be increased by substituting machine power for heavy or repetitive manual labor; the need to compete for a labor force; and union intervention to improve working conditions in addition to wages and hours.

However, except where the improvement contributed to increased productivity, the effort to make work more pleasant has had to support a large burden of proof. It was permissible to seek the elimination of hazardous, unsanitary, unhealthful or otherwise objectionable conditions of work. The speed-up might be resisted—to a point. But the test was not what was agreeable but what was unhealthful or, at a minimum, excessively fatiguing. The trend toward increased leisure is not reprehensible, but we resist vigorously the notion that a man should work less hard while on the job. Here, older attitudes are involved. We are gravely suspicious of any tendency to expend less than the maximum effort, for this has long been a prime economic virtue.

In strict logic, there is as much to be said for making work pleasant and agreeable as for shortening hours. On the whole, it is ostensibly as important for a wage earner to have pleasant working conditions as to have a pleasant home. To a degree, he can escape the latter but not the former—though no doubt the line between an agreeable tempo and what is flagrant featherbedding is difficult to draw. Moreover, it is a commonplace of the industrial scene that the dreariest and most burdensome tasks, requiring as they do a minimum of thought and skill, frequently have the largest numbers of takers. The solution to this problem lies, as we shall see presently, in drying up the supply of crude manpower at the bottom of the ladder. Nonetheless the basic point remains: The case for more leisure is not stronger on purely *prima facie* grounds than the case for making labor-time itself more agreeable. The test, it is worth repeating, is not the effect on productivity. It is not seriously argued that the shorter work week increases productivity—that men produce more in fewer hours than they would in more. Rather, it is whether fewer hours are always to be preferred to more but more pleasant ones.

III

Another of the obvious possibilities with increasing affluence is for fewer people to work. This tendency has also been operating for many years, although in a remarkably diverse form. Since 1890, when one boy in four and one girl in ten between the ages of ten and fifteen were gainfully employed, large numbers of juveniles have been retired from the labor force and their number now is negligible. At the same time, a large number of women have been added. In 1890, 19.5 percent of the female population ten years and over was in the labor force[3] and by 1974, this proportion had risen to 46 percent.[4] However, this change reflects in considerable measure the shift of tasks—food preparation, clothing manufacture, even child-rearing—out of the home. Women who previously performed them have gone along to other work. The woman who takes charge of a day nursery has joined the labor force, as have the women whose children she cares for. These changes, one would gather from all current pressures to enlarge the economic role of women, will continue.[5]

For seventy-five years, the proportion of the male population in the labor force has been constant at around 75 percent of those over ten years of age. There are a smaller percentage of the very young and of those over sixty-five, but this has been offset by the increase in population in the ages between twenty and sixty-five where the proportion of workers to the total is very high.[6]

With diminishing marginal urgency of goods, it is logical that the first to be spared should be old and young. We have yet, however, to view this tendency consistently and comprehensively. We are able to dispense with the labor of those who have reached retiring age because the goods they add are at a low order of urgency, whereas a poor society

---

[3] Dewhurst, pp. 726–727.
[4] U.S. Department of Labor, *Monthly Labor Review,* Vol. 98, No. 3 (March 1975), p. 88.
[5] A matter I have taken up in more detail in *Economics and the Public Purpose* (Boston: Houghton Mifflin, 1973).
[6] Dewhurst, pp. 725–726.

must extract the last ounce of labor effort from all. But we have ordinarily subjected those who retire to a drastic reduction in income and living standards. Obviously, if the retirement can be afforded because the product is no longer urgent, a satisfactory—meaning, for most purposes, the customary—living standard can be accorded to the retired employee for the same reason. Similarly, we have excluded youngsters from the labor market, partly on the ground that labor at too early an age is unduly painful and injurious to health, and partly to make way for educational opportunity. But while we have felt it possible to dispense with the goods that the youngsters produce, we have yet to provide them, at least in full and satisfactory measure, with the education that their exemption from labor was designed to make possible. If we are affluent enough to dispense with the product of juvenile labor, it again follows that we are affluent enough to provide the education that takes its place.

In addition to releasing the old and young, it may be that we need not use all of the labor force at all times. This possibility was explored in Chapter XX. If the marginal urgency of goods is low, then so is the urgency of employing the last man or the last million men in the labor force. By allowing ourselves such a margin, in turn, we reduce the standards of economic performance to a level more nearly consonant with the controls available for its management. And in so widening the band of what is deemed tolerable performance lies our best hope of minimizing the threat of inflation with its further and persistent threat to social balance.

Such a step requires that there be a substitute for production as a source of income—and that it be ample. But this accords wholly with the logic of the situation. It is also a point which even conservatives, in effect, accept. They are always open to the suggestion that unemployment is better than inflation. This means that they do not worry about the output so lost. So they cannot be too seriously perturbed by providing people who do not produce with income. If we do not miss what these non-producers do not make when they are unemployed, we will not miss what they eat and wear and otherwise need for something approximating their accustomed standard of living.

IV

However, the greatest prospect that we face—indeed what must now be counted one of the central economic goals of our society—is to eliminate toil as a required economic institution. This is not a utopian vision. We are already well on the way. Only an extraordinarily elaborate exercise in social camouflage has kept us from seeing what has been happening.

Nearly all societies at nearly all times have had a leisure class—a class of persons who were exempt from toil. In modern times and especially in the United States, the leisure class, at least as an easily indentifiable phenomenon, has disappeared. To be idle is no longer considered rewarding or even entirely respectable.

But we have barely noticed that the leisure class has been replaced by another and much larger class to which work has none of the older connotation of pain, fatigue or other mental or physical discomfort. And the continuing revolution in job quality being wrought by the computer is accelerating its growth. We have failed to appreciate the emergence of this New Class, as it may be called, largely as the result of one of the oldest and most effective obfuscations in the field of social science. This is the effort to assert that all work—physical, mental, artistic or managerial—is essentially the same.

This effort to proclaim the grand homogeneity of work has commanded, for different reasons, the support of remarkably numerous and diverse groups. To economists, it has seemed a harmless and, indeed, an indispensable simplification. It has enabled them to deal homogeneously with all of the different kinds of productive effort and to elaborate a general theory of wages applying to all who receive an income for services. Doubts have arisen from time to time, but they have been suppressed or considered to concern special cases.[7] The inden-

---

[7] Alfred Marshall defined labor as "any exertion of mind or body undergone partly or wholly with a view to some good other than the pleasure derived directly from the work." *Principles of Economics*, 8th ed. (London: Macmillan, 1927), p. 65. This definition obviously recognizes a category of individuals for whom work is a reward in itself.

tity of all classes of labor is one thing on which capitalist and communist doctrine wholly agree. The president of the corporation is pleased to think that his handsomely appointed, comfortably upholstered office is the scene of the same kind of toil as the assembly line and that only the greater demands in talent and intensity justify his wage differential. The communist officeholder cannot afford to have it supposed that his labor differs in any significant respect from that of the comrade at the lathe or on the collective farm with whom he is ideologically one. In both societies, it serves the democratic conscience of the more favored groups to identify themselves with those who do hard physical labor. A lurking sense of guilt over a more pleasant, agreeable and remunerative life can often be assuaged by the observation, "I am a worker too," or, more audaciously, by the statement that "mental labor is far more taxing than physical labor." Since the man who does physical labor is intellectually disqualified from comparing his toil with that of the brainworker, the proposition, though outrageous, is uniquely unassailable.

For, in fact, the differences in what labor means to different people could not be greater. For some, and probably a majority, it remains a stint to be performed. It may be preferable, especially in the context of social attitudes toward production, to doing nothing. Nevertheless, it is fatiguing or monotonous or, at a minimum, a source of no particular pleasure. The reward rests not in the task but in the pay.

For others, work, as it continues to be called, is an entirely different matter. It is taken for granted that it will be enjoyable. If it is not, this is a legitimate source of dissatifaction, even frustration. No one regards it as remarkable that the advertising man, tycoon, poet or professor who suddenly finds his work unrewarding should seek the counsel of a psychiatrist. One insults the business executive or the scientist by suggesting that his principal motivation in life is the pay he receives. Pay is not unimportant. Among other things, it is a prime index of prestige. Prestige—the respect, regard and

However, this group, having been introduced, plays little or no further part in Marshall's analysis. it has played almost no formal role in economic theory since.

esteem of others—is in turn one of the more important sources of satisfaction associated with this kind of work. But, in general, those who do this kind of work expect to contribute their best regardless of compensation.[8] They would be disturbed by any suggestion to the contrary.

Such is the labor of the New Class. No aristocrat ever contemplated the loss of feudal privileges with more sorrow than a member of this class would regard his descent into ordinary labor where the reward was only the pay. From time to time, grade school teachers leave their posts for substantially higher paid factory work. The action makes headlines because it represents an unprecedented desertion of an occupation which is assumed to confer the dignity of the New Class.[9] The college professor, who is more securely a member of the New Class than the school teacher, would never contemplate such a change even as an exercise in eccentricity and no matter how inadequate he may consider his income.[10]

In keeping with all past class behavior, the New Class seeks energetically to perpetuate itself. Offspring are not expected to plan their lives in order to make a large amount of money. (Those who go into business are something of an exception at least partly because income, in business, is uniquely an index of prestige.) From their earliest years, the

8 We have here an important reason why the income tax, despite frequent warnings of the damage to incentive, has so far had no visibly deleterious effect. The surtax rates fall almost entirely on members of the New Class. These are people who, by their own claim except when they are talking about the effect of income taxes, are not primarily motivated by money. Hence the tax, which also does not disturb the prestige structure—people are rated by before-tax income—touches no vital incentive. Were high marginal rates to be placed on, say, the overtime income of automobile workers, we would expect a substantial withdrawal of effort. Here pay, as an incentive, remains important.

9 Equally dramatic has been the American reaction to the Chinese Cultural Revolution. Almost no reputable spokesman has defended its central tenet, which is that everyone should be sent out to do common labor. Yet, were all work identical, such a movement should have great appeal. The argument that it is inefficient is presumed sufficient to end all debate.

10 Since the earlier editions of this book, a college president—of Haverford College—did take several months off to experimnt with manual labor. His temporary desertion of the New Class attracted much attention.

children of the New Class are carefully indoctrinated in the importance of finding an occupation from which they will derive satisfaction—one which will involve not toil but enjoyment. One of the principal sources of sorrow and frustration in the New Class is the son who fails to make the grade—who drops down into some tedious and unrewarding occupation. The individual who meets with this misfortune—the son of the surgeon who becomes a garage hand—is regarded by the community with pity not unmixed with horror. But the New Class has considerable protective powers. The son of the surgeon rarely does become a garage hand. However inadequate, he can usually manage to survive, perhaps somewhat exiguously, on the edge of his caste. And even if, as a salesman or an investment counselor, he finds little pleasure in his work, he will be expected to assert the contrary in order to affirm his membership in the New Class.

V

The New Class is not exclusive. While virtually no one leaves it, thousands join it every year. Overwhelmingly, the qualification is education.[11] Any individual whose adolescent situation is such that sufficient time and money are invested in his preparation, and who has at least the talents to carry him through the formal academic routine, can be a member. There is a hierarchy within the class. The son of the factory worker who becomes an electrical engineer is on the lower edge; his son who does graduate work and becomes a univer-

---

[11] Political capacity is another qualification, and it is of especial importance to those who seek to make their escape after reaching their adult years. The intensity of the campaigns for local political offices—city councilors, school committeemen and county supervisors—is to be explained by this fact, as also the enduring interest in appointive political office. Those who are already members of the New Class aften fail to see how such posts are valued as an entrée. They look askance at the competition for such posts between the less well educated members of the community. They fail to realize that such posts provide the greatest opportunity for such individuals and that it is upon such people that we depend for much good (as well as some bad) civic enterprise. The union is another important opportunity for the individual of political capacity. Cf. the interesting sketches by Harvey Swados in *On the Line* (Boston: Atlantic-Little, Brown, 1957).

sity physicist moves to the higher echelons; but opportunity for education is, in either case, the open sesame.

There can be little question that in the last hundred years, and even in the last few decades, the New Class has increased enormously in size. In early nineteenth-century England or the United States, excluding the leisure class and considering the New Class as a group that lived on what it has carefully called earned income, it consisted only of a handful of educators and clerics, with, in addition, a trifling number of writers, journalists and artists. In the United States of the eighteen-fifties, it could not have numbered more than a few thousand individuals. Now the number whose primary identification is with their job, rather than the income it returns, is in the millions.

Some of the attractiveness of membership in the New Class, to be sure, derives from a vicarious feeling of superiority—another manifestation of class attitudes. However, membership in the class unquestionably has other and more important rewards. Exemption from manual toil; escape from boredom and confining and severe routine; the chance to spend one's life in clean and physically comfortable surroundings; and some opportunity for applying one's thoughts to the day's work are regarded as unimportant only by those who take them completely for granted. For these reasons, it has been possible to expand the New Class greatly without visibly reducing its attractiveness.

This being so, there is every reason to conclude that the further and rapid expansion of this class should be a major, and perhaps next to peaceful survival itself, *the* major social goal of the society. Since education is the operative factor in expanding the class, investment in education, assessed qualitatively as well as quantitatively, becomes very close to being the basic index of social progress. It enables people to realize a dominant aspiration. It is an internally consistent course of development.

Recent experience has shown that the demand for individuals in the occupations generally identified with the New Class increases much more proportionately with increased income and well-being. Were the expansion of the New Class a deliberate objective of the society, this, with its emphasis on education and its ultimate effect on intellectual, literary, cultural and artistic demands, would greatly broaden the opportunities for membership. At the same time, the shrinking in the number of those who engage in work *qua* work is something to be regarded not alone with equanimity but with positive approval. One of the inevitable outlets for the intellectual energies and inventiveness of the New Class is, in fact, in finding substitutes for routine and repetitive manual labor. To the extent that such labor is made scarce and more expensive, this tendency will, of course, be accelerated. This is a highly plausible social goal.

It is a measure of how little we need worry about the danger from reducing the number of people engaged in work *qua* work that, as matters now stand, our concern is not that we will have too few available for toil but too many. We worry lest such technical advances as automation, an already realized dividend of the expansion of the New Class, will proceed so rapidly as to leave a surplus of those who still merely work. This, indeed, is probably the greater danger.

VI

I venture to suggest that the unprofessional reader will find rather reasonable and rational the ideas here offered. Why should men struggle to maximize income when the price is many dull and dark hours of labor? Why especially should they do so as goods become more plentiful and less urgent? Why should they not seek instead to maximize the rewards of all the hours of their days? And since this is the plain and obvious aspiration of a great and growing number of the most perceptive people, why should it not be the central goal of the society? And now to complete the case, we have a design for progress. It is education or, more broadly, investment in human as distinct from material capital.

But in the more sophisticated levels of the conventional wisdom, including, regrettably the more stolid and reputable of the professional economists, any such goal will seem exceedingly undesirable. The production of material goods, urgent or otherwise, is the accepted measure of our progress. Investment in material capital is our basic engine of such progress. Both this product and the means for increasing it are measurable and tangible. What is measurable is better. To talk of transferring increasing numbers of people from lives spent mostly in classical toil to lives which, for the most part, are spent pleasantly has less quantitative precision. Since investment in individuals, unlike investment in a blast furnace, provides a product that can be neither seen nor valued, it is inferior. And here the conventional wisdom unleashes its epithet of last resort. Since these achievements are not easily measured as a goal, they are "fuzzy." What economics finds inconvenient, it invariably so attacks and it is widely deemed to be a fatal condemnation. The precise, to be sure, is usually the old and familiar. Because it is old and familiar, it has been defined and measured. Thus does insistence on precision become another of the tautological devices by which the conventional wisdom protects itself. Nor should one doubt its power.

Yet anyone who finds this analysis and these proposals sensible should not be entirely discouraged. We are here in one of the contexts where circumstance has marched far beyond the conventional wisdom. We have seen how general are the efforts to join the New Class and how rapid is its expansion. We are not here establishing a new economic and social goal but identifying one that is already widely if but tacitly accepted. In this situation, the conventional wisdom cannot resist indefinitely. The economist of impeccable credentials in the conventional wisdom, who believes that there is no goal in life of comparable urgency with the maximization of total and individual real income, would never think of applying such a standard to himself. In his own life, he is an exponent of all the aspirations of the New Class. He educates and indoctrinates his own children with but one thing in mind. It is not that they should maximize their income. This is abhorrent. He wants above all that they will have an occupation that is interesting and rewarding. On this, he hopes, indeed, that they will take their learned parent as their model.

CHAPTER XXIV

On Security and Survival

In our society, the increased production of goods—privately produced goods—is, as we have seen, a basic measure of social achievement. This is partly the result of the great continuity of ideas which links the present with a world in which production indeed meant life. Partly, it is a matter of vested interest. Partly, it is a product of the elaborate obscurantism of the modern theory of consumer need. And partly, we have seen, the preoccupation with production is forced quite genuinely upon us by the tight nexus between production and economic security. However, it is a reasonable assumption that most people pressed to explain our concern for production—a pressure that is not often exerted—would be content to suggest that it serves the happiness of most men and women. That is sufficient.

The pursuit of happiness is admirable as a social goal. But the notion of happiness lacks philosophical exactitude; there is agreement neither on its substance nor its source. We know that it is "a profound instinctive union with the stream of life,"[1] but we do not know what is united. As just noted, precision in scholarly discourse not only serves as an aid in the communication of ideas, but it acts to eliminate unwelcome currents of thought, for these can almost invariably be dismissed as imprecise. To have argued simply that our present preoccupation with production of goods does not best aid in the pursuit of happiness would have got nowhere. The concepts to which one would have been committed would have been far too vague.

Any direct onslaught on the identification of goods with

[1] Bertrand Russell, *The Conquest of Happiness* (London: Allen & Unwin, 1930), p. 248.

happiness would have had another drawback. Scholarly discourse, like bullfighting and the classical ballet, has its deeper rules and they must be respected. In this arena, nothing counts so heavily against a man as to be found attacking the values of the public at large and seeking to substitute his own. Technically, his crime is arrogance. Actually, it is ignorance of the rules. In any case, he is automatically removed from the game. In the past, this has been a common error of those who have speculated on the sanctity of present economic goals—those who have sought to score against materialism and philistinism. They have advanced their own view of what adds to human happiness. For this, they could easily be accused of substituting for the crude economic goals of the people at large the more sensitive and refined but irrelevant goals of their own. The accusation is fatal.

The reader will now appreciate the care with which the defenses against such an attack have been prepared. The question of happiness and what adds to it has been evaded, for indeed only mathematicians and a few others are required to solve problems that can as sensibly be sidestepped. Instead, the present argument has been directed to seeing how extensively our present preoccupations, most of all that with the production of goods, are compelled by tradition and by myth. Released from these compulsions, we become free for the first time to survey our other opportunities. These at least have a plausible relation to happiness. But it will remain with the reader, and (since many of the opportunities can be served only by action of the state) one hopes with democratic process, to reconcile these opportunities with his own sense of what makes life better.

II

A society has one higher task than to consider its goals, to reflect on its pursuit of happiness and harmony and its success in expelling pain, tension, sorrow and the ubiquitous curse of ignorance. It must also, so far as this may be possible, ensure its own survival.

Once, in the not distant past, there was a simplistic association of security with an expanding economy—with a "healthy" increase in the production of private consumer goods. This is no longer believed. As noted, ideas, along with the ability of the Soviet Union to extract awesome space accomplishments from a far less productive economy, joined to defeat this error and now it is hard to remember that we once believed such nonsense. But a danegrous, indeed an infinitely more dangerous, association of production with military policy still exists. The basic stabilization apparatus of the modern economy consists in a large public sector sustained by a large volume of taxation, which, being progressive, increases more than in proportion with increases in production and income, and releases income for private use when the rate of expansion is slower. Close to half of the expenditures which currently (in the mid-seventies) justify this taxation and thus justify this regulatory process are for military or related purposes. Economists have been quick to aruge that other public expenditures would serve. But the fact cannot be eluded; as matters now stand, the stability of production depends on a large volume of military expenditures, quite a few of them for weapons thoughtfully designed to destroy all life.

Additionally, the weapons culture which underlies the macroeconomic stabilization of the economy also plays a deeply functional role in underwriting technology. If the notion that security depends on winning a race with the Soviet Union for increased production has been abandoned, the same cannot be said for the belief that it depends on winning a competition in technological innovation. Or rather, though the race is recognized as having no rational relation to the security of the participants, the commitment to it has been in nowise lessened. And one reason is that the race has, in fact, a deeply organic relation to economic performance. A consumer good economy is limited in the resources it can allocate to research and development. The weapons competition sustains such effort on a vastly greater scale. This is interesting to the participant producers for its own sake. It also finances development with application to the consumer goods sector—the development of air transport and computer technology. And it is also a cover by which the cost of research and development for civilian purposes which is too expensive or too risky to be afforded by private firms can, on occasion, be conducted at public cost. Were we deeply concerned about survival, we would question the wisdom of these arrangements and we would work relentlessly to persuade the Soviet Union, as the principal focus of this competition, of their danger. But if economic performance is our primary concern—if production *qua* production is the thing that counts—then survival naturally takes second place. And so it does. Only as we get matters into better perspective will our priorities become more consistent with life itself.[2]

There are other if lesser problems which our present preoccupation with production leaves unsolved. Were the Russians to disappear from the world, or, even more remarkably, become overnight as tractable as church mice, there would remain vast millions of hungry and discontented people in the world. Without the promise of relief from that hunger and privation, disorder would still be inevitable. The promise of such relief requires that we have available or usable resources. If such is the nature of our system that we have production only because we first create the wants that require it, we will have few resources to spare. We will be rich but never quite rich enough to spare anything much for the poor—including our own. We shan't present a very enchanting picture to the world or even to ourselves. If we understand that our society creates the wants that it satisfies, we may do better.

Even when the arms race ends, as it must be made to end, the scientific frontier will remain. Either as an aspect of international competition, or in pursuit of the esteem and satisfaction which go with discovery, we shall want to seek to cross it and be in on the crossing. In the field of consumer satisfaction, as we should by now agree, there is little on which one can fault the American performance. But this is not all and, as we should now, hopefully, also agree, an economy that is preoccupied however brilliantly with the production of private consumer products is supremely ill fitted for many of

2 These are matters which I discuss at great length, and I think with greater precision, in *The New Industrial State*, 2nd ed., rev. (Boston: Houghton Mifflin, 1971) and *Economics and the Public Purpose* (Boston: Houghton Mifflin, 1973). Indeed, the feeling that this somber and transcendent issue needed more attention was one of the inducements to these further books.

these frontier tasks. Under the best of circumstances, its research will be related to these products rather than to knowledge. The conventional wisdom will provide impressive arguments to the contrary. No one should be fooled.

And not only does a great part of modern scientific work lie outside the scope of the market and private enterprise but so does a large area of application and development. Private enterprise did not get us atomic energy. It has shown relatively slight interest in its development for power for the reason that it could not clearly be fitted into commercial patterns of cost and profit. Though no one doubts the vigor with which it addresses itself to travel on highways within the United States, General Motors has little interest in travel through space.

As matters now stand, we have few civilian arrangements that are by central design and purpose directed to large-scale participation in modern scientific and technological progress and its large-scale application in advance of knowledge that these will be commercially feasible. Much has been accomplished by research and development not immediately subject to commercial criteria under the inspiration of military need. This has done more to save us from the partial technological stagnation that is inherent in a consumer goods economy than we imagine. But this is a hideously inefficient way of subsidizing general scientific and technical development, as nearly all scientists agree. And it has the further effect of associating great and exciting scientific advances with an atmosphere of fear and even terror.

III

Nor is this all. The day will not soon come when the problems of either the world or our own polity are solved. Since we do not know the shape of the problems, we do not know the requirements for solution. But one thing is tolerably certain. Whether the problem be that of a burgeoning population and of space in which to live with peace and grace, or whether it be the depletion of the materials which nature has stocked in the earth's crust and which have been drawn upon more heavily in this century than in all previous time together, or whether it be that of occupying minds no longer committed to the stockpiling of consumer goods, the basic demand on America will be on its resources of ability, intelligence and education. The test will be less the effectiveness of our material investment than the effectiveness of our investment in men. We live in a day of grandiose generalization. This one can be made with confidence.

Education, no less than national defense or foreign assistance, is in the public domain. It is subject to the impediments to resource allocation between private and public use. So, once again, our hope for survival, security and contentment returns us to the problem of guiding resources to the most urgent ends.

To furnish a barren room is one thing. To continue to crowd in furniture until the foundation buckles is quite another. To have failed to solve the problem of producing goods would have been to continue man in his oldest and most grievous misfortune. But to fail to see that we have solved it, and to fail to proceed thence to the next tasks would be fully as tragic.

Index

Abramovitz, Moses, 99n
Acceptability, 6-7; conventional wisdom and, 7-10; of ideas, 7
Advertising, 103, 124n, 201; auto industry, 201; competition and 124n; debt creation and, 142; dependence effect and, 124-126; diminishing returns of, 144; expenditures for, 124; investment and, 201; privately produced goods and, 108; production and, 221; social balance and, 189-190; virtuosity in, 144; wants and, 123, 142
Affluence, 221; causes of, xxviii; conventional wisdom and, 243; effect of increasing, 116; employment and, 213; in Europe, 1-2; family life as manifestation of, 236; full employment and, 213-214; ideas and, 1-2; labor and, 242-246; problems of, 205-212; public costs of, xxi; sales tax and, 227-228; Social Darwinism and, 50-51; wants and 126. *See also* Wealth
Affluent consumer, market behavior of, xxviii
Affluent society, the, 1-4; consumer behavior and, 115; education and, 204; elimination of toil, 245-246; minimum income, 238; New Class and, 251-252; poverty in, xxii, 238-240, price stability and, 171;
sales tax and, 226-229; social balance and, 226-230; symbols of prestige in, 123; wants and, xxvi
Affluent Society, The, xxi-xxviii; origin of title, xxiv; publisher's attitude toward, xxv; reviews of, xxii, xxiii, xxv; third edition of, xxvi-xxviii
Aggregate demand for goods, xvii; means of regulating, 171; tax cuts and, 175
Agriculture, xxi-xxii, Appalachian region, 87, 235-236; bankrupt farmers, 211; competition in, 153; farm price supports, 90; hazards inherent in, 89; income, 87, 159; inflation and, 153; innovations in, 100; monetary policy and, 171; poverty and, 235-236; research in, 100. *See also* Farmers; Farm support prices
Alcott, William A., 211n
American Capitalism: The Concept of Countervailing Power, 32n, 34n, 100n, 153n, 201n
American Economic Review, 103n
American Federation of Labor —Congress of Industrial Organizations (AFL—CIO), 6
Antitrust laws, 76, 105
Appalachia, 87, 235
Arkwright, Richard, 197
Asia, 21
Atomic energy, 258

Holmes, Justice Oliver Wendell, 47
Honolulu, 160
Hoover, Herbert, 13, 134
Hopkins, Sheila V., 16n
Housing, 233, 239; public, xiii; social balance and, 186-187
Houthakker, H. S., 123n
Humphrey, Hubert, xiv

Idleness: condemnation of, 213; involuntary, 92, 104; voluntary, 215
Income: agriculture, 87, 159; alternative sources of, 216; consumer demand and, 118, 119n; consumption and, 140n; disposable personal, 143; fiscal policy and, 176; guaranteed, xxvi-xxvii, 217, 238, 238n; inequality and, 67-70; inflation and, 157n, 192-193; median (1955), 143-144; minimum, 238; monetary policy and, 170, 171; poverty and, xxvi-xxvii, 233-234, 236-239; production and, 213-219, 246; redistribution of, 65, 76-77; savings and, 66-67; taxes and, 223-226; upper limits on, 28-29
Income taxes, 191-192; efficiency and, 209; inequality and, 64-69; negative, 217; the New Class and, 249n; social balance and, 224-229; as a stabilizer, 228. *See also* Taxes
Increased national output, 99n, 243; economic security and, 94; inflation and, 154; measures for, 109. *See also* Output
Increased production, xix, 207, 254; in advanced countries, 77; in backward countries,

76; economic insecurity and, 91-95; economic security and, 90-95, 255-257; England, 103; inflation and, 154; investment and, 202-203; Keynesian fiscal policy and, xxiii; major threat to, 92; redistribution and, 76-77; Russia, xxvi, 256-257; stylized efforts for, 109-110; unemployment and, 134-135, 141; wants and, xxiii n; war and, 105; working conditions and, 244
India, xxiii n, 27, 74
Indifference curves, 119n
Indochina, 57
Indonesia, 27
Industrial Revolution, 17, 197
Inequality, 64-78; capital and, 66; capital formation and, 65-67; case for, 65; conservatives and, 67-68, 191; conventional wisdom and, 66, 67-68, 77-78; decline of interest in, 67-72, 77-78; economics and, 21; education and, 65; income and, 67-70; income tax and, 66-69; labor and, 65; liberals and, 67-68; Marx on, 63; poverty and, 237-238; social balance and, 190-192; trade unions and, 70; Veblen on, 43-44; wealth and, 21, 22, 70-75
Inflation, xxvi-xxvii, 150-161; agriculture and, 153; competition and, 155-156; conservatives and, 178; consumer demand and, 153-157, 161; control of, 161; conventional wisdom and, 150, 151, 160, 220; debt creation and, 146-147; depression and, 151, 152; economic security and, 90; farmers and, 159; fiscal

MENTOR Titles of Interest

(0451)

☐ **YOUR CAREER: How to Plan It—Manage It—Change It by Richard H. Buskirk.** Whether you're in school, on your first job, or in a position that is dead-end or wrong-way, this remarkable and practical guide is for you. The product of wide professional experience, filled with fascinating case histories, this book is meant not just to be read but to be used. Its goal is yours: the career and success you deserve. (620593—$2.50)

☐ **THE PRINCE by Niccolò Machiavelli.** The classic work on statesmanship and power, the techniques and strategy of gaining and keeping political control. (618572—$1.95)

☐ **CONCEPT OF THE CORPORATION by Peter F. Drucker.** An up-to-date edition of the classic study of the organization and management policies of General Motors—the company that has become the model for modern large-scale corporations across the world. (618203—$2.50)

☐ **HOW TO START AND MANAGE YOUR OWN BUSINESS by Gardiner G. Greene.** If you run a small business, you need all the help you can get—and this is the book that gives it all to you. It includes information on financial strategies, selecting professional services, developing and marketing your product, the psychology of negotiating, contracting with the government, and everything else you need to know to be your own boss, create your own company, and make a good profit! (620755—$3.50)

☐ **CORPORATE ETIQUETTE by Milla Alihan.** Why do some executives quickly rise on the corporate ladder, while others, seemingly just as qualified, remain bogged down on the lower echelons? An eminent business consultant clearly spotlights all the trouble areas where minor gaffs can turn into major roadblocks to advancement in this essential guide to getting ahead in the fast-changing business world of today. (619188—$2.50)

Buy them at your local bookstore or use this convenient coupon for ordering.

THE NEW AMERICAN LIBRARY, INC.,
P.O. Box 999, Bergenfield, New Jersey 07621

Please send me the books I have checked above. I am enclosing $_____ (please add $1.00 to this order to cover postage and handling). Send check or money order—no cash or C.O.D.'s. Prices and numbers are subject to change without notice.

Name_____

Address_____

City _____ State _____ Zip Code _____

Allow 4-6 weeks for delivery.
This offer is subject to withdrawal without notice.